The 8086 and Assembly Langua

The 8086 and Assembly Language Programming

R.W. TURPIN

BSP PROFESSIONAL BOOKS
OXFORD LONDON EDINBURGH
BOSTON PALO ALTO MELBOURNE

Copyright © R.W. Turpin 1987

All rights reserved. No part of this publication may be reproduced, stored in a retrieval system, or transmitted, in any form or by any means, electronic, mechanical, photocopying, recording or otherwise without the prior permission of the copyright owner.

First published 1987

British Library
Cataloguing in Publication Data
Turpin, R.W.
  The 8086 and assembly language programming.
  1. Intel 8086 (Microprocessor) — Programming   2. Assembler language
  (Computer program language)
  I. Title
  005.2'65   QA76.8.I292
ISBN 0-632-01892-5

BSP Professional Books
Editorial offices:
Osney Mead, Oxford OX2 0EL
  (*Orders*: Tel. 0865 240201)
8 John Street, London WC1N 2ES
23 Ainslie Place, Edinburgh EH3 6AJ
52 Beacon Street, Boston
  Massachusetts 02108, USA
667 Lytton Avenue, Palo Alto
  California 94301, USA
107 Barry Street, Carlton
  Victoria 3053, Australia

Printed and bound in Great Britain

To Susan

CONTENTS

Preface ix

CHAPTER 1 INTRODUCING THE 8086

Microprocessor Basic System 1
8086 Microprocessor Programming Model 2
Memory Segmentation 7
Machine Language and Assembly Language 10
Addressing Modes 13
Segment Register Selection 16

CHAPTER 2 THE 8086 ARCHITECTURE

8086 Microprocessor Internal Architecture 18
The 8086 Microprocessor Pin Definitions 21

CHAPTER 3 THE 8086 INSTRUCTION SET

Symbolic Addressing 27
Instruction Set Alphabetical Listing 29

CHAPTER 4 INSTRUCTION CATEGORIES

Data Transfer Instructions 67
Arithmetic Instructions 73
Bit Manipulation Instructions 81
String Instructions 84
Program Transfer Instructions 86

CHAPTER 5 ASSEMBLY LANGUAGE

Software Development Procedure 90
Segmentation 94
Assembly Language Constituents 95
Summary of Directives and Operators 97
Macros 105
Assembler Errors 108

CHAPTER 6 MEMORY INTERFACING

8086 Minimum Mode System   112
8086 Memory Organization   120

CHAPTER 7 INPUT/OUTPUT INTERFACING

8255A Programmable Peripheral Interface PPI   136
Serial Communication - Microprocessor and I/O Device   144
8251A Programmable Communication Interface 146
8086 Interrupts   154
8259A Programmable Interrupt Controller   160

CHAPTER 8 8086 ASSEMBLY LANGUAGE PROGRAMS   168

CHAPTER 9 INTRODUCING THE 80186 AND 80286 MICROPROCESSORS

The 80186 Microprocessor   199
The 80286 microprocessor   214

APPENDIX A

Diagnostic Listing of Error Program   229

APPENDIX B

RS-232C Interface Pin Assignments   231

APPENDIX C

Procedure for 8086 Machine Instruction Encoding   232
Single Operand Instructions   232
Two Operand Instructions   236
Addressing Modes and the Object Code   248
Instruction Execution Times   250

APPENDIX D

8086 Bus Timing   252

APPENDIX E

The ASCII character Set   256

INDEX   257

PREFACE

This book is intended as an introduction to the 16 bit 8086 microprocessor family and to the assembly language programming of these devices. The material is intended for engineering students and practitioners of the subject. The approach is tutorial in manner. The text is principally about the 8086 microprocessor, a knowledge of which is desirable or perhaps necessary, before proceeding to the study of the more advanced 16 bit microprocessors in this family.

The device architecture of the 8086 microprocessor is examined in detail in chapters 1 and 2. Chapters 6 and 7 deal with interfacing this microprocessor to commonly used memory and peripheral devices. Chapter 9 presents an introduction to the architecture of the more advanced 80186 and 80286 microprocessors.

A complete list of the assembly language instruction set accompanied by a brief explanation of each instruction is provided in chapter 3. The reason for its inclusion in this book is that such a list provides the new user of the assembly language with both a convenient and invaluable reference. Further examination of the instruction set is given in chapter 4, where the instructions are considered in their respective categories. The assembly language itself i.e. the use of directives and operators is explained in chapter 5. This information applies to assemblers ASM86 and MASM. Chapter 8 consists of introductory assembly language program examples. These programs are related to the engineering aspects of using the 8086 microprocessor.

I am indebted to the Intel corporation for permission to use their data books as source material and to reproduce several diagrams relating to this material. It has been my students of the past three years who have, by their interest in the material in my 8086 course, stimulated me to write this book and for this I thank them. Finally I should like to acknowledge my gratitude to my family for the patience with which they have endured the constant rattle of the printer.

CHAPTER 1
Introducing the 8086

MICROPROCESSOR BASIC SYSTEM

The most basic microprocessor system whether it is described as a microcomputer or a microcontroller comprises, a microprocessor or group of microprocessors in which data operations are performed and decisions are carried out, a memory block in which programs are stored, an in/out facility so that the system is capable of external communication and a bus system for internal communication between these three areas. Figure 1.1 shows such a fundamental system for an 8086 microprocessor in which the bus system is divided into address bus, data bus and control bus.

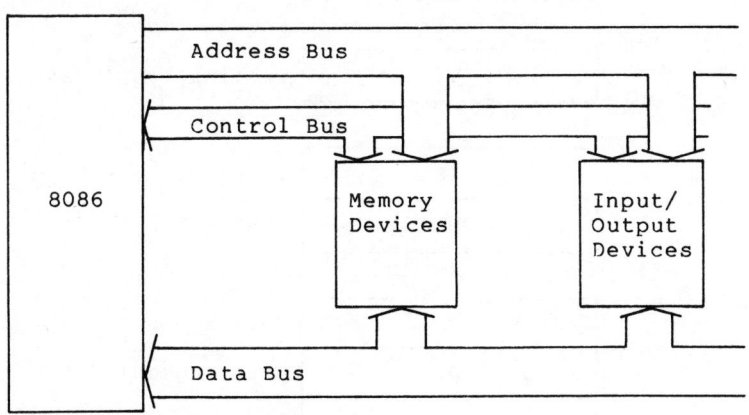

Figure 1.1 Basic microprocessor system.

The 8086 microprocessor has 20 address lines and can therefore access directly 2^{20} bytes (1,048,576 or 1 Mbyte).

2 The 8086 and Assembly Language

It can also access 2^{16} I/O port addresses (65,536 or 64 K bytes). The address bus is unidirectional i.e. address information is transferred from the microprocessor to the other devices within the system. The 16 data lines of the 8086 microprocessor form a 16 bit data bus which is bidirectional, i.e. data information can be transferred to and from the microprocessor. The control bus contains such lines as read control, write control, memory/IO select, data enable, data transmit/receive, and address latch enable lines.

8086 MICROPROCESSOR PROGRAMMING MODEL

The 8086 microprocessor is a single integrated circuit device which can be modelled for programming purposes as

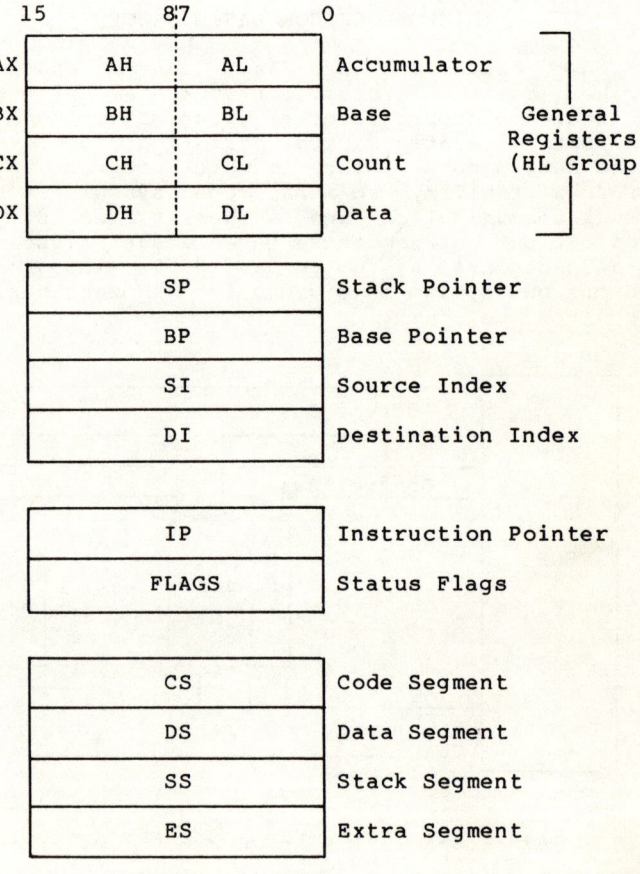

Figure 1.2 8086 Microprocessor programming model.

shown in figure 1.2. This model contains 14 registers arranged in four groups. A brief explanation of the usage of each of these groups of registers is given and a more detailed explanation of the individual register usage follows.

The first group consists of the general purpose registers which can be used in both arithmetic and logical operations, and are usually employed to hold immediate data. The pointer and index registers form the second group, these are the addressing registers. They can be used for some general purpose operations but are more frequently used with the more complex instructions to access specific memory locations. The third group is formed by the instruction pointer and the flag registers and can be regarded as registers indicating the status of the microprocessor operation. The final group consists of the segment registers which have a very specific function in relation to the identification of the memory areas used by the microprocessor.

Segment Registers CS, DS, SS and ES

The 1 Mbyte of memory locations that can be accessed by the 8086 microprocessor is divided into segments, and at any one time the microprocessor can access four such segments. It is the segment registers which provide selection of these four active 64 Kbyte segments.

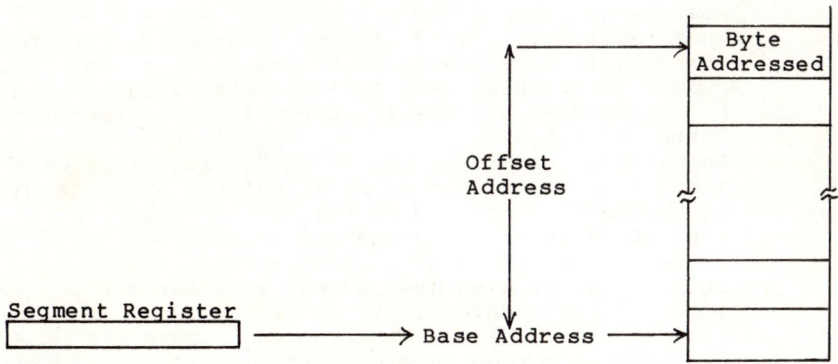

Figure 1.3 Accessing information in memory.

The segments are known as code, data, stack and extra segments. The 16 bit base address or starting address of each of these segments is stored in the associated segment register. The CS register holds the base address of the current code segment, the DS register holds the base address of the current data segment, the SS register holds the base address of the stack segment, and the ES register

4 The 8086 and Assembly Language

holds the base address of the current extra data segment. An 'offset' address refers to the number of bytes from the base of a segment. So, to access a byte the microprocessor uses both the base address and the offset address of that byte. Figure 1.3 shows that a byte within memory is reached via a base address for the segment and an offset address for its position within that segment. Segmentation is explained in detail later in this chapter.

General Registers AX, BX, CX and DX

These registers can be used as 16 bit registers manipulating words or as two 8 bit registers separately addressable as high and low halves H and L manipulating bytes. Operations can occur between 16 bit registers and memory words or between 8 bit registers and memory bytes. However, operations between 16 bit registers and bytes or between 8 bit registers and words are illegal and cannot be performed. These registers can be used as either the source or destination of data in both arithmetic and logical operations. However, each of these general purpose registers has one or more dedicated uses associated with particular instructions, so they have names which indicate these uses.

AX — Accumulator: the use of this register is assumed in all multiplication and division operations. It is also used as the data source or destination in what is termed 'accumulator I/O' input and output operations.

BX — Base register: used as an addressing register pointing to data in memory in what is termed the 'based addressing mode'. It is also used to point to the base of a table in memory in the translate instruction XLAT.

CX — Count register: commonly used by instructions which involve a count. For example register contents can be shifted and rotated by the count value held in the CL register. Loop and string instructions also assume the CX register to hold a count value.

DX — Data register: used in indirect I/O instructions to select a port address. It is also used in word multiply and divide instructions where the DX-AX register pair are regarded as a single 32 bit register.

All the other registers are addressable as 16 bit word registers only.

Pointer and Index Registers SP, BP, SI and DI

These registers can be used to store offset addresses. An instruction which relates to data in memory need only specify the associated pointer or index register in order

Introducing the 8086 **5**

to access that data. The pointer registers SP and BP relate to data stored in the current stack segment of memory. A stack is a list of data stored in memory which can only be accessed in a last on first off manner. So the stack pointer SP is used to point to the most recent data placed on the stack list. It is modified automatically with all stack instructions, for example the register contents are incremented or decremented respectively each time data is placed on the stack or removed from the stack. The base pointer BP is used by instructions which refer to parameters passed to a subroutine via the stack, it is used to point to data other than that most recently placed on the stack list. The index registers SI and DI are used implicitly with string instructions, where data taken from memory in the data segment uses the source index register, and data placed in memory in the extra segment uses the destination index register. Pointer and index registers can be used to define the locations used in most arithmetic and logical instructions.

Data Pointers

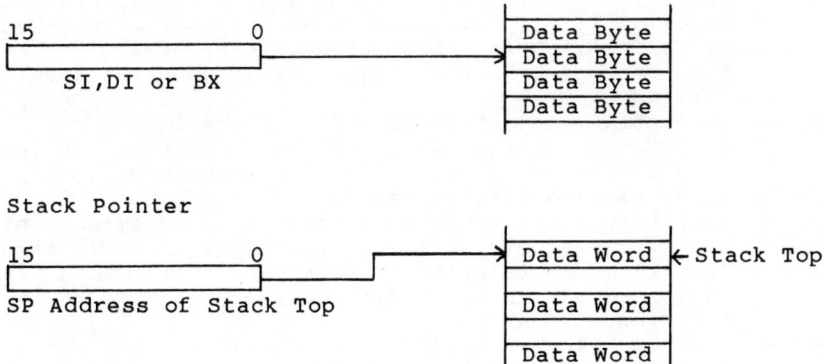

Figure 1.4 Registers as address pointers.

Figure 1.4 shows the data pointers SI, DI and also BX indicating offset addresses of data bytes in memory, and the stack pointer SP indicating the address of the most recent word in the current stack, i.e. of the stack top.

Single Bit Flag Registers

The 8086 microprocessor flag word has nine single bit flag registers arranged as shown in figure 1.5. Six of these flag registers, namely ZF, SF, PF, CF, AF and OF, are status registers indicating the result of arithmetic or logical operations. The remaining three flag registers DF, IF and TF are used as control registers to alter microprocessor operations.

6 The 8086 and Assembly Language

```
* * * * O D I T S Z * A * P * C
```

Figure 1.5 Flag register word.

The words 'set' and 'reset' are the flag condition terminolgy. A flag bit is said to be set when it has the value '1', and said to be reset when it has the value '0'. Certain instructons, such as arithmetic or logical instructions, affect the flags and after the execution of these instructions the flags are either set or reset.

ZF - Zero flag: if the result of an instruction is zero this flag is set, otherwise it is reset.
SF - Sign flag: this flag is set if the most significant bit of the instruction result is '1'; otherwise the flag is reset. So the flag is set if the result is negative and reset if the result is positive. This applies to both byte and word operations.
PF - Parity flag: if the parity of an instruction result is even, i.e. it contains an even number of bits at logic '1', then this flag is set; otherwise the flag is reset. So the flag is reset when the result has odd parity.
CF - Carry flag: this flag is set if there is a carry out of, or a borrow into, the high order bit of the result (whether it is a 16 bit or an 8 bit result); otherwise the flag is reset.
AF - Auxiliary carry flag: when there is a carry out of bit 3 into bit 4 of the instruction result this flag is set; otherwise it is reset. This flag is used when binary coded decimal arithmetic is employed.
OF - Overflow flag: this flag is set when the logical exclusive-or operation performed on the carry into and the carry out of the most significant bit of the result yields '1'; otherwise the flag is reset. When the flag is set it indicates that the signed result is out of range, this is explained in detail in chapter 4.

The following diagram figure 1.6 shows, for an operation involving two 8 bit operands, the relation between the condition of the flags and the 8 bit result of the operation. For example the carry in and out of the most significant bit determine the condition of the overflow flag, whereas all the bits in the result are used in determining the condition of the parity flag.

DF - Direction flag: when this flag is reset string instructions autoincrement and when it is set such instructions autodecrement.

Introducing the 8086 **7**

IF - Interrupt enable flag: this flag when set allows the microprocessor to recognize interrupt requests, and when reset it disables such interrupts.
TF - Trap flag: when this is set the microprocessor is placed in the single step mode.

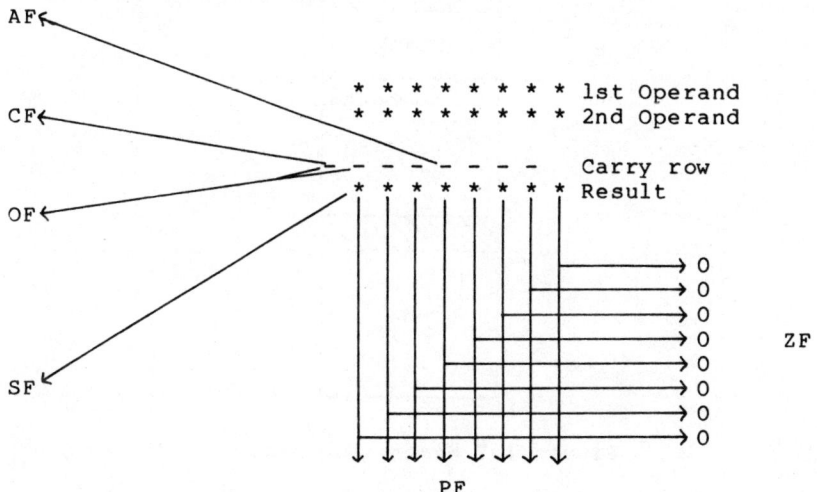

Figure 1.6 Instruction result and status flags.

Instruction Pointer IP
The instruction pointer is the 16 bit register which holds the offset address of the next instruction due to be executed. Each instruction when executing causes the instruction pointer to be updated such that it points to the next instruction in the sequence.

MEMORY SEGMENTATION

Viewed by the microprocessor the memory currently in use consists of four segments. These segments are first the code segment which is used to store program instructions, second the data segment which is used for the storage of data, third the extra data segment and fourth the stack segment. Each segment can be up to 64Kbytes in length, that is one-sixteenth of the 1 Mbyte of addressable memory. Each segment begins on a 16 byte memory boundary. A typical arrangement of these segments is shown in figure 1.7.

Referring to the programming model of the 8086 shown in figure 1.2, the registers used to hold program addresses are 16 bits in length and are hence each only capable of addressing 2^{16}, i.e. 64 Kbytes of memory. So within any program the logical addressing range is that which can be

8 The 8086 and Assembly Language

expressed with 16 bits, which in the hexadecimal notation is 0000H to FFFFH. Hence each segment is limited in size to 64Kbytes.

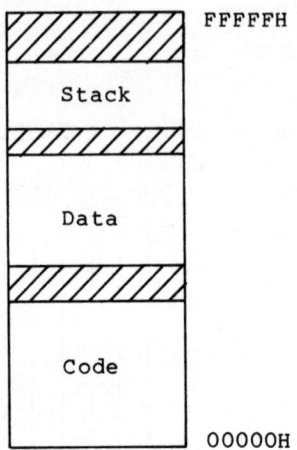

Figure 1.7 Memory segments.

The microprocessor address bus consists of 20 lines giving an addressing capability of 2^{20} bytes, i.e. 1024 Kbytes or 1 Mbyte. So the total addressing range of the 8086 microprocessor expressed in the hexadecimal notation is 00000H to FFFFFH. The memory organisation task, carried out within the microprocessor, is to convert all 16 bit program logical addresses to 20 bit physical addresses. The 8086 microprocessor achieves this by combining 16 bit segment addresses with 16 bit offset addresses to form 20 bit physical addresses as shown in figure 1.8(a). The base address of a segment is stored in the corresponding segment register. The offset address is contained in either the instruction pointer in the case of code or the stack pointer for stack addressing or other registers in the case of the data. In each case the offset address refers to the distance in bytes of the memory location from the base of the segment in which it is situated; this is clearly shown in figure 1.3. So by definition the segment register must contain the 16 most significant bits of the 20 bit physical address of the segment base, i.e. it points to the base of the segment where the offset is zero. So, using hexadecimal notation, if the CS register contains 10A0H then the physical address of the segment base must be 10A00H.

To continue this example, an instruction within this code segment is reached by using a logical offset address held in the IP, so the least significant bits of the 20 bit address must depend on the IP. If the IP contains 0048H then the offset address within the segment is 0048H.

Introducing the 8086 9

Consequently the physical address is obtained by adding the offset address to the 20 bit base address of the segment. The addition of the hexadecimal addresses is as follows:

```
  10A00  -  contents of CS shifted left 4 binary places to
            give segment base address
+ 0048   -  contents of IP indicating the offset within
            the segment
  10A48  -  physical address of instruction
```

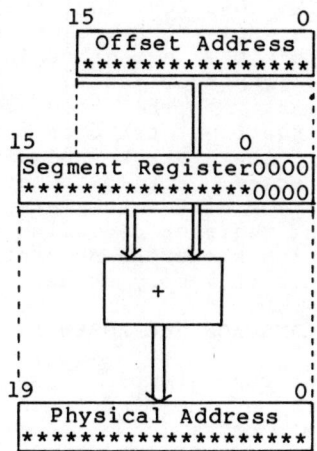

(a) Physical Address Generation from Segment Register
    Contents and Offset Address

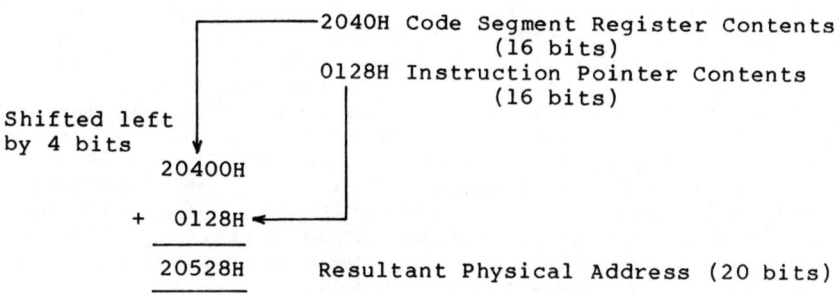

(b) Calculation of the Physical Address of an Instruction

Figure 1.8 Physical address generation.

The formation of the 20 bit physical address takes place

as follows:

(a) The 16 bit segment address is shifted four places to the left to form a 20 bit address.
(b) This shifted segment address is added to an offset address to form a complete 20 bit physical address.

This process is illustrated in figure 1.8(a) and an example of the 20 bit address calculation is shown in figure 1.8(b). Because the segment register contents are always shifted left four places, a segment can begin at any physical address which is a multiple of 16. So using hexadecimal notation we can see that segments can begin at addresses such as 0H, 10H, 20H, 30H etc. and so on up to FFFF0H, covering the whole of the 1 Mbyte range.

The selection of the segment register is done by the microprocessor. All instructions are fetched from the current code segment so the code segment register is selected in an instruction fetch operation. In the case of stack operations, the stack segment register is automatically selected. For data access the segment register chosen will be either the data segment register or the extra segment register depending on the instruction involved. Figure 1.9 shows the segment register selected for the various types of memory access.

MACHINE LANGUAGE and ASSEMBLY LANGUAGE

The machine language consists of a set of instructions that can be executed by the microprocessor. Each of these instructions consists of a code constructed from the binary digits 1 and 0. This machine code can be represented in either binary form or in hexadecimal form. A list of machine code instructions forming a program is often referred to as object code.

Assembly language instructions are written using letters forming a mnemonic (or memory aid) each mnemonic corresponding to a machine language instruction. The following are examples of easily remembered mnemonics: MOV, ADD, JMP, OUT and IN. The 8086 assembly language instruction statements use mnemonics and operands to specify machine instructions. The mnemonic informs the microprocessor of the task to be performed and the operand indicates the nature of the data on which the task is to be carried out. A typical example of an instruction statement would be: AND BX,007FH where AND is the part of the statement which informs the microprocessor that the logical AND operation must be carried out between the operands. The operands in this case are the contents of register BX and the immediate data 007FH. Note that the immediate data is expressed in hexadecimal format using four digits rather than in binary format which would require 16 digits.

A machine code instruction specifies the operation to be performed, which operands are to used, where the operands are located for example in a register or in

Introducing the 8086 11

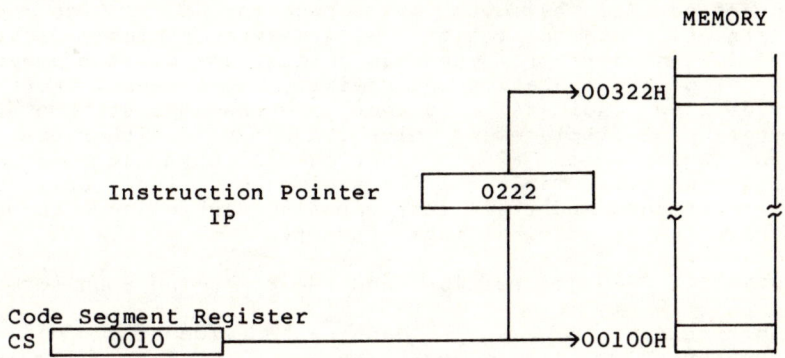

(a) Instructions are Fetched from the Code Segment

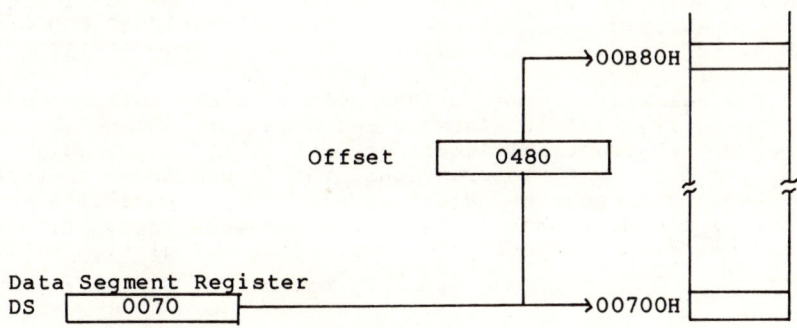

(b) Data is typically accessed in the Data Segment

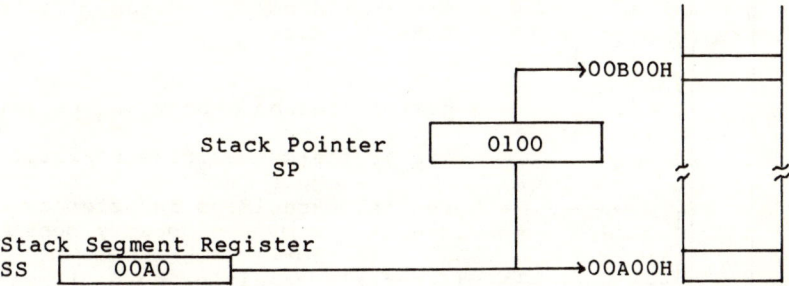

(c) Accessing the stack always involves the Stack Segment

Figure 1.9 Selection of segment registers depending on the type of memory access.

12 The 8086 and Assembly Language

memory, and if an operand is in memory how the address is generated. For the 8086 microprocessor a machine code instruction can consist of a single byte (8 binary digits) or any number of bytes up to six. The first two bytes represent the operation and specify the operands. Further bytes can indicate a direct address consisting of two bytes, or a displacement which can comprise either one or two bytes or a combination of both address and displacement. Table 1.1 shows examples of 8086 instructions, and their corresponding machine code in both binary and hexadecimal (HEX) format.

Table 1.1 8086 Instructions and their machine code format.

| Instruction Statement | Machine Code (Object Code) | |
	Hex Format	Binary Format
OUT DX,AL	EE	11101110
DEC BX	4B	01001011
MOV DS,BX	8E DB	10001110 11011011
ADC AL,[DI]	12 05	00010010 00000101
RCL BX,1	D1 D3	11010001 11010011

The general format of the 8086 machine instruction is shown in figure 1.10. This format does not include all the possible instruction variations, but it is applicable to the majority of instructions. The figure shows that the byte or bytes for the object code specify opcode bits and various fields representing operand length, register, mode of operation, effective address (EA) calculation method etc.

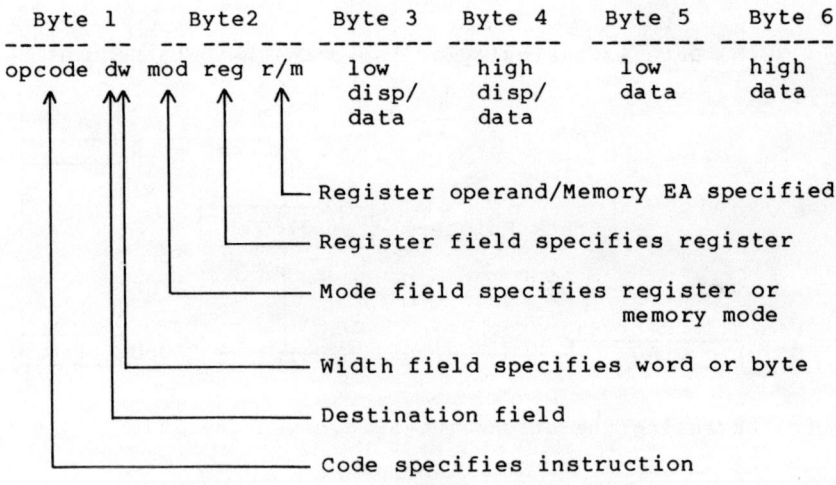

Figure 1.10 Format of the 8086 machine instruction.

Introducing the 8086   13

The detailed procedure for the encoding of an assembly language instruction to its equivalent object code, can best be explained by working through a series of examples for a wide range of instruction types, this is done in appendix C.

ADDRESSING MODES

Instructions executed by the microprocessor are usually performed on specifically identified data. The data specified in the instruction is referred to as the operand or operands. The operand can be part of the instruction, held in a register within the microprocessor, stored at an address in memory or accessed at an I/O port. There is a wide range of methods for obtaining these operands and they are known as addressing modes. Immediate addressing and register addressing do not access an operand in a memory location and so do not cause the microprocessor to start a memory access cycle. Each of the other modes provides a different way of evaluating the memory access address. Different authors and different manufacturers give a variety of names to the wide range of addressing modes, however in this text the names given by Intel will be used.

As we have seen, the 8086 microprocessor registers are 16 bits wide so logical addresses are also 16 bits in length. Two logical addresses are used in the generation of the physical address, one of these is the address held in a segment register and the other is an offset address or effective memory address EA. A constant can be used in the evaluation of the effective memory address. This constant, known by the term displacement, appears in the instruction itself.

The memory addressing modes available on the 8086 microprocessor are: immediate addressing, register addressing, register indirect addressing, indexed addressing, based addressing and based indexed addressing. The remainder of this introductory chapter is devoted to the explanation of memory addressing modes.

Immediate Addressing

In this case the operand takes the form of a byte or two bytes within the instruction and represents a data constant. So it is not necessary for the microprocessor to evaluate a memory address in order to obtain the operand. Note that the low order byte of the operand precedes the high order byte when a 16 bit immediate operand is stored in memory as part of an instruction. A typical example of an instruction involving an immediate operand is: SUB AX,045AH, where SUB is the mnemonic for subtraction and this is the operation that will occur. It is the immediate operand 045AH which will be subtracted from the contents of the AX register.

14 The 8086 and Assembly Language

Register Addressing

Again the operand is obtained without the microprocessor accessing memory, this is because the operand is held in an internal register within the microprocessor. An example of such an instruction is: DEC CX. The operand is the CX register contents and DEC is the mnemonic for decrement so the execution of the instruction will cause the operand to be decremented, i.e. have one subtracted from its value.

Direct Addressing

This is the most straightforward of the memory addressing modes, in which an effective memory address EA is provided by two bytes in the instruction. This address is the offset address of the operand stored in the data segment. A typical example of an instruction using direct addressing is: MOV AX,VARE. MOV is the mnemonic for move; so in this case the contents of the memory location, whose offset is given by the identifier VARE, will be copied into the AX register. VARE will have previously been designated as the offset address identifier for a word variable within the data segment.

Register Indirect Addressing

The effective memory address EA is contained in either a base register BX or BP, or in an index register SI or DI. Because there is neither a direct address nor a displacement within the instruction this type of addressing is often referred to as implied addressing. An example of this type of addressing mode is: SUB AX,[SI]. The contents of the location addressed by SI are subtracted from the contents of the AX register.

Indexed Addressing

In this type of addressing an index register SI or DI is specified within the instruction and also optionally an 8 bit or a 16 bit displacement. The effective memory address EA calculated by the microprocessor is the sum of the index register contents and the displacement. A typical example of this form of addressing is: ADD CX,VARC [SI + 0A3BH]. In this example the word added to the contents of CX has an effective address EA or offset address given by the sum of VARC plus the contents of SI plus the displacement 0A3BH.

Based Addressing

In this case the effective memory address calculated by the microprocessor is the sum of the base register, BX or BP, contents, and either an 8 bit or a 16 bit displacement value. A typical example of this type of instruction is:

Introducing the 8086 **15**

INSTRUCTION ADDRESSING MODE	8086 REGISTERS	MEMORY

MOV AX,1234H Immediate	AX 1234 ←
	PC 04C5
		Code Segment
		← 12
		  34
		  B8 04C2

MOV AX,CX Register	AX 7778 ← BX 0F01 CX 7778 ─┘	
MOV AX,NUMB1 Direct Offset address of variable is 0284	AX 6A7B ←	Data Segment ← 6A 7B 0284

MOV AX,[SI]   Register
               Indirect
	AX 3231 ←
	SI 0872
		Data Segment
		← 32
		  31 0872

MOV AX,[SI+4] Indexed	AX 5278 ←
	SI 0992
		Data Segment
		  0A
		  52
		  78
		  00
		  00
		  00
		  00 0992

MOV AX,[BX+2] Based	AX 5522 ←
	BX 0444
		Data Segment
		  66
		  55
		  22
		  00
		  00 0444

MOV AX,[SI+BX+4]   Based
                   Indexed
	AX A429 ←
	SI 0A40
	BX 0050
		Data Segment
		← A4
		  29
		  A2
		  00
		  00
		  11 0A90
		       Offset
		       Address

Figure 1.11 Addressing modes illustrated using the 8086 move instruction.

16 The 8086 and Assembly Language

SUB AX,[BX + 14H]. In this example a word operand in memory is added to the contents of the AX register. The effective address of the memory operand is given by the sum of the contents of register BX and displacement 14H, this effective address is the offset address in the data segment. However, specifying BP as the base pointer automatically involves the use of the SS stack segment register and hence provides a method of accessing stack data.

Based Indexed Addressing

This final method of addressing generates an effective memory address EA by adding the contents of the base register, the contents of the index register and the displacement value. Because two address components can be varied in this mode of addressing, it is used to access two dimensional arrays of data. An example of such an instruction is: ADD AX,[SI + BX + 04]. In this example a word in memory is added to the contents of the AX register. The effective address of this word data is given by the sum of the contents of the SI register and the contents of the BX register and the displacement 04. Based addressing, indexed addressing and based indexed addressing are often included under the general heading of register indirect addressing.

The move instruction, the mnemonic for which is MOV, has the general form MOV destination,source. The instruction copies the source operand to the destination operand. Variations of the MOV instruction in which the destination is the AX accumulator are shown in figure 1.11 to illustrate the addressing modes and to point out the source of the data moved to the accumulator. The generation of the effective address EA in each of the various addressing modes is related to the format of the machine instruction in figure C.1 in Appendix C. It should be mentioned that string instructions do not use the usual addressing modes. In their case the index registers are used implicitly.

SEGMENT REGISTER SELECTION

The discussion in this section on addressing modes has mainly revolved around the generation of the effective address EA and there has been little mention of the segment address. How then is the segment register selected? The reader, at this point, is reminded that this is done automatically by the microprocessor depending on the type of memory access required by the instruction. Once an instruction has selected an offset or evaluated an effective memory address then the choice of segment register is straightforward. So whenever the instruction pointer IP is used, the CS code segment register is selected as the accompanying segment register. Generally when an effective memory address is evaluated the

Introducing the 8086 17

operation involves the DS data segment register. Stack operations, where the offset address is obtained from the stack pointer, involve the SS stack segment register.

Table 1.2 Offset address and corresponding segment register.

Memory Reference Type	Segment Base Address	Offset Address
Instruction Fetch	CS	Instruction Pointer
Data Operations	DS	Effective Address EA
Stack Operation	SS	Stack Pointer
Data on Stack using Base Pointer BP	SS	Effective Address EA
String Source	DS	SI
String destination	ES	DI

When the BP is used in obtaining the effective address the SS stack segment register is again used to compute the physical address. Table 1.2 shows the offset address source and corresponding segment register for the various types of memory reference. However the 8086 instruction set does provide the facility to change the segment to be used with an instruction. This is done using a segment override prefix as part of the instruction, this prefix occupies a single byte. Hence the segment register to be used with an instruction can be specified by the programmer.

Questions

(1.1) What are the pointer and index registers of the 8086 microprocessor? How are these registers used?

(1.2) If the result of an arithmetic byte operation affecting the status flags is 97H; give the condition of the flags: SF, ZF and PF. What further information would be required to determine the state of the overflow flag?

(1.3) Explain what is meant by memory segmentation. What are the advantages of using memory segmentation?

(1.4) Evaluate the physical address used by the 8086 microprocessor in each of the memory references:
(a) Instruction fetch, CS = 8800H and IP = 0484H
(b) Instruction fetch, CS = 0400H and IP = 0400H
(c) Data operation, CS = 0400H, DS = 0A20H and the effective offset address = 888H
(d) Stack operation, SS = 1000H and SP = 40H

CHAPTER 2
The 8086 architecture

8086 MICROPROCESSOR INTERNAL ARCHITECTURE

The 8086 microprocessor is divided internally into two separate processing parts. They are called the bus interface unit (BIU) and the execution unit (EU). The BIU carries out the bus operations; namely it fetches instructions, reads memory operands, writes operands to memory and transfers data to and from input/output devices. The EU, as the name suggests, has the main task of decoding and executing instructions. The two sections of the microprocessor operate asynchronously to give an overlap of instruction fetch and instruction execution. A diagram of the internal structure of the 8086 microprocessor which shows clearly the two processing sections is given in figure 2.1.

Bus Interface Unit

This unit performs all external bus operations. It presents to the outside world a 16 bit bidirectional data bus and a 20 bit unidirectional address bus. It contains bus control logic, internal communication registers, the instruction pointer, segment registers and a summation unit to form the 20 bit address. An example of the physical address formed by this adder can be the 20 bit address for the next instruction. This is formed by combining the IP contents and the CS contents. The unit also generates bus control signals for reading and writing to both memory and IO.

The BIU also contains the instruction stream queue. This is a RAM array which stores six bytes of instruction object code. Under most conditions the queue will have prefetched instructions readily available for execution by the EU and so the EU does not have to wait for instructions to be fetched from memory. Whenever there are two empty bytes within the queue the BIU, provided it is not being requested by the EU to read or write to memory, will fill the empty spaces by fetching the next sequential instruction. The BIU fetches two bytes in a single memory access via the 16 bit data bus. The bytes loaded into the queue at the input end automatically move through the queue towards the output end because it operates on a first in, first out (FIFO) basis.

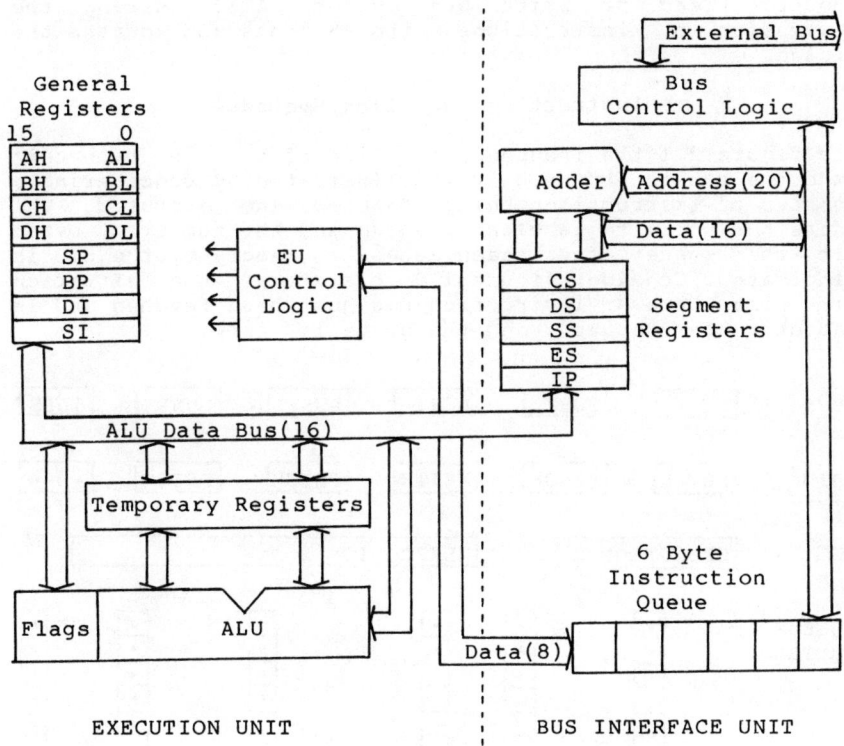

Figure 2.1 Internal architecture of the 8086 microprocessor.

When the queue is full and the EU is not requesting access to operands in memory or IO, the BIU remains idle. When the BIU is fetching instruction bytes to fill the queue and it is requested by the EU to access memory or IO, it first completes the byte fetch process before servicing the EU. If the EU executes a jump instruction then the bytes in the queue will not be from the new address, so the BIU resets the queue, fetches two bytes for the EU, and then proceeds to fill the queue.

Execution Unit

This section of the CPU contains an arithmetic and logic unit (ALU), eight general registers, the flag registers, temporary registers and queue control logic. The EU takes

20 The 8086 and Assembly Language

instructions from the output end of the queue, decodes them and executes them. If the queue is empty the EU will wait while the BIU fetches further instruction object code. If during instruction execution it is necessary to access memory or IO then the EU requests the BIU to undergo read or write bus cycles. Also, during the execution of instructions, the EU tests and updates the flags.

Instruction Execution Sequence

In figure 2.1 the independent action of the execution unit and the bus interface unit is illustrated by considering a series of instructions being fetched and executed. The data bus activity is clearly shown and the number of bytes in the queue after each access of memory by the BIU is indicated. Consider figure 1.9 to start at the situation in time where an instruction has just been fetched and is about to be executed, and the queue is empty.

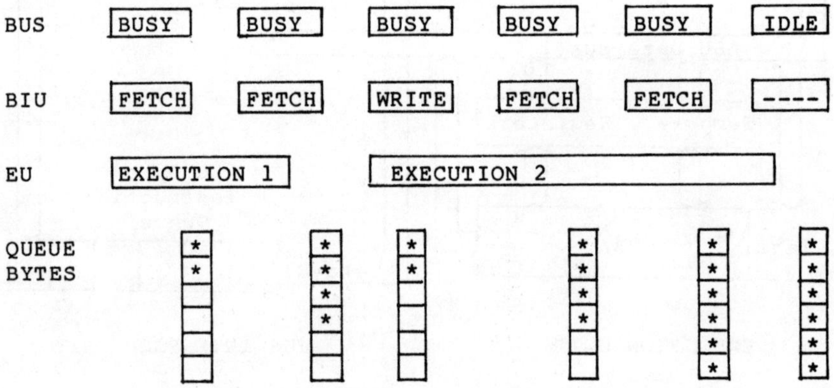

```
BUS    [BUSY]  [BUSY]  [BUSY]  [BUSY]  [BUSY]  [IDLE]

BIU    [FETCH] [FETCH] [WRITE] [FETCH] [FETCH] [----]

EU     [EXECUTION 1  ] [   EXECUTION 2            ]
```

QUEUE
BYTES

Figure 2.2 Overlapping of instruction fetch and instruction execution.

The following points explain the asynchronous operation of instruction fetch and instruction execution shown in figure 2.1:

(1) While the first instruction is executing in the EU, the BIU is fetching a second instruction and the data bus is busy. Assume this second instruction to consist of two bytes. At the end of this bus cycle the queue will have two bytes waiting to be used by the EU.

(2) As the execution has not been completed when the second instruction is placed in the queue, the BIU will again access memory and bring a further two bytes. Assume this to be two single byte

8086 Architecture 21

instructions. There will now be four bytes in the queue making up three instructions to be executed.
(3) Assume that the EU now requests the BIU to write to memory as part of the execution of the first instruction. While the BIU is writing to memory the bus is again busy, and the EU will execute the second instruction. There will now be two bytes in the instruction queue.
(4) Again in this example, the execution of the second instruction takes longer than the memory write cycle, so the BIU will be able to fetch two more bytes for the queue. If the execution is still taking place when this memory access has completed then the BIU will fetch a further two bytes to fill the queue.
(5) Consider that the execution of the second instruction is not complete when the queue is full; then the BIU and the data bus will remain idle until the execution is finished and there are two empty places in the queue, or until the EU requests the BIU to access memory.

THE 8086 MICROPROCESSOR PIN DEFINITIONS

The 8086 microprocessor is enclosed in a 40 pin dual in-line package, the pin layout of which is shown in figure 2.3 along with the pin definitions and signals. The

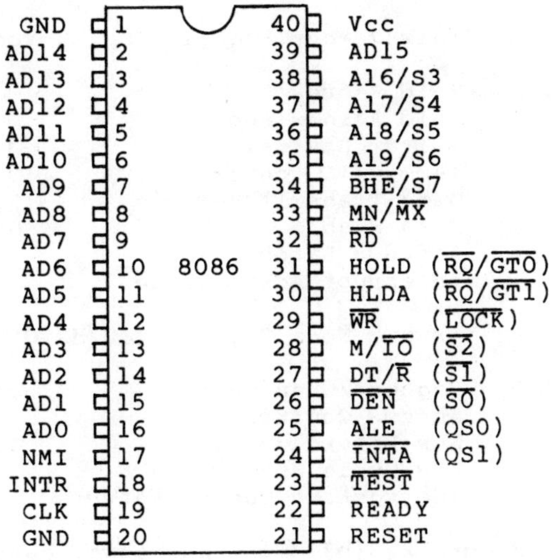

```
      GND  [ 1        40 ]  Vcc
      AD14 [ 2        39 ]  AD15
      AD13 [ 3        38 ]  A16/S3
      AD12 [ 4        37 ]  A17/S4
      AD11 [ 5        36 ]  A18/S5
      AD10 [ 6        35 ]  A19/S6
       AD9 [ 7        34 ]  BHE/S7
       AD8 [ 8        33 ]  MN/MX
       AD7 [ 9        32 ]  RD
       AD6 [10  8086  31 ]  HOLD  (RQ/GT0)
       AD5 [11        30 ]  HLDA  (RQ/GT1)
       AD4 [12        29 ]  WR    (LOCK)
       AD3 [13        28 ]  M/IO  (S2)
       AD2 [14        27 ]  DT/R  (S1)
       AD1 [15        26 ]  DEN   (S0)
       AD0 [16        25 ]  ALE   (QS0)
       NMI [17        24 ]  INTA  (QS1)
      INTR [18        23 ]  TEST
       CLK [19        22 ]  READY
       GND [20        21 ]  RESET
```

Figure 2.3(a) 8086 Pin definitions.

device is manufactured using HMOS (high-performance metal oxide semiconductor) technology, and has approximately

22 The 8086 and Assembly Language

29,000 transistors. It can be considered to be a true 16-bit microprocessor because it has both a 16 bit internal data bus and a 16-bit external data bus. The device has two operating modes namely the minimum mode and

Common Signals

Name	Function	Type
AD15/AD0	Address/Data Bus	Bidirectional,3-State
A19/S6 AD16/S3	Address/ Status	Output,3-State
BHE/S7	Bus High Enable/ Status	Output,3-State
MN/MX	Minimum/Maximum Mode Control	Input
RD	Read Control	Output,3-State
TEST	Wait on Test Control	Input
READY	Wait State Control	Input
RESET	System Reset	Input
NMI	Non-Maskable Interrupt Request	Input
INTR	Interrupt Request	Input
CLK	System clock	Input
Vcc	+5V	Input
GND	Ground	

Minimum Mode Signals (MN/MX=Vcc)

HOLD	Hold Request	Input
HLDA	Hold Acknowledge	Output
WR	Write Control	Output,3-State
M/IO	Memory/IO Control	Output,3-State
DT/R	Data Transmit/Receive	Output,3-State
DEN	Data Enable	Output,3-State
ALE	Address Latch Enable	Output
INTA	Interrupt Acknowledge	Output

Maximum Mode Signals (MN/MX=GND)

RQ/GT1,0	Request/Grant Bus Access Control	Bidirectional
LOCK	Bus Priority Lock	Output,3-State
S2-S0	Bus Cycle Status	Output,3-State
QS1-QS0	Instruction Queue Status	Output

Figure 2.3(b) 8086 Pin signal assignments.

the maximum mode. The selection of the mode of operation is accomplished by the choice of logic level applied to pin 33 of the microprocessor which is labelled MN/MX. If this pin is held at logic '1' the minimum mode is selected and if it is held at logic '0' the maximum mode

8086 Architecture **23**

is chosen. As shown in figure 2.3(b), the assignments for eight of the pins on the microprocessor depend on the mode of operation selected, for example pin 29 provides a write control signal WR in the minimum mode of operation and a LOCK output signal in the maximum mode of operation.

Minimum Mode of Operation

The 8086 minimum mode of operation is for use in small systems where only a single microprocessor is employed. In this mode the microprocessor supplies the control signals for all memory and I/O devices within the system. Consequently in the minimum mode the 8086 is effectively operating a stand-alone mode. The signals from the 8086 can be arranged into the groups as follows: power and clock, address/data, control, interrupt and finally DMA. these groups are indicated in figure 2.4

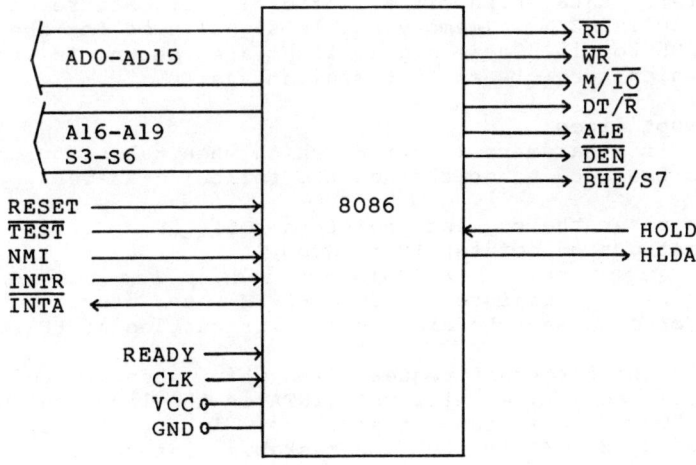

Figure 2.4 8086 Minimum mode block diagram.

Address/Data Lines
The 20 line address bus A0 to A19 provides the 8086 with a 1 MByte memory address capability. The 16 line data bus D0 to D15 provides 16 bit word transfer to and from memory. This is achieved by the simultaneous transfer of two 8 bit bytes from two separate banks of memory, this is shown diagrammatically in figures 6.9 to 6.12. The data bus is time division multiplexed with lines A0 to A15 of the address bus. Time division multiplexing implies that these 16 lines at one time transmit address information and at another time transfer data to or from the microprocessor.

Status lines
The status lines S3 to S6 are multiplexed with address

24 The 8086 and Assembly Language

lines A16 to A19. These signals occupy the lines at the same time as the data is transferred on the other multiplexed lines. S3 and S4 identify the segment register in use and S5 indicates the state of the internal interrupt enable flag.

Control lines
The read control line RD is taken to logic '0' by the microprocessor indicating that the data bus is being read. The data enable line DEN is used to inform external devices to apply data to the bus, and is used in conjunction with the read signal. ALE is the address latch enable pulse applied to external devices indicating that a valid address is on the bus and that the address should be latched on the trailing edge of the pulse. The type of bus cycle being operated by the microprocessor is indicated by the signals M/IO and DT/R. The M/IO signal is used to select either a memory device or an IO device. While the DT/R signal indicates the direction of the data transfer, data transmit at logic '1', or data receive at logic '0'. BHE is a memory enable signal used for the data lines D8 to D15. These signal lines are shown in figure 6.7, which depicts an 8086 minimum system.

Interrupt lines
RESET is a hardware interrupt which when taken to logic 0 causes the 8086 to go through the following stages:

(1) To reset the segment registers DS, SS, ES and the instruction pointer IP to 0000.
(2) To clear the flag registers and to set the control segment register to FFFFH so forcing the microprocessor to execute the instruction at FFFF0H.

INTR is the interrupt request line which when at logic '1' indicates an active interrupt. INTA is the line on which the 8086 indicates that the interrupt has been acknowledged. NMI is the non-maskable interrupt request input.
TEST is an input relating to the WAIT instruction.

Direct Memory Access - DMA
The direct memory access lines of the 8086 are HOLD and HLDA. Direct memory access is the process by which a peripheral device can access memory directly without interference from the microprocessor.

Maximum Mode of Operation

The maximum mode of operation is one designed for use in large systems, i.e. in a multi-processor or co-processor environment. In this case the 8086 microprocessor employs an 8288 bus controller to provide all bus control and command outputs. A multi-processor system is one which has more than one microprocessor each executing its own program. However to provide system operation the microprocessors communicate with each other via a commonly accessible memory. A co-processor system is one in which there is a another processor present but the two devices access the bus at separate times. The signals from the 8086 can be arranged into groups and these are shown in figure 2.5

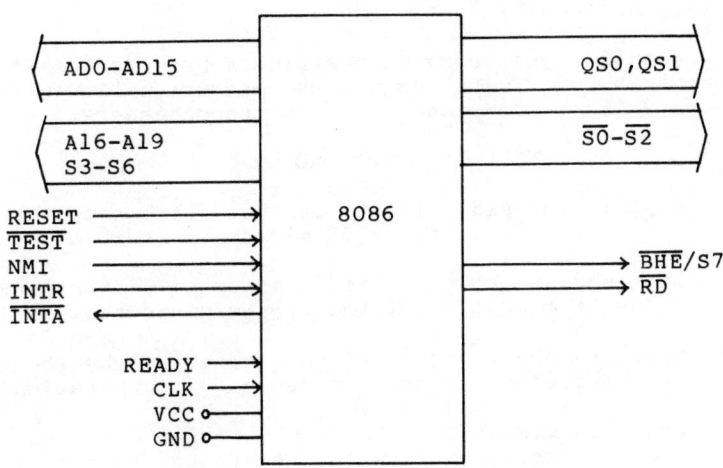

Figure 2.5 Maximum mode block diagram.

Bus Control Lines
Three status lines S0, S1,and S2 provide the external bus controller device, the 8288, with signals to identify the type of bus cycle to follow. The bus controller 8288 decodes the status signals and then generates timed command and control signals associated with the type of bus cycle requested. These status signals can also be taken to a bus arbiter device 8289, it is this device which facilitates the use of multiple processors in the maximum mode operation.

Queue Status Lines
The queue status outputs QS0 and QS1 form a code which in turn informs the external circuitry what happened in the queue during the last bus cycle, e.g. code 01 indicates that the byte taken from the queue was the first byte of an instruction.

8088 Microprocessor
The 8088 microprocessor is almost identical from an architectural point of view, and is identical from a

26 The 8086 and Assembly Language

programming point of view, to the 8086 microprocessor. The few differences which relate mainly to the 8 bit external data bus of the 8088 microprocessor are listed as follows:

(1) The 8088 microprocessor has an 8 bit external data bus. Therefore always accesses bytes both in memory and IO. So instructions are fetched one byte at a time.
(2) The 8088 microprocessor instruction queue holds only 4 bytes and its BIU fetches another byte whenever there is a byte empty in the queue.

The reason for producing a 16 bit microprocessor with an external 8 bit data bus was the provision of continuity between 8 bit systems and 16 bit microprocessors.

Questions

(2.1) Explain the significance of the instruction queue in the operation of the 8086 microprocessor.

(2.2) Distinguish between the minimum and the maximum modes of operation of the 8086 microprocessor.

(2.3) What are the control signals generated by the 8086 microprocessor in the minimum mode of operation?

(2.4) Draw a simplified block diagram of the 8086 microprocessor and with reference to the diagram explain the independent action of the BIU and the EU after the execution of a jump instruction.

CHAPTER 3
The 8086 instruction set

SYMBOLIC ADDRESSING

Assembly language instructions have a one-to-one relationship with machine code instructions, i.e. one machine code instruction is generated by each assembly language instruction. An assembler is a program which converts assembly language instructions to machine code instructions. The assembly language instruction format is:

   Label: Operation Mnemonic, Operand ;Comment

Using an assembler allows the programmer to use symbols for addresses and constants. Whereas programming in machine code necessitates the evaluation of absolute addresses. Many of the instruction examples used in explaining the instruction set involve symbols to represent addresses. For example the instruction CALL 0554H can in assembly language be written as CALL DELB where DELB is a symbolic address. Symbols are also used to represent the address of a data variable defined in the data segment, for example by the define word directive DW, as in NEWVAL DW 2233H. In this case the offset address of the variable is NVAL and the variable has the initial value 2233H. So the instruction ADD NEWVAL,CX means add the contents of register CX to the memory location whose offset address is NVAL, hence if CX contained 0122H this would be added to the value of the variable 2233H to produce a new value 2355H.
   When two operands are quoted in an 8086 instruction the first represents the destination operand and the second represents the source operand, in the above example the destination operand is memory location NEWVAL. In the instruction MOV CX,BX the source operand is the register BX and its contents are copied to CX the destination operand. In yet another example ADD CX,STVAL the source operand is at location STVAL and the contents of this location are added to the operand in the CX register, the destination of the sum is the CX register. When a relative address is used with a jump instruction the machine code

28 The 8086 and Assembly Language

programmer must evaluate the number of intervening locations required by the instruction. However, the assembler uses symbolic addressing and will automatically produce the required address. For example in the instruction NEXT: MOV DX,P1B the instruction address label is NEXT and another instruction such as JMP NEXT will automatically provide the correct address for the jump. Symbols are also used to represent constants ,this makes the reading of the program much easier. If the constant COUNT is defined as equal to 120 by the statement COUNT EQU 120, then the instruction MOV CX,COUNT will move the constant value 120 into the CX register. Whenever the assembler reads the symbol COUNT it will replace it by the constant 120.

The complete instruction set is presented in alphabetic order in this chapter. Each instruction is accompanied by a brief explanation of its operation. This enables the reader to have an organised readily available reference for every instruction. The format adopted in this listing is as follows:

(1) The instruction mnemonic is given in capital letters.
(2) A single line explaining its meaning is provided.
(3) Variations of the instruction in terms of the possible operands it can employ are given.
(4) A description of the action taken when the instruction is executed is next provided.
(5) The effect of the instruction on the flags is given using the notation shown below. No mention is made of flags for those instructions which do not affect the flags, or leave the flags undefined.
(6) The instruction times are quoted in terms of the number of clock periods which elapse during the instruction execution. For the instructions which have a large number of variations the minimum and maximum number of clock periods is given. The number of clock periods per instruction often refers to the time taken to evalute the effective memory address EA. A section on the evaluation of instruction execution times including the EA is given in Appendix C.
(7) An example (or examples) of the operation is provided.

Abbreviations used in the instruction set listing:
```
ac------------accumulator
data----------8 or 16 bits of immediate data
displ---------8 bit signed binary displacement.
displ 16------16 bit binary displacement.
mem-----------memory operand.
mem/reg-------memory or register operand.
reg-----------register operand.
segreg--------segment register operand.
```

Notation used for the effect on the flags:
  0 the flag is reset to zero.
  1 the flag is set to one.
  x the flag is set according to the instruction result.

ASSEMBLY LANGUAGE INSTRUCTION SET ALPHABETICAL LISTING

AAA ASCII adjust of addition result
This instruction is used in unpacked binary coded decimal (BCD) arithmetic. In the ASCII character code a BCD digit is represented by the least significant 4 bits of the byte and the most significant 4 bits contain 0011. This is a form of unpacked BCD representation. Unpacked BCD representation is that in which a byte represents a single binary digit. For example the ASCII representation of the decimal value 6 is 0011 0110 (36H), but the unpacked BCD representation is 0000 0110 . After binary addition, in which the result is in the AL register, the AAA instruction is used to adjust the result to the unpacked BCD format. Binary coded decimal notation, both packed and unpacked, is explained further in chapter 4.

```
Flags affected:    A  C     Clock periods
                   x  x          4
Example 3.1
      ADD   AL,CL
      AAA
      OR    AL,30H
```

Consider AX contains 0037H (00000000 00110111) and CX contains 0038H, the ASCII equivalents of decimal numbers 7 and 8 respectively. Then the ADD instruction leaves 6FH in AL (not the equivalent of decimal 15). The AAA instruction converts the value 006FH in AX to its BCD equivalent 0105H, i.e. the BCD representation of decimal 15. The instruction OR AL,30H restores the low byte to the ASCII character 35H in AL. A further instruction OR AH,30H will restore the high byte to the ASCII format 31H in upper register AH. The result is that AX now contains 3135H, the ASCII representation of decimal 15. (Note the ASCII code is given in table 4.7 and the character set in Appendix E).

AAD ASCII adjust of the AX register before division
This instruction is used when AX register contains two unpacked BCD operands, the most significant in AH and the least significant in AL. The instruction converts this data into its equivalent binary value and stores it in the AX register. The result can now be used in a division operation.

```
Flags affected:    S  Z  P     Clock periods
                   x  x  x          60
Example 3.2
      AAD
```

Consider register AX contains 0508H, i.e. the unpacked BCD representation of decimal 58. Then after execution of the instruction AAD it will contain the binary equivalent of decimal 58 which is represented by the hexadecimal number 003AH.

AAM ASCII adjust of multiplication result
This instruction is used when two unpacked BCD numbers have been multiplied and the result is in the AL register. It then converts this result to two unpacked BCD digits, placing the most significant digit in AH and the least significant digit in AL.

Flags affected: S Z C   Clock periods
                 x x x   83

Example 3.3
    MUL CL
    AAM

Consider AL contains 09H and CL contains 06H then after the MUL instruction AX contains 0036H, the binary equivalent of decimal 54. The instruction AAM converts this value to 0504H in the AX register, the unpacked BCD equivalent of decimal 54.

AAS ASCII adjust of subtraction result
After normal subtraction of two unpacked BCD digits and when the resulting difference is in the AL register, then the AAS instruction can be used to convert the result to unpacked BCD format.

Flags affected: A C   Clock periods
                 x x   4

Example 3.4
    SUB AL,CL
    AAS
    OR   AL,30H

Consider AL contains 33H (0011 0011) the ASCII equivalent of decimal 03, and CL contains 34H the ASCII equivalent of decimal 04. Then after the instruction SUB AL,CL has executed register AL will contain FFH. The instruction AAS will convert this to unpacked BCD format and AL will then contain 09H. This is now decimally correct for example consider a single column when decimal subtraction is taking place between two numbers, if 4 is subtracted from 3 the result in that column is 9. If it is further required to restore the ASCII character format, then the instruction OR AL,30H can be used to modify the contents to the ASCII character format 39H.

ADC Add with carry
The three variations of this instruction are:

ADC ac,data. Add with carry immediate data to the accumulator.

Instruction Set **31**

ADC mem/reg,data. Add with carry immediate data to a memory location or register.

ADC mem/reg1,mem/reg2.
Add with carry from - register to register
                    - register to memory
                    - memory to register

Considering the general form of this instruction to be :
ADC destination, source, then the instruction adds the two operands and the carry status and places the sum in the destination operand.

Flags affected: O S Z A P C   Clock periods
                 x x x x x x   3 to (17 + EA)
Example 3.5
        ADC AX,1127H
        ADC [SI],0123H
        ADC BX,CX
        ADC NEWVAL,CX ;NEWVAL is an address identifier
        ;for a variable defined in the data segment
        ADC CL,[SI]

Consider the example ADC AX,1127H and assume AX to contain 04A2H and the carry status to be 1 before the execution of the instruction. After the instruction has executed, the register AX will contain 15CAH and the flag setting will be:

                 O S Z A P C
                 0 0 0 0 1 0

ADD Integer Addition
The three variations of this instruction are:

ADD ac,data. Add immediate data to the accumulator.

ADD mem/reg,data. Add immediate data to a memory location or register.

ADD mem/reg1,mem/reg2. Add - register to register
                           - register to memory
                           - memory to register

Consider the general form as: ADD destination, source. The instruction adds two operands and places the sum in the destination operand. It can be an 8 bit or a 16 bit operation.

Flags affected: O S Z A P C   Clock periods
                 x x x x x x   3 to (17 + EA)
Example 3.6
        ADD AX,1127H
        ADD MAXIM, 0402H ;MAXIM is an address identifier
        ;for a variable in the data segment.

32 The 8086 and Assembly Language

```
ADD   [SI],0402H
ADD   CX,MAXIM
ADD   [DI + 124],BX
```

Consider the instruction ADD [SI],0402H and assume the word location pointed to by the source index register before the instruction is executed contains 2217H. After the instruction is executed this word memory location will contain 2619H and the flag setting will be:

```
O  S  Z  A  P  C
0  0  0  0  0  0
```

AND Logical AND
The three variations of this instruction are:

AND ac,data. AND immediate data with the accumulator contents.

AND mem/reg,data. AND immediate data with a memory location or register contents.

AND mem/reg1,mem/reg2. AND - register with register
                             - register with memory
                             - memory with register

Consider the general form as: AND destination, source. The instruction performs the AND operation on two operands and places the result in the destination operand. The operation may be on an 8 bit or 16 bit operand.

Flags affected: O S Z P C   Clock periods
                 0 x x x 0   3 to (17 + EA)

Example 3.7
```
AND   AX,3030H
AND   [BX],00FFH
AND   CL,BL
AND   MINIM,CX  ;MINIM is an address identifier
;for a word variable in the data segment
AND   CX,[BX + SI + 66]
```

A typical example of this instruction is AND [BX],00FFH. Assume the word location pointed to by the BX register contains 1727H before the instruction is executed. After the instruction is executed this word memory location will contain 0027H and the flag setting will be:

```
O  S  Z  P  C
0  0  0  1  0
```

CALL Call the subroutine specified
INTRA-SEGMENT CALL i.e. specified within the current code segment.

Instruction Set **33**

There are two variations of this instruction namely:

CALL displ 16. Call the subroutine whose address is specified by bytes two and three of the instruction.

CALL mem/reg. Call the subroutine specified by the memory location or register.

In the first variation of the instruction, the contents of the second and third bytes are considered as a 16 bit unsigned number and added to the IP contents to produce the target address. In the second variation the target address is specified by the operand. In both cases the current IP contents, i.e. address of the instruction, which follows the CALL instruction, is placed on the stack.

Clock periods 19 to (21 + EA)
Example 3.8
```
        ADC     AX,1432H
        CALL    DELB
        ADD     AX,BX
          -
 DELB:  PUSH    SI
        MOV     BX,[DI + 22]
```

In this example, after the CALL instruction has been executed the next instruction to be executed is PUSH SI the first instruction of the subroutine DELB. During the execution of an instruction the IP is incremented to point to the address of the next instruction. So that in this case it is the current IP contents, i.e. address of the instruction ADD AX,BX which is stored on the stack when the CALL instruction is executed. The colon after DELB is necessary to indicate an intrasegment or NEAR label.

CALL Call the subroutine specified
INTERSEGMENT CALL in which both offset and segment addresses are specified.
Again there are two variations:

CALL offset 16 seg addr 16. Call the subroutine whose offset address is specified by bytes two and three and whose segment address is specified by bytes four and five. Instruction bytes two and three are placed in the IP register, whereas bytes four and five are placed in the CS register.

CALL mem. Call the subroutine whose offset and segment register addresses are specified by the operand.

The operation takes place by replacing the values in both the IP and CS registers, so transferring control to another segment. Both the code segment address and the offset address of the instruction, which follows the CALL instruction, are stored on the stack.

34 The 8086 and Assembly Language

Clock periods   28 to (37 + EA)
Example 3.9
    CALL   DWORD PTR [SI]
    CALL   SROUT1

In the example CALL SROUT1, the subroutine SROUT1 must be designated as a FAR subroutine, so that the CALL instruction will save both IP and CS contents on the stack. The instruction CALL DWORD PTR [SI] will call a subroutine whose offset address is the word stored in the location pointed to by SI and whose segment address is the word stored in the location indicated by SI + 2. The assembler must be informed that SI must be pointing to a location designated as storing a double word, hence the use of the DWORD PTR within the instruction. The use of the assembler operator PTR is explained in chapter 5.

CBW   Convert byte to word, sign extending AL into AH
The accumulator data is converted from 8 to 16 bits, while the sign is maintained by placing FF in AH if the most significant bit in AL is 1, or by placing 00 in AH if it is 0.

Clock periods   2
Example 3.10
    CBW

Consider register AL contains an 8 bit signed number, e.g. 84H, before the instruction CBW is executed, after execution AH will contain FFH. In this case the negative number in the AL register has been extended to the same negative number in the AX register. Now a 16 bit multiplication instruction can be carried out.

CLC   Clear the carry flag
This instruction resets the carry flag to zero; it does not affect any other flags.

Flags affected: C = 0   Clock periods   2

CLD   Clear the direction flag
This instruction resets the direction flag to zero; it does not affect any other flags. When this flag is cleared the pointers are incremented during a repeated string instruction.

Flags affected: D = 0   Clock periods   2

CLI   Clear the interrupt enable flag
The interrupt flag is reset to zero by this instruction and so all maskable interrupts are disabled.

Flags affected: I = 0   Clock periods   2

Instruction Set 35

CMC   Complement the carry flag
The instruction changes the state of the carry flag, e.g. if it had been at 1 then the instruction would convert it to 0, and vice versa.

Flags affected: C = x   Clock periods   2

CMP   Compare Two Operands
The three variations of this instruction are:

CMP   ac,data.   Compare immediate data with the accumulator contents

CMP   mem/reg,data. Compare immediate data with a memory location or register contents

CMP   mem/reg1,mem/reg2. Compare - register with register
                                  - register with memory
                                  - memory with register

Consider the instruction to have the general form: CMP first operand, second operand. The comparison is carried out by subtracting the second operand from the first operand and the result is used to set the flags. Neither operand is affected by the operation, so the purpose of the operation is simply to set the flags. A comparison instruction is frequently followed by a conditional jump instruction.

Flags affected: O S Z A P C   Clock periods
                  x x x x x x   3 to (10 + EA)

Example 3.11

```
MEZZRO  DW    079BH ;Data definition
        -
        -
        CMP   AX,0180H
        CMP   MEZZRO,0A00H ;MEZZRO is an address identifier
                           ;for a word variable in the data segment
        CMP   BL,CL
        CMP   AX,DX
        CMP   [SI],BX
        CMP   BX,[SI + 286H]
```

As an example consider the instruction CMP BL,CL when register BL contains A4H and register CL contains 29H. The instuction effectively performs binary subtraction and the result causes the setting of the flags as shown:

$$A4H = 1010\ 0100$$
$$29H = 0010\ 1001$$

Subtraction result = 0111 1011

36 The 8086 and Assembly Language

From the result the flag setting is as follows:

C = 0 no carry out of most significant bit
P = 1 the number of one's in result is six, i.e. even
A = 1 carry from bit 3 to bit 4
Z = 0 the result is not zero
S = 0 most significant bit of result is zero

```
          O S Z A P C
          x 0 0 1 1 0
```

Consider a second example: CMP MEZZRO,0A00H. Assume that the word variable at location MEZZRO has the value 079BH; the instruction will subtract 0A00H from this value and without altering the value of the variable the result will be used to set the flags.

```
          079BH = 0000 0111 1001 1011
          0A00H = 0000 1010 0000 0000
```

Subtraction result = 1111 1101 1001 1011

From the result the flag setting is as follows:

C = 1 carry out of bit 15
P = 1 as the number of ones is twelve, i.e. even
A = 0 no carry from bit 3 to bit 4
Z = 0 the result is not zero
S = 1 most significant bit of result is 1
O = 1 carry into and out of bit 15

```
          O S Z A P C
          0 1 0 0 1 1
```

CMPS/CMPSB/CMPSW Compare memory contents with memory contents
This instruction compares the contents of the memory location in the ES extra segment addressed by the DI register with the contents of the memory location in the DS data segment addressed by the SI register. The contents of these locations remain unaffected by the comparison. The SI and DI registers are incremented or decremented depending on the setting of the DF direction flag as 0 or 1 respectively. The value in these registers is changed by one for a byte instruction and by two for a word instruction.

Flags affected: O S Z A P C   Clock periods
                 x x x x x x   22

Instruction Set 37

Example 3.12

```
    CMPSW
    CMPSB
```

Suppose that before the execution of CMPSW the state of the registers is as follows: DS = 0A00H, SI = 0048H, ES = 0B40H, DI = 0066H and DF = 0. Consider that the word stored at location 0A048H is 3B97H and the word stored at 0B466H is 4880H; then the instruction will carry out the following subtraction:

```
            3B97H = 0011 1011 1001 0111
            4880H = 0100 1000 1000 0000

        Difference = 1111 1011 0001 0111
```

From this result the flag setting is as follows:

C = 1 carry out of bit 15
P = 0 the number of ones in result is eleven
A = 0 no carry from bit 3 to bit 4
Z = 0 result not zero
S = 1 most significant bit of result is 1
O = 0 carry into and out of bit 15

```
            O  S  Z  A  P  C
            0  1  0  0  0  1
```

CWD Convert word to doubleword, sign extending AX into DX.
The accumulator 16 bit data is converted into 32 bits, while the sign is maintained by placing FFFFH in DX if the most significant bit in AX is 1, or by placing 0000H in DX if it is 0.

Clock periods 5
Example 3.13

```
        MOV  DX,0000H
        MOV  AX,8000H
        CWD
```

In this example, the most significant bit in the register AX before execution of CWD is at 1, so after the execution of the instruction CWD register DX will contain FFFFH, maintaining the sign into the 32 bit number.

DAA Decimal Adjust of Accumulator contents after addition
When two packed BCD numbers are added using ADD or ADC, and the result is in the AL register, then DAA is used to convert that result into packed BCD format.

38 The 8086 and Assembly Language

Flags affected: O   S   Z   A   P   C   Clock periods
                 x   x   x   x   x   x   4

Example 3.14
    ADD   AL,CL
    DAA

If before the addition instruction register AL contains 47H (0100 0111) the packed BCD equivalent of decimal 47, and register CL contains 47H, again the packed BCD equivalent of decimal 47, then after binary addition instruction ADD AL,CL is executed register AL contains 8EH which is the binary equivalent of decimal 142 - obviously not the required result, i.e. it is not in BCD format. The DAA instruction converts this result to 94H (1001 0100) which is the packed BCD representation of decimal 94. If in the lower four bits the value is greater than 9 or if the auxiliary carry flag AF is set, then the instruction adds 06 to produce the correct decimal digit. If in the high order four bits the value is greater than 9 or carry flag CF is set, then the instruction adds 60H.

DAS Decimal Adjust of accumulator after Subtraction
When two packed BCD numbers are subtracted using SUB or SBB, and the result is in the AL register, then DAS is used to convert that result into packed BCD format.

Flags affected: S   Z   A   P   C   Clock periods
                 x   x   x   x   x   4

Example 3.15
    SUB   AL,CL
    DAS

If before the subtraction register AL contains 74H and this represents a packed BCD number equivalent to decimal 74, and register CL contains 25H equivalent to decimal 25, then after the subtraction AL contains 4FH which is not the required equivalent decimal result. This result is not in BCD format but is converted to such by the use of the instruction DAS; the result then becomes 49H, the packed BCD equivalent of decimal 49. The instruction DAS acts as follows: if the lower four bits have a value greater than 9 or if AF is set then DAS subtracts 06H from the result. Also, if the upper four bits have a value greater than 9 or CF is set then the instruction subtracts 60H, thus achieving a packed BCD format.

DEC Decrement the operand
There are two variations of this instruction:

DEC   reg. Decrement a 16 bit register.

DEC   mem/reg. Decrement the contents of a memory location or register. This can be an 8 bit or 16 bit operation.

Instruction Set

This instruction causes 1 to be subtracted from the specified operand.

Flags affected: O S Z A P   Clock periods
                 x x x x x   2 to (15 + EA)

Example 3.16
```
BIOPH   DW    23000
        DEC   BX
        DEC   BIOPH ;BIOPH is an address identifier
              ;for a variable in the data segment.
        DEC   [SI + BX + 138H]
```

Consider the instruction DEC CX when register CX contains 4A00H. After execution of the instruction CX will contain 49FFH.

DIV Division of unsigned numbers
The two variations of this instruction are:

DIV AX by mem/reg
DIV DX:AX by mem/reg

As indicated by the instruction, either an 8 bit or a 16 bit operation occurs. In the 8 bit operation the AX register contents are divided by an 8 bit operand from a memory location or register, and the 8 bit quotient is stored in the AL register while the 8 bit remainder is stored in the AH register. In the 16 bit operation the doubleword in the DX:AX register is divided by a 16 bit operand from a memory location or register. The quotient is stored in the AX register and the 16 bit remainder is stored in the DX register. If the dividend and the divisor are both 16 bits in length then the dividend is first extended to 32 bits by using the CWD instruction.

In either of these cases, if the quotient is too large for the designated register then a type 0 interrupt is generated. This will allow the overflow to be accommodated.

Flag values are undetermined after a division instruction.

Clock periods 80 to (96 + EA) and 144 to (168 + EA)
Example 3.17
```
        MOV   AX,105
        CWD
        MOV   CX,24
        DIV   CX
```

In this case, where register AX contains 0069H, the equivalent of decimal 105, it is converted to a doubleword by CWD, which ensures that DX will contain 0000H. Also, register CX contains 0018, the equivalent of decimal 24. After the instruction DIV CX has executed the AX contains the quotient 0003H and DX contains the remainder 0009H.

40 The 8086 and Assembly Language

ESC Escape to coprocessor
ESC   mem
This instruction allows other processors to receive their instructions from the 8086 instruction stream and to use the 8086 addressing modes. The contents of the memory location, specified in the instruction, are placed on the data bus.

Clock periods   2 to (8 + EA)

HLT Halt the microprocessor
This instruction causes the microprocessor operations to stop. A reset or external interrupt will initiate restart.

Clock periods   2

IDIV Division of signed numbers
The two variations of this instruction are:

IDIV   AX by mem/reg
IDIV   DX:AX by mem/reg

As indicated by the instruction, either an 8 bit or a 16 bit signed binary operation occurs. In the 8 bit operation the AX register contents are divided by an 8 bit operand from a memory location or register, and the 8 bit quotient is stored in the AL register while the 8 bit remainder is stored in the AH register. In the 16 bit operation the doubleword in the DX:AX register is divided by a 16 bit operand from a memory location or register. The quotient is stored in the AX register and the 16 bit remainder is stored in the DX register. If the dividend and the divisor are both the same length then the dividend is first extended. For a byte operation the extension is to 16 bits by using the CWB instruction, and for a word operation to 32 bits by using the CWD instruction.
   In either of these cases, if the quotient is too large for the designated register, then a type 0 interrupt is generated. This will allow the overflow to be accommodated.
   Flag values are undetermined after a division instruction.

Clock periods   110 to (118 + EA) and 165 to (190 + EA)
Example 3.18
        MOV   AL,F3H
        CBW
        MOV   CL,04H
        IDIV CL

In this example, as register AL contains F3H (equivalent to decimal -13), on execution of CBW the upper half of the accumulator register AH will contain FFH, the signed number F3H has been extended to the signed number FFF3H.

Instruction Set **41**

Register CL contains a positive number 04H (equivalent to decimal +04) as a result of the move instruction. Then after IDIV CL has been executed the register AL contains FDH (equivalent to decimal -3) and register AH contains the remainder FFH, the equivalent of decimal -1.

IMUL   Multiplication of signed numbers
The two variations of this instruction are:

IMUL AL by mem/reg
IMUL AX by mem/reg

As indicated by the instruction either an 8 bit or a 16 bit signed binary operation takes place. In the 8 bit operation the AL register contents are multiplied by an 8 bit operand, from a memory location or register, and the word result is stored in AX. In the 16 bit operation the AX register contents are multiplied by a 16 bit operand, from a memory location or register, and the doubleword product is stored in the DX:AX register combination.

Flags affected: O C   Clock periods
                 x x   80 to (160 + EA)
Example 3.19
     MOV AL,04H
     MOV CL,0FFH
     IMUL CL

When registers AL and CL contain respectively 04H and FFH, then after execution of IMUL CL the contents of AX will be FFFCH. The decimal equivalents of these signed twos complement numbers are +4, -1 and -4 respectively and multiplying 4 by -1 results in -4.

IN   Input byte or word to the accumulator
There are two variations of this instruction namely:

IN ac,DX. Input to the accumulator from the port specified by DX.

IN ac,port. Input to the accumulator from the port specified in the instruction.

This instruction causes a byte or word to be transferred from a port to the accumulator.

Clock periods 8 and 10
Example 3.20
     IN AL,DX
     IN AX,22H

For the instruction IN AL,DX if the DX register contains 0FFF9H and port 0FFF9H has an I/O buffer containing 4A20H then after execution of the instruction AX contains 4A20H.

42 The 8086 and Assembly Language

INC Increment the operand
The two variations of the instruction are:

INC   reg. Increment a 16 bit register.

INC   mem/reg. Increment the contents of memory location or register. This can be an 8 bit or 16 bit operation.

This instruction causes 1 to be added to the specified operand.

Flags affected: O S Z A P   Clock periods
                 x x x x x   2 to (15 + EA)
Example 3.21
     INC CX
     INC MEXXD ;MEXXD is an address identifier

Consider the instruction INC CX when register CX contains 26FFH. After execution of the instruction register CX will contain 2700H.

INT Software Interrupt
INT type
In this instruction the microprocessor pushes the flag register contents onto the stack, and clears the interrupt flag IF and the trap flag TF. It then performs an indirect call in which the 2nd byte of the machine instruction is utilised. This involves placing the CS contents onto the stack and loading the CS register with a new value loc1 where loc1 = (2nd byte * 4) + 2; then placing the IP contents onto the stack and loading the IP with a new value loc2 where loc2 = (2nd byte * 4). The address to which the call is directed is given by loc1 and loc2 and is known as a vector.

Flags affected: I T   Clock periods
                 0 0   51 or 52
Example 3.22
     INT 32
     INT 34

In the example INT 34 the interrupt vector type number is 34. The instruction when executed causes flags CS and IP to be saved, clears IF and TF, then transfers control to the vector routine, the IP address of which is stored in location 00088H and the code segment address of which is stored in next word location 0008AH. This is further explained in chapter 7, where table 7.4 shows the interrupt vectors.

INTO Software interrupt
This is a variation of the INT instruction, which performs a type 4 interrupt when the overflow flag OF = 1. If the OF is clear then no action is taken.

Clock periods   53 or 4

Instruction Set **43**

IRET   Return from interrupt
This instruction returns control to the program which had been interrupted. The instruction transfers the top two bytes of stack to IP, the next two bytes to CS and the next two bytes to the flag register, so restoring to these registers the values which were saved when the interrupt occured.

Clock periods   24

Jump On Condition Instructions
In the list of conditional instructions below those which are paired are identical. The different mnemonics apply to alternative interpetations of the same instruction.

JA	Jump if above / **JNBE** Jump if neither below nor equal
JAE	Jump if above or equal / **JNB** Jump if not below
JB	Jump if below / **JNAE** Jump if neither above nor equal
JBE	Jump if below or equal / **JNA** Jump not above
JC	Jump if carry is set
JCXZ	Jump if CX register is zero
JE	Jump if equal / **JZ** Jump if zero
JG	Jump if greater / **JNLE** Jump if neither less nor equal
JGE	Jump if greater or equal / **JNL** Jump not less than
JL	Jump if less / **JNGE** Jump if neither greater nor equal
JLE	Jump if less or equal / **JNG** Jump not greater than
JNC	Jump if no carry
JNE	Jump if not equal / **JNZ** Jump if not zero
JNO	Jump if no overflow
JNP	Jump if no parity / **JPO** Jump if parity odd
JNS	Jump if no sign (jump if positive)
JO	Jump if overflow is set
JP	Jump if parity is set / **JPE** Jump if parity even
JS	Jump if sign is set

The conditional jump machine code instructions have as a second byte a signed displacement, the value of which is added to the IP to obtain the destination address. So the range of the conditional jump is 127 bytes ahead and 126 bytes behind the instruction.

These instructions test a combination of flags for a particular condition, except for JCXZ which tests the CX register. If this condition holds then a jump occurs, otherwise the next instruction is executed. Hence they usually follow a flag setting instruction such as a compare instruction. When a conditional jump follows a compare instruction, which has a first operand and a second operand, the condition refers to the first operand. For example, if the instruction is JL, then a jump will take place if the first operand is less than the second, for JGE a jump will occur if the first operand is greater than or equal to the second operand.

Clock periods   16 or 4   (JCX 18 or 4)

44 The 8086 and Assembly Language

Example 3.23
```
      CMP  AX,[SI]
      JG   NEXL
       -
       -
       -
NEXL: MOV  CX,[SI]
```

If in this case AX contains 04AAH and the word location pointed to by SI contains 04A9H, then the JG instruction will cause a jump to the location whose label is NEXL.

```
NEWM: MOV  AX,OAOAH
       -
       -
       -
      AND  AX,[SI + 2]
      JZ   NEWM
```

In this example, if the result of the logical AND between the contents of AX and the contents of the location pointed to by SI + 2 is zero, then the conditional jump instruction JZ will cause a jump to the location whose label is NEWM. Otherwise the next instruction will be executed.

JMP   Jump to the location specified
INTRA-SEGMENT JMP, i.e. specified within the current code segment
There are three variations of this instruction namely:

JMP displ. Jump to the location whose address is formed by adding the contents of the second byte, an 8 bit signed number, to the IP plus 2.

JMP displ 16. Jump to the location whose address is specified by bytes two and three of the instruction.

JMP mem/reg. Jump to the location specified by the memory location or register.

In the first variation, the contents of the second byte are considered as a signed 8 bit displacement to be added to the IP contents plus 2 to produce the target address. In the second variation of the instruction, the contents of the second and third bytes are considered as a 16 bit unsigned number and added to the IP contents to produce the target address. In the third variation the target address is specified by the operand.

Clock periods 15 to (18 + EA)
Example 3.24
```
      SUB  AX,1132H
      JMP  BECO
```

Instruction Set 45

```
          ADD     AX,BX
BECO:   PUSH    AX
          MOV     BX,[DI + 22]
```

In this example the instruction which will be executed after the jump instruction is PUSH AX. The colon after BECO is necessary to indicate an intrasegment or NEAR label

JMP Jump to the location specified
INTERSEGMENT JUMP in which both offset and segment addresses are specified
There are two variations:

JMP offset 16 seg addr 16. Jump to the location whose offset address is specified by bytes two and three and whose segment address is specified by bytes four and five. Instruction bytes two and three are placed in the IP register, whereas bytes four and five are placed in the CS register.

JMP mem. Jump to the location whose offset and segment register addresses are specified by the operand.

The operation takes place by replacing the values in both the IP and CS registers, so transferring control to another segment. In each case the target location must be given a label whose type is FAR rather than NEAR. This is explained in the chapter 5 dealing with assembly language.

Clock periods   15 to (24 + EA)
Example 3.25
```
          JMP     DOWNL
          JMP     DWORD PTR [SI]
```

In this example the first JMP instruction will jump to a location which has been labelled as type FAR. Hence a new code segment address and a new offset address will be placed in the registers CS and IP respectively; these addresses relate to the name DOWNL. The second JMP instruction will jump to a location whose offset address is the word stored in the location pointed to by SI and whose segment address is the word stored in the location indicated by SI + 2.

LAHF Load AH register with low byte of flag register
This instruction transfers the low order 8 bits of the flag register into the high byte of the accumulator in the following format: 7 6 5 4 3 2 1 0
                                   S Z - A - P - C
Clock periods   4

46 The 8086 and Assembly Language

LDS/LES   Load register and segment register DS/ES

LDS   reg,mem
LES   reg/mem

These instructions cause the specified memory word to be loaded into the designated register and the memory word following the specified word to be loaded into the DS or ES registers.

Clock periods   16 + EA
Example 3.26
DOTTR   DD   01234H,8899H
          -
          LDS   SI,[0120H]
          LES   DI,DOTTR ;DOTTR is the address of a
          ;double word variable in the data segment

On the execution of the LDS SI,[0120H] instruction the registers SI and DS will be loaded with the contents of the word locations whose offset addresses in the data segment are 0120H and 0122H respectively. Hence if the DS register initially contained 2020H then the contents of word location 20320H would be placed in SI and the contents of word location 20322H would be placed in the DS register; whereas on the execution of LES DI,DOTTR the first word of the variable is placed in the DI register and the second word in the ES register.

LEA   Load effective address of memory operand
LEA reg/mem. Load the specified register with the 16 bit offset address of the specified memory operand.

Clock periods   2 + EA
Example 3.27
STAR   DW   120H
         -
         -
         LEA BX,STAR

The offset address of the data variable of value 120 is given by the identifier STAR, it is this address which is placed in the BX register. Another method of loading the offset address is to use the assembler operator OFFSET, an example of this is given in the instruction:
MOV BX, OFFSET STAR.

LOCK   Assert Bus Lock
This is a one byte prefix which can precede any instruction. It is used to cause the 8086 microprocessor to output its LOCK signal low, for the duration of the next instruction. This is an instruction prefix used in multiple processor systems sharing a particular resource e.g. a data bank. It ensures that the resource is only

Instruction Set 47

available to the 8086 microprocessor whose instruction carries the prefix.

Clock periods 2

LODS/LODSB/LODSW Load memory contents into accumulator. This instruction causes the contents of the memory location pointed to by the SI register to be loaded into the accumulator. The source index register is then incremented or decremented depending on the setting of the DF direction flag as 0 or 1. For a word instruction, the AX register is loaded and the index register is changed by 2. For a byte instruction it is the AL register which is loaded and the index register is changed by 1. This instruction does not affect the flag registers.

Clock periods 12
Example 3.28
    LODSB
    LODSW

Suppose that before the execution of LODSW the state of the registers is as follows: AX = 5555, DS = 0060, SI = 0048 and DF = 1. If the word stored at 00648 is 3B97H then after the instruction has executed the register state will be AX = 3B97, DS = 0060, SI = 0046 and DF = 1.

LOOP Decrement CX, jump if CX non-zero
LOOPE/LOOPZ Decrement CX, jump if CX non-zero and ZF=1
LOOPNE/LOOPNZ Decrement CX, jump if CX non-zero and ZF=0
Before these instructions are used an unsigned number must be placed in the CX register to act as an iteration count. When the loop instruction is executed the CX register is decremented and a branch to the target location takes place, if the condition specified is true; otherwise, the next instruction is executed. These machine instructions have as a second byte a signed displacement similar to the conditional jump instructions.

```
                    LOOP      LOOPZ     LOOPNZ
Clock periods     17 or 5    18 or 6   19 or 5
```

Example 3.29
    DLOAD   LODSB
    -
    -
    CMP   [BP]
    LOOPNZ   DLOAD

In this example the loop will be repeated until the BX register has been decremented to 0 and the zero flag is not set.

48 The 8086 and Assembly Language

MOV Move data
There are seven variations of this instruction:

MOV   mem/reg1,mem/reg2. Move register or memory location contents to or from register.

MOV   reg,data. Move immediate data into register.

MOV   mem/reg,data. Move immediate data to a memory location or register.

MOV   ac,mem. Move memory location contents into accumulator.

MOV   mem,ac. Move accumulator contents to a memory location.

MOV   segreg,mem/reg. Move memory location or register contents to a segment register.

MOV   mem/reg,segreg. Move segment register contents to a memory location or a register.

The instruction general form is: MOV destination, source. The instruction copies the source operand to the destination operand. These instructions do not affect the flags.

Clock periods 2 to (10 + EA)
Example 3.30
        MOV   CL,AH
        MOV   BX,0889H
        MOV   VARY1,2076
        MOV   AX,LOTT
        MOV   LOCO,AX
        MOV   ES,CX
        MOV   BX,DS

In these instruction examples, VARY1, LOTT and LOCO are identifiers for the offset addresses of word variables in the data segment of memory.

MOVS/MOVSB/MOVSW Move memory contents from location to location
This instruction causes the contents of the memory location pointed to by the SI register in the data segment to be moved to the memory location pointed to by the DI register in the extra segment. The source index and destination index registers are then incremented or decremented depending on the setting of the DF direction flag as 0 or 1. For a word instruction the index registers are changed by two. For a byte instruction the index registers are changed by one. This instruction does not affect the flag registers.

Clock periods 18 to 28

Instruction Set **49**

Example 3.31
   MOVSW

Suppose that before the execution of of MOVSW the state of the registers is as follows: DS = 0000H, SI = 0048H, ES = 0B00H, DI = 0120H and DF = 1. If the word stored at 00048H is 4A79H then after the instruction has executed the register state will be DS = 0000H, SI = 0046H, ES = 0B00H, DI = 011EH, DF = 1 and the word stored at 0B120H will now be 4A79H. This instruction is usually used with the loop instructions.

MUL Multiplication of unsigned numbers
The two variations of the instruction are:

MUL   AL by mem/reg
MUL   AX by mem/reg

As indicated by the operand in the instruction either an 8 bit or a 16 bit operation occurs. In the 8 bit operation the AL register contents are multiplied by an 8 bit operand from a memory location or a register and the resultant product word is stored in the AX register. In the 16 bit operation the AX register contents are multiplied by a 16 bit operand from memory or register and the double word product is stored in the DX:AX register combination. In each case the CF and OF flags will be set to 1 if the product is larger than the operands producing it, e.g. if the product of an 8 bit multiplication is larger than a single byte then the flags are set to 1.

Flags affected: O C   Clock periods
                  x x   70 to (139 + EA)

Example 3.32
   MUL   CX

Consider the AX register to contain 8000H and the CX register 0003H before execution of the instruction; then after execution the DX and AX registers will contain respectively 0003H and 0018H, the result being 00180003H.

NEG Negate the contents of a memory location or register
NEG mem/reg
This instruction forms the two's complement of the indicated operand. It then replaces it with this new value i.e. with the negative of the original operand. The operation can be either in 8 bit or 16 bit format.

Flags affected: O S Z A P   Clock periods
                  x x x x x   3 or (16 + EA)

Example 3.33
   NEG   WN014

Consider that, before these instructions are carried out, the register AL contains 04H and the variable, whose location in the data segment is given by WN014, has the

50 The 8086 and Assembly Language

value FFFEH. After execution of the instructions the AL register contains FCH and the variable at WN014 has the value 0002H. It is immediately apparent that the sign of each operand has changed as the most significant bit of each operand has changed. The new operands are the negatives of the initial values using the signed twos complement notation.

NOP No operation
No operation is performed. The code which is 90H occupies a byte and only affects the instruction pointer IP. It is often used to pad out sections of a program.

Clock periods 3

NOT Formation of the ones complement of the operand specified.

NOT mem/reg
This instruction complements the contents of the specified operand.

Clock periods 3 or (16 + EA)
Example 3.34
    NOT   CX

Consider CX to contain 14E5H before execution of the instruction, then afterwards it will contain EB1AH.

OR Logical OR
The three variations of this instruction are:

OR   ac,data. OR immediate data with the accumulator contents.

OR mem/reg,data. OR immediate data with a memory or register contents.

OR   mem/reg1,mem/reg2. OR - register with register
                                             - register with memory
                                             - memory with register

Consider the general form as: OR destination, source. The instruction performs the OR operation on two operands and places the result in the destination operand. The operation may be on an 8 bit or 16 bit operand.

Flags affected: O S Z P C   Clock periods
                       0 x x x 0   3 to (17 + EA)
Examples 3.35
      OR   AX,3000H
      OR   BL,CL
      OR   [DI + 22],CX
      OR   CX,[BX + SI + 4]

Instruction Set **51**

```
    OR  WESTH,0F51H ;WESTH is address identifier
                   ;for a variable in the data segment
```

A typical example is: OR WESTH,0F51H. Assume the word variable located at WESTH has the value 10A6H before the instruction is executed. After the instruction is executed the new value of the variable will be 1FF7H and the flag setting will be:

```
              O  S  Z  P  C
              0  0  0  1  0
```

OUT Output byte or word from the accumulator
There are two variations of this instruction namely:

OUT DX,ac. Output from the accumulator to the port specified by DX.

OUT port,ac. Output from the accumulator to the port specified in the instruction.

This instruction causes a byte or word to be transferred from the accumulator to the port. The flags are not affected by this instruction.

Clock periods 8 or 10
Example 3.36
```
      OUT  DX,AL
      OUT  22H,AX
```

For the instruction OUT DX,AL if the DX register contains 0FFF9H and the AL register contains 37H then after execution of the instruction the port 0FFF9H I/O buffer will contain 37H.

POP Transfer a word from the top of the stack
The three variations of this instruction are:

POP reg. The word on the top of the stack is transferred to a register.

POP segreg. The word on the top of the stack is transferred to a segment register.

POP mem/reg. The word on the top of the stack is transferred to a memory location.

The top two bytes of stack replace the register or memory location contents, and the stack pointer is incremented by two. The third variation is used to pop data into memory locations in the data segment and not into registers.

Clock periods 8 to (17 + EA)

52 The 8086 and Assembly Language

Example 3.37
```
        POP    CX
        POP    DS
        POP    NVAL   ;NVAL is an address identifier
               ;for a word variable in the data segment
```

A typical example is : POP CX. Assume the contents of the registers are CX = 0808H, SS = 0A00H, SP = 0140H and the contents of the stack locations 0A140H and 0A13FH are 22H and 44H respectively. Then after the execution of the instruction CX will contain 4422H and SP = 013EH. A diagrammatic representation of the action of this instruction is given in chapter 4.

POPF Transfer a word from the top of the stack to the flags register
The top byte of the stack is transferred to the low byte of the flag register and the next stack byte to the high byte of the flag register. The stack pointer is incremented by two.

Clock periods   8

PUSH Transfer a word to the top of the stack
The three variations of this instruction are:

PUSH   reg. The word in the register is transferred onto the top of the stack.

PUSH   segreg. The word in the segment register is transferred onto the top of the stack.

PUSH   mem/reg. The word in the memory location is transferred onto the top of the stack.

The register or memory location contents are placed on the stack, and the stack pointer is decremented by two. The third variation is used to push data from memory locations and not from registers.

Clock periods   10 to (16 + EA)
Example 3.38
```
        PUSH   BX
        PUSH   ES
        PUSH   [DI + 16]
```

A typical example is: PUSH BX. Assume the contents of the registers are BX = 0448H, SS = 0A00H, SP = 0136H, then after the instruction is executed the contents of the stack locations 0A137H and 0A138H are 04H and 48H respectively and SP = 0138H. A diagrammatic representation of the action of this instruction is given in chapter 4.

Instruction Set **53**

PUSHF Transfer the word from the flags register to the top of the stack.
The stack pointer is incremented by 2 and the top two bytes of the stack store the flags register contents.

Clock periods 10

RCL Rotate left through carry
RCL mem/reg,count. Rotate the memory location or register contents left through carry.
This instruction causes the contents of the memory location or register to be rotated left through carry by 1 or by the count number contained in the CL register. The instruction can specify either an 8 bit or a 16 bit operand.

Flags affected: O C   Clock periods
                 x x   2 to (20 + EA)
Example 3.39
      RCL   AL,1
      RCL   AX,CL

In the example RCL AX,CL consider, before execution of the instruction, the register contents to be AX = 70F2H, CF = 1 and CL = 03H. Then after the instruction has been carried out AX = 8795H and CL = 1.

RCR Rotate right through carry
RCR mem/reg,count. Rotate the memory location or register contents right through carry.
This instruction causes the contents of the memory location or register to be rotated right through carry by 1 or by the count number contained in the CL register. The instruction can specify either an 8 bit or a 16 bit operand.

Flags affected: O C   Clock periods
                 x x   2 to (20 + EA)
Examples 3.40
      RCR   BX,CL
      RCR   BL,1
      RCR   WHU11,1 ;WHU11 is an address identifier

In the example RCR BX,CL consider, before execution of the instruction, the register contents to be BX = 70F2H, CF = 1 and CL = 03H. Then after the instruction has been carried out BX = AE1EH and C = 0.

REP Repeat prefix used with string instructions
REP/REPE/REPZ
REPNE/REPNZ
These prefixes cause the following string instructions to be repeated until the count value in the CX register reaches zero.

Clock periods 2

54 The 8086 and Assembly Language

Example 3.41
```
      REP     MOVSW
      -
      -
REPZ  CMPSB
```

Consider the first of these examples REP MOVSW. The string operation is preceded by the prefix and the result, a re-executing loop, has been initialised. REP causes the string operation to repeat itself until CX is zero. The CX register is automatically decremented by REP.
REPZ and REPNZ are variations of the prefix used with the string instructions CMPS and SCAS. They cause the string operation to repeat itself until CX is zero or the ZF flag is 0 or 1 respectively.

RET Return from subroutine
RET   displ 16   Return from subroutine and add to stack pointer
This instruction transfers control from the subroutine back to the program which called it. When the return is within a segment the top two bytes of the stack are placed in the IP register. When the return is between segments (intersegment) the top two bytes of the stack are placed in the IP and the next bytes in the CS register. The assembler will differentiate between these two returns automatically. If within the instruction there are two further bytes stipulated as a displacement then at execution, after the IP and CS values have been obtained from the stack, these two bytes are added to the stack pointer. The result of adding to the stack pointer is to move it past entries placed on the stack prior to the call instruction. This allows a set of values to be passed to the subroutine, used by the subroutine and then to be effectively discarded on return to the calling program.

Clock periods 8 to 18

ROL Rotate left
ROL   mem/reg,count. Rotate the memory location or register contents left
This instruction causes the contents of the memory location or register to be rotated left by 1 or by the count number contained in the CL register. The instruction can specify either an 8 bit or a 16 bit operand.

Flags affected: O C   Clock periods
                  x x   2 to (20 + EA)

Example 3.42
```
      ROL    AX,CL
      ROL    NUMBW,CL  ;NUMBW is an address of
      ;a variable in the data segment.
      ROL    AL,1
```

Instruction Set **55**

In the example, ROL NUMBW,CL consider, before execution of the instruction, the memory variable, whose address is given by NUMBW, to have the value 70F2H, and the register contents to be CF = 1 and CL = 03H. Then after the instruction has been carried out the memory variable will be 8793H and register CF = 1.

ROR Rotate right
ROR mem/reg,count. Rotate the memory location or register contents right
This instruction causes the contents of the memory location or register to be rotated right by 1 or by the count number contained in the CL register. The instruction can specify either an 8 bit or a 16 bit operand.

Flags affected: O C   Clock periods
                 x x   2 to (20 + EA)
Example 3.43
        ROR   BX,CL
        ROR   NUMBV,1 ;NUMBV is an address of
        ;a variable in the data segment.
        ROR   BL,1

In the example ROR BX,CL consider, before execution of the instruction, the register contents to be BX = 70F2H, CF = 1 and CL = 03H. Then after the instruction has been carried out the register contents will be BX = 4E1EH and C = 0.

SAHF Store AH register contents in the low byte of flag register
This instruction copies the contents of the AH register into the low order flag register in the following format:

 Bit7 Bit6 Bit5 Bit4 Bit3 Bit2 Bit1 Bit0
  SF   ZF   --   AF   --   PF   --   CF

Flags affected: S Z A P C   Clock periods
                 r r r r r   4
(r implies restored from previously saved value)
Example 3.44
        LAHF
        PUSH AX
        -
        POP AX
        SAHF

This example illustrates the method that can be used to store the flag register contents on the stack. LAHF transfers the flag contents to the AH register; this is then pushed onto the stack. At a later time the stack contents are popped back to the AH register and then copied to the flags using SAHF.

SAL/SHL Arithmetic/Logical shift left
SAL/SHL   mem/reg,count. Shift the memory location or register contents left
This instruction causes the contents of the memory location or register to be shifted left by 1 or by the count number contained in the CL register; zeros are shifted into the least significant bit. The instruction can specify either an 8 bit or a 16 bit operand.

Flags affected: O   C   Clock periods
                  x   x   2 to (20 + EA)
Example 3.45
         SAL   AX,CL
         SHL   [SI],1
         SAL   NVAL,CL ;NVAL is an address identifier
         ;of a variable in the data segment.

In the example SAL NVAL,CL consider, before execution of the instruction, the memory contents to be 62E2H, and the register contents to be CF = 0 and CL = 02H. Then after the instruction has been carried out the memory contents will be AX = 9B88H and register CF = 1. It is worth noting that this instruction has caused the value of the memory variable to be multiplied by four.

SAR Arithmetic shift right
SAR   mem/reg,count. Shift the memory location or register contents right
This instruction causes the contents of the memory location or register to be shifted right by 1 or by the count number contained in the CL register. Bits equal to the most significant bit are shifted in from the left, so maintaining the sign. The instruction can specify either an 8 bit or a 16 bit operand.

Flags affected: O   S   Z   P   C   Clock periods
                  x   x   x   x   x   2 to (20 + EA)
Example 3.46
         SAR   BX,CL
         SAR   [SI + 6],1
         SAR   NVAL,1 ;NVAL is an address identifier
         ;of a variable in the data segment.

In the example SAR BX,CL consider, before execution of the instruction, the register contents to be BX = 80F8H, CF = 1 and CL = 03H. Then after the instruction has been carried out the register contents will be BX = F01FH and CF = 0.

SBB Subtract with borrow
The three variations of this instruction are:

SBB   ac,data. Subtract with borrow immediate data from the accumulator

Instruction Set 57

SBB   mem/reg,data.   Subtract with borrow immediate data from a memory location or register

SBB   mem/reg1,mem/reg2
Subtract with borrow   - register from register
                       - register from memory
                       - memory from register

Consider the general form of this instruction to be SBB destination, source; then the instruction subtracts the source operand and the original value of the carry flag from the destination operand and places the difference in the destination operand.

Flags affected: O S Z A P C   Clock periods
                   x x x x x x   3 to (17 + EA)
Example 3.47
       SBB   BX,CX
       SBB   AX,1B27H
       SBB   [BX],0A60H
       SBB   AX,MAXV ;MAXV is an address identifier
       SBB   [DI],CX
       SBB   CL,[SI]

Consider the example SBB AX,2222H and assume AX to contain 2222H and the carry flag to be 1. After the execution of the instruction the register AX will contain FFFFH and the flag setting will be:

            O S Z A P C
            0 0 0 0 1 1

SCAS/SCASB/SCASW   Compare memory contents with register AL or AX.
This instruction compares the contents of the memory location in the ES extra segment addressed by the DI register with the contents of the AL or AX register. The comparison is carried out by subtracting the memory contents from the register contents and using the result to set the flags. The memory and register contents remain unaffected by the comparison. The DI register is incremented or decremented depending on the setting of the DF direction flag as 0 or 1 respectively and the change in its value is by one for the byte instruction and by two for the word instruction.

Flags affected: O S Z A P C   Clock periods
                   x x x x x x   15 to 24
Example 3.48
       SCASW

Suppose that before the execution of SCASW the state of the registers is as follows: ES = 0450H, DI = 0036H and DF = 0. Consider that the word in the AX register is 7567H

58 The 8086 and Assembly Language

and the word stored at 04536H is 4880H then the instruction will carry out the following subtraction:

```
     7567H = 0111 0101 0110 0111
     4880H = 0100 1000 1000 0000
Difference = 0010 1100 1110 0111
```

From this result the flag setting is as follows:

C = 1 no carry out of bit 15
P = 0 the number of one's in result is nine
A = 1 no carry from bit 3 to bit 4
Z = 0 result not zero
S = 0 most significant bit of result is 0
O = 0 no carry out of either bit 14 or bit 15

```
O S Z A P C
0 1 0 1 0 1
```

The DI register will now contain 0038H.

SHR Logical shift right
SHR   mem/reg,count. Shift the memory location or register contents right
This instruction causes the contents of the memory location or register to be shifted right by 1 or by the count number contained in the CL register. Zeros are shifted in from the left. The instruction can specify either an 8 bit or a 16 bit operand.

Flags affected: O C   Clock periods
                 x x   2 to (20 + EA)

Example 3.49
    SHR   BX,CL
    SHR   [SI + 6],1
    SHR   NEWVAL,CL ;NEWVAL is the offset address
          ;of a variable in the data segment.

In the example SHR NEWVAL,CL consider, before execution of the instruction, the variable at the offset address NEWVAL to have the value 80F8H, and register values to be CF = 1 and CL = 03H. Then after the instruction has been carried out the variable at location NEWVAL will be 101FH and and flag register CF = 0.

STC Set the carry flag
This instruction sets the carry flag to 1; it does not affect any other flags.

Flags affected C=1   Clock periods 2

STD Set the direction flag
This instruction sets the direction flag to 1; it does not affect any other flags.

Flags affected D=1   Clock periods 2

Instruction Set **59**

STI Set the interrupt enable flag
This instruction sets the interrupt enable flag to 1 after the execution of the next instruction. Interrupt service routines frequently end with the two instructions:

    STI
    RET

The fact that the instruction RET must be executed before the preceding instruction STI re-enables the interrupts, ensures that the service routine is completed before a new service routine can be entered.

Clock periods   2

STOS/STOSB/STOSW   Store AL or AX register contents in memory
This instruction causes the contents of the accumulator to be stored in the memory location pointed to by the DI register. The destination index register is then incremented or decremented depending on the setting of the DF direction flag as 0 or 1. For a word instruction the AX register is stored and the index register is changed by two. For a byte instruction it is the AL register which is stored and the index register is changed by one. This instruction does not affect the flag registers.

Clock periods   11 to 19
Example 3.50
    STOSB
    STOSW

Suppose that before the execution of STOSW the state of the registers is AX = 5555, ES = 0500, DI = 0034. After the instruction has BEEN executed the word stored at 05034H will be 5555H and the register state will be AX = 5555, ES = 0500, DI = 0036 and DF = 1. This instruction is frequently used with the loop instructions.

SUB   Integer Subtraction
The three variations of this instruction are:

SUB ac,data. Subtract immediate data from the accumulator.

SUB   mem/reg,data. Subtract immediate data from a memory location or register.

SUB   mem/reg1,mem/reg2 Subtract - register from register
                                   - register from memory
                                   - memory from register

Consider the general form of this instruction to be SUB destination, source. Then the instruction subtracts the source operand from the destination operand and places the difference in the destination operand.

60 The 8086 and Assembly Language

Flags affected: O S Z A P C   Clock periods
                 x x x x x x   3 to (17 + EA)

Example 3.51
      SUB CX,BX
      SUB AX,1B27H
      SUB [SI],0A60H
      SUB AX,VALUE1 ; VALUE1 is the address indentifier
      ;of a variable in the data segment.
      SUB [DI],CX
      SUB CL,[SI]

Consider the example SUB [SI],0A60H and assume DS to contain 04A8H and SI to contain 0122H. Consider before execution of the instruction that the location 04BA2H contains 18C7H and after execution this location will contain 0E67H and the flag setting will be:

          O S Z A P C
          0 0 0 0 1 0

TEST Logical compare
The three variations of this instruction are:

TEST ac,data. AND immediate data with the accumulator.

TEST mem/reg,data. AND immediate data with memory location or register.

TEST reg,mem/reg. AND register contents with the contents of the specified memory location or register.

Consider the general format to be TEST destination, source; the instruction performs the logical AND operation on the two operands and the result is simply used to set the flags. Neither of the operands is affected by the test.

Flags affected: O S Z P C   Clock periods
                 0 x x x 0   3 to (11 + EA)
Example 3.52
      TEST AX,0666H
      TEST [SI+2],0060H
      TEST BX,CX
      TEST AL,BL

A typical example could be TEST BX,CX. Consider that before the instruction is carried out the register state is BX = FE87H and CX = 066FH then the instruction will carry out the following test:

          FE87H = 1111 1110 1000 0111
          066FH = 0000 0110 0110 1111
Logical AND result = 0000 0110 0000 0111

Instruction Set **61**

From this result the flag setting is as follows:

C = 0
P = 0 the number of 1's in the result is five
Z = 0 result not zero
S = 0 most significant bit of the result is zero
O = 0

WAIT   Wait until TEST signal is active
This instruction causes the microprocessor to enter a wait state until the TEST signal line is active. However if the interrupts are enabled an interrupt service routine can be processed, the return being to the wait condition. This instruction can be used to synchronise the 8086 microprocessor and a coprocessor.

Clock periods   3 + 5n

XCHG   Exchange memory or register contents with register contents
The two variations of this instruction are:

XCHG   ac,reg. Exchange register contents with accumulator contents.

XCHG   reg,mem/reg. Exchange register contents with register or memory contents.

This instruction switches the contents of the two operands the instruction can specify either an 8 bit or 16 bit operand.

Clock periods   3 to (17 + EA)
Example 3.53
        XCHG   AL,CL
        XCHG   AX,CX
        XCHG   AX,NVAL1 ;NVAL1 is an address identifier
        ;of a variable in the data segment.
        XCHG   CX,[SI]

XLAT   Transfers a byte from a lookup table to the AL register
This instruction transfers, from a table in memory, a byte of data to the AL register. The DS segment offset address of this data byte is obtained by adding the initial contents of the AL register to the 16 bit contents of the BX register. So the first address of the lookup table must be kept in the BX register and the byte initially in the AL register is used as an index to this table.

Clock periods   11

Example 3.54
```
      MOV   BX,0A00H
      MOV   AL,4
      XLAT
```

In this example consider the DS register to contain 0000H and the locations beginning at 00A00H to contain 30H, 41H, 52H, 63H, 74H, 85H etc. Then after execution of the instruction XLAT the AL register will contain 74H because the offset address from which the accumulator was loaded was calculated by adding BX contents 0A00H and AL contents 04H.

XOR Logical exclusive-OR
The three variations of this instruction are:

XOR ac,data. Exclusive-OR immediate data with the accumulator contents.

XOR mem/reg,data. Exclusive-OR immediate data with a memory location contents or register contents.

XOR mem/reg1,mem/reg2
   Exclusive-OR - register with register
                 - register with memory
                 - memory with register

Consider the general form as: XOR destination, source. The instruction performs the logical exclusive-OR operation on two operands and places the result in the destination operand. The operation may be on an 8 bit or 16 bit operand.

```
Flags affected:  O  S  Z  P  C   Clock periods
                 0  x  x  x  0   3 to (17 + EA)
```
Example 3.55
```
      XOR   AL,BL
      XOR   AX,3000H
      XOR   [BX],0F51H
      XOR   AX,LOT1  ;LOT1 is an address identifier
                    ;for a variable in the data segment
      XOR   [SI + 2],CX
      XOR   CX,[BX + SI + 8]
```

A typical example is: XOR [SI],00FFH. Assume the word location pointed to by the SI register contains 10A6H before the instruction is executed. After the instruction is executed this word memory location will contain 1059H and the flag setting will be:

```
              O  S  Z  P  C
              0  0  0  1  0
```

Instruction Set **63**

Table 3.1 8086 Instruction Set with Clock Periods

Instruction	Operands	Clock periods	Bytes
AAA		4	1
AAD		60	2
AAM		83	1
AAS		4	1
ADC	reg,reg	3	2
	reg,mem	9+EA	2-4
	mem,reg	16+EA	2-4
	reg,data	4	3-4
	mem,data	17+EA	3-6
	ac,data	4	2-3
ADD	reg,reg	3	2
	reg,mem	9+EA	2-4
	mem,reg	16+EA	2-4
	reg,data	4	3-4
	mem,data	17+EA	3-6
	ac,data	4	2-3
AND	reg,reg	3	2
	reg,mem	9+EA	2-4
	mem,reg	16+EA	2-4
	reg,data	4	3-4
	mem,data	17+EA	3-6
	ac,data	4	2-3
CALL	(Intraseg)Displ 16 bit	19	3
	mem(16 bit ptr)	21+EA	2-4
	reg(16 bit)	16	2
CALL	(Interseg)Displ 32	28	5
	mem(32 bit ptr)	37+EA	2-4
CBW		2	1
CLC		2	1
CLD		2	1
CLI		2	1
CMC		2	1
CMP	reg,reg	3	2
	reg,mem	9+EA	2-4
	mem,reg	9+EA	2-4
	reg,data	4	3-4
	mem,data	10+EA	3-6
	ac,data	4	2-3
CMPS	dest,source	22	1
	(rep)dest,source	9+22/rep	1
CWD		5	1
DAA		4	1
DAS		4	1
DEC	reg 16/8	2/3	1-2
	mem	15+EA	2-4
DIV	reg 8/16	80-90/144-162	2
	mem 8/16	(86-96)+EA/(150-168)+EA	2-4
ESC	data,mem	8+EA	2-4
	data,reg	2	2
HLT		2	1

64 The 8086 and Assembly Language

Table 3.1(Continued)

Instruction	Operands	Clock periods	Bytes
IDIV	reg 8/16	101-112/165-184	2
	mem 8/16	(107-118)+EA/(171-190)+EA	2-4
IMUL	reg 8/16	80-98/128-154	2
	mem 8/16	(86-104)+EA/(134-160)+EA	2-4
IN	ac,data	10	2
	ac,DX	8	1
INC	reg 16/8	2/3	1-2
	mem	15+EA	2-4
INT	data(type 3/type n)	52/51	2-1
INTO		53 or 4	1
IRET		24	1
JA-JS	Conditional jumps(jump/no jump)	16 or 6	2
JCXZ		18 or 4	2
JMP	(Intraseg)Displ 8 bit	15	2
	displ 16 bit	15	3
	mem(16 bit ptr)	18+EA	2-4
	reg(16 bit)	11	2
JMP	(Interseg)Displ 32	15	5
	mem(32 bit ptr)	24+EA	2-4
LAHF		4	1
LDS/LES		16+EA	2-4
LEA		2+EA	2-4
LOCK		2	1
LODS	source-string	12	1
	(rep)source-string	9+13/rep	1
LOOP		17/5	2
LOOPE/LOOPZ		18/6	2
LOOPNE/LOOPNZ		19/5	2
MOV	mem/ac	10	3
	ac,mem	10	3
	reg,reg	2	2
	reg,mem	8+EA	2-4
	mem,reg	9+EA	2-4
	reg,data	4	2-3
	mem,data	10+EA	3-6
	segreg,reg16	4	2
	segreg,mem16	8+EA	2-4
	mem,segreg	9+EA	2-4
MOVS	dest-string,source-string	18	1
	(rep)dest-string,source-string	9+17/rep	1
MUL	reg 8/16	70-77/118-133	2
	mem 8/16	(76-83)+EA/(124-139)+EA	2-4
NEG	reg	18	2
	mem	16+EA	2-4
NOP		3	1
NOT	reg	18	2
	mem	16+EA	2-4

Table 3.1(Continued)

Instruction	Operands		Clock periods	Bytes
OR	reg,reg		3	2
	reg,mem		9+EA	2-4
	mem,reg		16+EA	2-4
	reg,data		4	3-4
	mem,data		17+EA	3-6
	ac,data		4	2-3
OUT	data,ac		10	2
	DX,ac		8	1
POP	reg(CS illegal)		8	1
	mem		17+EA	2-4
POPF			8	1
PUSH	reg(CS legal)		11	1
	mem		16+EA	2-4
PUSHF			10	1
RCL	reg,1		2	2
	reg,CL		8+4/bit	2
	mem,1		15+EA	2-4
	mem,CL		20+EA+4/bit	2-4
RCR	reg,1		2	2
	reg,CL		8+4/bit	2
	mem,1		15+EA	2-4
	mem,CL		20+EA+4/bit	2-4
REP			2	1
REPE/REPZ			2	1
REPNE/REPNZ			2	1
RET	(Intra-segment)	no POP	8	1
		POP	13	3
	(Inter-segment)	no POP	18	1
		POP	17	3
ROL	reg,1		2	2
	reg,CL		8+4/bit	2
	mem,1		15+EA	2-4
	mem,CL		20+EA+4/bit	2-4
ROR	reg,1		2	2
	reg,CL		8+4/bit	2
	mem,1		15+EA	2-4
	mem,CL		20+EA+4/bit	2-4
SAHF			4	1
SAL/SHL	reg,1		2	2
	reg,CL		8+4/bit	2
	mem,1		15+EA	2-4
	mem,CL		20+EA+4/bit	2-4
SAR	reg,1		2	2
	reg,CL		8+4/bit	2
	mem,1		15+EA	2-4
	mem,CL		20+EA+4/bit	2-4

66 The 8086 and Assembly Language

Table 3.1(Continued)

Instruction	Operands	Clock periods	Bytes
SBB	reg,reg	3	2
	reg,mem	9+EA	2-4
	mem,reg	16+EA	2-4
	reg,data	4	3-4
	mem,data	17+EA	3-6
	ac,data	4	2-3
SCAS	dest-string	15	1
	(rep)dest-string	9+15/rep	1
SHR	reg,1	2	2
	reg,CL	8+4/bit	2
	mem,1	15+EA	2-4
	mem,CL	20+EA+4/bit	2-4
STC		2	1
STD		2	1
STI		2	1
STOS	dest-string	11	1
	(rep)dest-string	9+10/rep	1
SUB	reg,reg	3	2
	reg,mem	9+EA	2-4
	mem,reg	16+EA	2-4
	reg,data	4	3-4
	mem,data	17+EA	3-6
	ac,data	4	2-3
TEST	reg,reg	3	2
	reg,mem	9+EA	2-4
	reg,data	5	3-4
	mem,data	11+EA	3-6
	ac,data	4	2-3
WAIT		3+5n	1
XCHG	ac,reg16	3	1
	mem,reg	17+EA	2-4
	reg,reg	4	2
XLAT		11	1
XOR	reg,reg	3	2
	reg,mem	9+EA	2-4
	mem,reg	16+EA	2-4
	reg,data	4	3-4
	mem,data	17+EA	3-6
	ac,data	4	2-3

CHAPTER 4
Instruction categories

In the previous chapter a brief explanation of each individual 8086 instruction has been given, but it is a valuable exercise to examine the instruction set within categories which describe their operation and that is the purpose of this chapter. The categories that will be considered are: data transfer instructions, arithmetic instructions, bit manipulation instructions, string instructions, program transfer instructions, interrupt instructions, flag instructions and external synchronisation instructions.

DATA TRANSFER INSTRUCTIONS

These instructions are further divided into groups which are shown in tabular form in table 4.1

Table 4.1 Data transfer instructions.

General purpose transfers	MOV PUSH POP XCHG XLAT	Move data Push word onto stack Pop off the stack Exchange word or byte Translate byte
Input/Output transfers	IN OUT	Input byte or word Output byte or word
Address transfers	LEA LDS LES	Load effective address Load register and DS register Load register and ES register
Flag transfers	LAHF SAHF PUSHF POPF	Load AH register from flags Store AH register in flags Push flags onto stack Pop flags off stack

68 The 8086 and Assembly Language

The general purpose transfer instructions move data from register to register or between memory locations and registers. The wide range of MOV instructions is illustrated by the following list of assembled instructions in program 4.1. (Note that this list does not form a program of any meaning but simply illustrates the variety of move instructions available). Each instruction is followed by a comment indicating the type of data transfer. It should be pointed out at this stage that when using a symbolic assembler the use of numeric characters in an instruction implies an immediate operand.

Program 4.1

```
;      Title:    The 8086 Move Instruction
;      Filename: DMOV.A86
;      Registers used: DS,ES,AX,BX,CX,SI,DI
;      Purpose: The instructions in the code segment are
;all MOVE instructions. This list of instructions
;while not forming a meaningful program, gives
;some idea of the wide variety of addressing
;modes available with the 8086 microprocessor
;**************************************************************
       ASSUME  CS:PCODE,DS:PDATA
;**************************************************************
       PDATA   SEGMENT
               ORG     8040H;Sets the offset within data segment
       ADDR1   DW      ?
       ADDR2   DW      0000
       ADDR3   DW      ?
       ADDR4   DW      ?
       PDATA   ENDS
;**************************************************************
       PCODE   SEGMENT
               MOV     AX,0123H ;Move immediate into accumulator
               MOV     ADDR1,AX ;Move AX contents to address
                                ;8040H in the data segment
               MOV     DS,AX    ;Transfer between registers
               MOV     CX,ES    ;Transfer between registers
               MOV     ADDR2,DS ;Move DS contents to address 8042H
               MOV     ES,ADDR3 ;Contents of 8044H transferred
                                ;to the ES register
               MOV     BL,04H   ;Move immediate instruction
               MOV     CX,0AAAAH;Move immediate instruction
               MOV     ADDR4,0FFFH;Move immediate to address 8046H
               MOV     [SI],4000H ;Move immediate to address
                                ;pointed to by the SI index register
               MOV     BX,[SI]  ;Move contents of address pointed
                                ;to by SI register into BX register
               MOV     BX,[SI+4AH]
               MOV     BX,[SI+0238H]
               MOV     [BX+DI+0401H],5FF0H
       PCODE   ENDS
;**************************************************************
               END
```

Instruction Categories 69

The segment registers cannot be used as operands with all instructions. This is to ensure that segment registers once set cannot easily be altered. However, the general purpose transfer instructions can be used to set data in the segment registers. To avoid setting a meaningless address, for the next instruction to be carried out, it is not permitted for an instruction to set the code segment register CS without setting the instruction pointer register IP. So a move instruction with CS as the operand is undefined. The following instructions indicate a direct way of setting the data and extra segment registers DS and ES to contain 0000H:

```
MOV     AX,0
MOV     DS,AX
MOV     ES,DS
```

To point to a specific location 0A048H in a data segment the following instructions can be used:

```
MOV     AX,0A00H
MOV     DS,AX ;Data Segment register holds 0A00H
MOV     SI,0048H
```

An alternative method of loading both the DS and SI registers is to use the LDS instruction to load the registers from specified memory locations:

```
LDS     SI,[0B00H]
```

The SI register will be loaded with the contents of the word location offset 0B00H in the present data segment and the DS register will be loaded with the contents of word location offset 0B02H. The instruction LDS is known as an address transfer instruction.

The instruction XLAT can be used most effectively to convert a value from one code to the corresponding value in another code. XLAT performs a lookup table translation. The following Gray coding of decimal digits 0 to 9 can be taken as an example:

Digit	Gray encoding	Offset address
9	1101	041DH
8	1100	041CH
7	0100	041BH
6	0101	041AH
5	0111	0419H
4	0110	0418H
3	0010	0417H
2	0011	0416H
1	0001	0415H
0	0000	0414H

The encoded values form a lookup table placed in the data

70 The 8086 and Assembly Language

segment. The address of the first value of the table must be kept in the BX register, in this case 0414H. The binary value of the decimal number to be translated must be placed in the accumulator, for example 5 (05H). Execution of the instruction XLAT will transfer the corresponding entry from the lookup table to the accumulator; for this example 0000 0111, i.e. 07H, the Gray equivalent of 5, will be placed in the accumulator. The following instructions can be used:

```
MOV   BX,0414H
MOV   AL,05
XLATB
```

The following set of instructions enable an input value in the form of a decimal number between 0 and 9 to be converted immediately to Gray code:

```
MOV   BX,0414H
IN    AL,DX
XLATB
```

The conversion can be in the opposite direction in the sense that an input value which is in Gray code can be converted to a binary or decimal value. In this case the lookup table will perform the reverse conversion.

Input Gray value	Binary value	Offset address
1101	1001	041DH
1100	1000	041CH
0100	0111	041BH
0101	0110	041AH
0111	0101	0419H
0110	0100	0418H
0010	0011	0417H
0011	0010	0416H
0001	0001	0415H
0000	0000	0414H

The lookup table is again located in the data segment with the offset address of the first value being 0414H. The following instructions can be used to convert an input Gray value to its equivalent binary value:

```
MOV   BX,0414H
IN    AL,DX
XLATB
```

The input/output instructions IN and OUT relate to the transfer of data between the accumulator and an I/O port. There are two forms of instruction: (1) a static form, where the 8 bit port address is part of the instruction, e.g. IN 4AH; and (2) a dynamic form, where the 16 bit address is held in the DX register and can be altered

Instruction Categories 71

during the running of the program, e.g. IN AL,DX. The instructions previously discussed to convert an input data value to a new code would have been preceded by an instruction placing the port address in the DX register, as follows:

```
MOV     DX,0FFF9H;Setting of port address
MOV     BX,0414H
IN      AL,DX
XLAT
```

The instruction LEA facilitates the transfer of a memory operand offset address to a 16 bit register. Hence it can be used to pass the offset address of a variable to a register within the main program or within a subroutine. The assembler operator OFFSET can be used to achieve the same effect. The following instructions pass the same data segment offset address, given by the identifier REXXO to both SI and DI registers:

```
REXXO   DW      ?
        -
        -
        LEA     SI,REXXO
        MOV     DI,OFFSET REXXO
```

The operation of the assembler operator OFFSET is explained in chapter 5.

The Stack

The stack is an area of memory organised on a last-in, first-out basis. Data is added to and removed from the top of the stack using the PUSH and POP instructions respectively. To save the contents of the 8086 registers

Example 4.1

```
        PUSH    AX
        PUSH    BX
        PUSH    CX      Saving
        PUSH    DX      register
        PUSH    BP      contents
        PUSH    SI
        PUSH    DI
        PUSH    DS

        POP     DS
        POP     DI
        POP     SI      Restoring
        POP     BP      register
        POP     DX      contents
        POP     CX
        POP     BX
        POP     AX
```

72 The 8086 and Assembly Language

the PUSH instruction can be used before entering a subroutine. The stack pointer is automatically adjusted by the microprocessor during the execution of the PUSH instruction. To restore these contents to their respective registers the POP instruction is used, again the stack pointer is auotomatically adjusted to point to the stack top. The order of the instructions as shown in example 4.1 illustrates the last-in, first-out organisation.

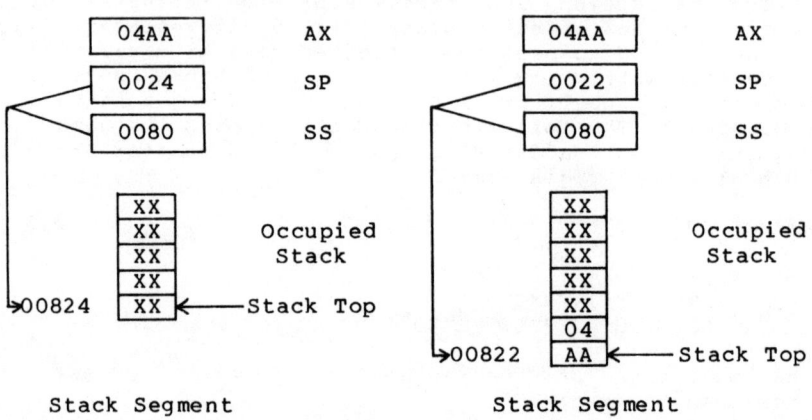

Figure 4.1 The action of pushing data onto the stack

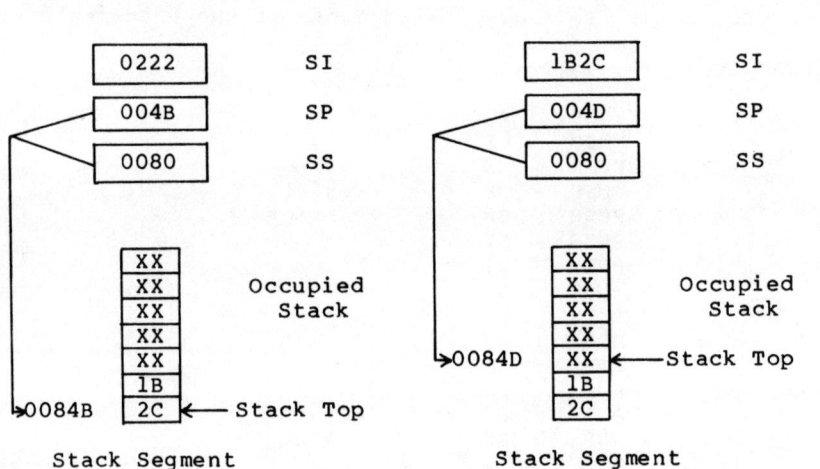

Figure 4.2 The action of popping data from the stack

Instruction Categories 73

The operation of transferring data to and from the stack is illustrated in the figures 4.1 and 4.2. The state of the microprocessor registers and the stack contents are shown both before and after the execution of the PUSH and POP instructions.

ARITHMETIC INSTRUCTIONS

These instructions are further divided into groups which are shown in tabular form in table 4.2.

The information or data can be interpreted by the user as either signed or unsigned; the actual arithmetic operation is the same in both cases. The number range of unsigned and signed numbers is shown in table 4.3 for both 8 bit numbers and 16 bit numbers. The difference between the interpretations between unsigned and signed numbers is in the detection of out of range results. The carry flag CF is set when an unsigned result is out of range. The overflow flag OF is set when the operation results in a signed number being out of range.

The 8086 handles BCD (binary coded decimal) arithmetic by performing binary arithmetic and providing instructions to convert the result to BCD form.

Table 4.2 Arithmetic instructions.

Addition	ADD	Add byte or word
	ADC	Add byte or word with carry
	INC	Increment byte or word by 1
	AAA	ASCII adjust after addition
	DAA	Decimal adjust after addition
Subtraction	SUB	Subtract byte or word
	SBB	Subtract byte or word with borrow
	DEC	Decrement byte or word by 1
	NEG	Negate bte or word
	CMP	Compare byte or word
	AAS	ASCII adjust subtraction result
	DAS	Decimal adjust after subtraction
Multiplication	MUL	Multiply unsigned byte or word
	IMUL	Multiply signed byte or word
	AAM	ASCII adjust multiplication result
Division	DIV	Divide unsigned byte or word
	IDIV	Divide signed byte or word
	AAD	ASCII adjust for division
	CWB	Convert byte to word
	CWD	Convert word to double word

74 The 8086 and Assembly Language

Table 4.3 Number range of 8 bit and 16 bit unsigned and signed binary numbers.

Range of unsigned numbers

8 bit numbers		16 bit numbers	
0	0000 0000	0	0000 0000 0000 0000
3	0000 0011	3	0000 0000 0000 0011
127	0111 1111	32,767	0111 1111 1111 1111
128	1000 0000	32,768	1000 0000 0000 0000
254	1111 1110	65,534	1111 1111 1111 1110
255	1111 1111	65,535	1111 1111 1111 1111

Range of signed numbers

8 bit numbers		16 bit numbers	
-128	1000 0000	-32,768	1000 0000 0000 0000
-64	1100 0000	-16,384	1100 0000 0000 0000
-1	1111 1111	-1	1111 1111 1111 1111
0	0000 0000	0	0000 0000 0000 0000
+1	0000 0001	+1	0000 0000 0000 0001
+63	0011 1111	+16,383	0011 1111 1111 1111
+127	0111 1111	+32,767	0111 1111 1111 1111

Unsigned Number Interpretation and the Carry Flag

As has already been pointed out, the arithmetic operations used by the 8086 microprocessor are independent of the number interpretation employed by the programmer. The following 8 bit binary additions labelled example 4.2, show how the carry flag indicates an out of range unsigned binary number:

Example 4.2

```
      01100110 (102)              01110010 (114)
    + 01010011  (83)            + 10110100 (180)
      10111001 (185)            1 00100110  (38)
no carry                        carry
```

In example 4.2 the 8 bit number result is correct in the first addition where there is not a carry out of the most significant bit and incorrect in the second example where there is a carry out of the most significant bit. In the second case the carry flag is set to 1 indicating that there is an overflow, which in turn shows that the result is incorrect. The conclusion is that in the case of unsigned binary number arithmetic a carry flag set to 1 indicates an out of range number.

Instruction Categories **75**

Signed Number Interpretation and the Overflow Flag

In this case, the following 8 bit binary addition examples can be used to show how the overflow flag OF indicates an out of range signed number.

```
Example 4.3                        Example 4.4

      10010011 (- 237)                   01100110 (+ 102)
    + 10000101 (- 251)                 + 01010101 (+  85)

    1 00011000 (+  24)                   10111011 (-  69)

Example 4.5                        Example 4.6

      10010011 (- 237)                   01100110 (+ 102)
    + 01010101 (+  85)                 + 11000000 (-  64)

      11101000 (- 152)                 1 00100110 (+  38)
```

The overflow flag contains the result of performing the logical exclusive-or between the the carry values into and out of the most significant bit. The most significant bit is bit 7 for an 8 bit operation and bit 15 for a 16 bit operation. The following examination of the carry values into and out of bit 7 for each of the above four examples illustrates how the overflow flag indicates an out of range signed number.
Example 4.3
The carry into bit 7 is 0 and the carry out of bit 7 is 1; the exclusive-or of these two values is 1 so the overflow flag is set. This indicates an incorrect 8 bit result, i.e. for the result of the addition to be negative 9 bits are required, hence the result is an out of range signed number.
Example 4.4
The carry into bit 7 is 1 and the carry out of bit 7 is 0; the exclusive-or of these two values is 1 so the overflow flag is set. This again indicates an an incorrect 8 bit result. For a positive result 9 bits are required so in this case the result is an out of range signed number.
Example 4.5
The carry into and out of bit 7 is 0, and the exclusive-or of these two values is 0. The overflow flag is reset to 0 by the addition instruction, indicating the result to be an in range signed number.
Example 4.6
The carry into and out of bit 7 is 1, and the exclusive-or of these two values is 0. Again the overflow flag is reset to 0 by the addition instruction. The overflow flag indicates that the result is an in range signed number, as can be seen by referring to the example above.
 It should be noted that examples using binary subtraction instructions yield similar results with regard to the setting of the overflow flag.

76 The 8086 and Assembly Language

Addition and Subtraction Instructions

These instruction operate with either 8 bit or 16 bit operands. For addition instructions the source operand is added to the destination operand, and for subtraction instructions the source operand is subtracted from the destination operand. The instructions ADC and SBB operate in a similar manner to the ADD and SUB instructions except that they involve the contents of the carry flag in the operation. The instructions INC and DEC are addition and subtraction instructions respectively, where 1 is used as the second operand. The size of the results for addition and subtraction instructions are shown in table 4.4 where the general format of the instruction is considered to be: opcode destination, source.

Table 4.4 Addition and subtraction operands.

	First operand (destination)	Second operand (source)	Result (destination)
Addition	8 bits 16 bits	8 bits 16 bits	8 bits 16 bits
Subtraction	8 bits 16 bits	8 bits 16 bits	8 bits 16 bits

Comparison Instruction CMP

Execution of the instruction causes the second operand to be subtracted from the first operand and the result is used to configure the flags OF, SF, ZF, and CF. A comparision instruction is normally followed directly by a conditional jump instruction, because the flag configuration produced by the comparision instruction is used by the conditional jump instruction. Consider the instruction to have the general form CMP first operand, second operand; then the flags will be configured as shown in table 4.5.

To illustrate the use of the comparison instruction and the resultant flag configuration refer to example 4.7, where a variety of data values in registers BL and CL are compared, firstly as signed and secondly as unsigned numbers. The results of CMP BL,CL and the consequent flag configuration are given: refer to the detailed explanation of the CMP instruction in chapter 3. These examples are then compared with and shown to verify the information given in table 4.5.

Instruction Categories 77

Table 4.5 Flag configuration after execution of compare instruction CMP first operand, second operand.

	OF	SF	ZF	CF
Signed and unsigned numbers				
First operand equals second operand	0	0	1	0
Signed numbers				
First operand greater than second	1 0	1 0	0 0	– –
First operand less than second	1 0	0 1	0 0	– –
Unsigned numbers				
First operand below second	–	–	0	1
First operand above second	–	–	0	0

Example 4.7

	First operand BL	Second operand CL	Result of CMP BL,CL	OF	SF	ZF	CF
(a)	A4H	29H	7BH	1	0	0	0
(b)	93H	B1H	E1H	0	1	0	1
(c)	7BH	B7H	–	–	–	–	–
(d)	88H	80H	–	–	–	–	–

Case (a). The signed number A4H represents decimal -91 and the signed number 29H represents decimal 41. The flag configuration when compared with a similar configuration in table 4.4 indicates that the 1st operand -91 is less than the second operand, which of course is the situation. The unsigned number A4H represents decimal 164 and 29H represents decimal 41. The flags when compared to table 4.4 indicate that the first operand 164 is above the second operand 41, which of course is the situation.

Case (b). The signed number 93H represents decimal -109 and B1H represents decimal -79. The flags indicate the first operand to be less than the second operand, and of course -109 is less than -79. Considering the data as unsigned numbers the flags indicate that the first operand is below the second operand. This is the situation as 93H represents decimal 145 and B1H represents decimal 177.

Cases (c) and (d) are left as an exercise for the reader.

Multiplication and Division Instructions

These instruction operate with either 8 bit or 16 bit operands. For multiplication of 8 bit numbers, the AL register contents can be multiplied by an 8 bit number specified in the instruction. The 16 bit result is stored in the AX register. In the case of multiplication of 16 bit numbers, the AX register contents is multiplied by a 16 bit number specified in the instruction. The 32 bit result is stored in the DX-AX register combination as shown in table 4.6.

Table 4.6 Multiplication operands and results.

8 bits in AL register	*	8 bit instruction operand	=	16 bits in AX register
16 bits in AX register	*	16 bit instruction operand	=	32 bits in DX-AX register

In the case of division instructions, the 16 bit number in the AX register is divided by the 8 bit number specified in the instruction, e.g. DIV CL. The resulting quotient is placed in the AL register, and the remainder is placed in the AH register. When the divisor specified in the instruction is a 16 bit number, the number to be divided into is the double precision number in the DX-AX register combination, e.g. DIV CX. In this case the quotient is placed in the AX register and the remainder in the DX register, as shown in table 4.7.

Table 4.7 Division operands and results.

16 bits in AX register	-	8 bit instruction operand	=	8 bit quotient in AL and 8 bit remainder in AH
32 bits in DX-AX combination	-	16 bit instruction operand	=	16 bit quotient in AX and 16 bit remainder in DX

With multiplication and division of binary numbers, the arithmetic methods that give the correct result for unsigned numbers give an incorrect result for signed numbers. Hence the 8086 microprocessor has not only instructions MUL and DIV for multiplication and division of unsigned numbers but also instructions IMUL and IDIV for multiplication and division of signed numbers. The following example 4.8 illustrates the multiplication of binary numbers:

Instruction Categories **79**

Example 4.8

```
        1111 1111           multiplicand
       *1010 1010           multiplier

        0000 0000
       1111 1111
      0000 0000
     1111 1111
    0000 0000
   1111 1111
  0000 0000
 1111 1111

1010 1001 0101 0110         product
```

The decimal representation of this example, considering the interpretation to be unsigned binary numbers, is 255 * 170 = 43,350, which is correct. However, the decimal representation considering the example to be interpretated as signed binary numbers is −1 * −86 = −22,186, which is certainly not correct. Consequently the algorithm to be used for multiplication of signed binary numbers must be different to that used for multiplication of unsigned binary numbers. So instructions applying only to signed multiplication and signed division must be used.

The following example 4.9 shows how, by first sign extending both the multiplicand and the multiplier to the same size as the product, the binary multiplication method used in the previous example could be satisfactory for signed number interpretation.

Example 4.9

```
         1111 1111 1111 1111       multiplicand
        *1111 1111 1010 1010       multiplier

         0000 0000 0000 0000
         1111 1111 1111 111
         0000 0000 0000 00
         1111 1111 1111 1
         0000 0000 0000
         1111 1111 111
         0000 0000 00
         1111 1111 1
         1111 1111
         1111 111
         1111 11
         1111 1
         1111
         111
         11
         1

         0000 0000 0101 0110       product
```

80 The 8086 and Assembly Language

The decimal representation of the signed numbers in this example is -1 * -86 = +86, which is correct. This illustrates that by first performing sign extension, multiplication of signed numbers can be achieved.

When using IMUL to divide signed numbers it should be noted that the 8086 microprocessor produces the result in such a manner that the sign of the quotient and the sign of the remainder is the same. For example, +36 divided by -8 results in a quotient of -5 with a remainder -4 and not a quotient of -4 accompanied by a remainder +4.

The size of the numbers in a division operation must be as shown in table 4.7. For example, it is not possible to divide a 16 bit number by another 16 bit number. The number to be divided into must first be extended to a 32 bit number by using the convert word to double-word instruction CWD. Similarly an 8 bit number must first be extended to a 16 bit number using CBW before division by another 8 bit number. For signed number operation these instructions automatically maintain the correct sign.

Binary Coded Decimal Arithmetic

The standard binary instructions so far discussed can be used in conjunction with the instructions DAA, DAS, AAA, AAS, AAM and AAD to perform binary coded decimal arithmetic. There are two forms of BCD which can be used with the 8086 microprocessor, namely packed BCD and unpacked BCD.

Table 4.8 Binary, ASCII and BCD number representations.

Decimal	Binary (unsigned)	ASCII code	BCD
0	0	00110000	0000
1	1	00110001	0001
2	10	00110010	0010
3	11	00110011	0011
4	100	00110100	0100
5	101	00110101	0101
6	110	00110110	0110
7	111	00110111	0111
8	1000	00111000	1000
9	1001	00111001	1001
10	1010	00110001 00110000	0001 0000
11	1011	00110001 00110001	0001 0001
12	1100	00110001 00110010	0001 0010
15	1111	00110001 00110101	0001 0101
16	10000	00110001 00110110	0001 0110
21	10101	00110010 00110001	0010 0001
64	1000000	00110110 00110100	0110 0100
99	1100011	00111001 00111001	1001 1001

Instruction Categories **81**

When a single byte of information contains two BCD digits the representation is known as packed BCD. When a byte of data contains a single BCD digit in the four least significant bits the representation is known as unpacked BCD. The ASCII representation is an example of unpacked BCD and it is the ASCII adjust instructions which are used with the binary instructions to perform unpacked BCD arithmetic. Packed BCD arithmetic is performed by using the decimal adjust instructions. Table 4.8 shows these number representations.

When the binary addition or subtraction instructions are used with packed BCD data the results are incorrect. These binary instructions must be followed by their corresponding decimal adjust instructions. This process works only for addition and subtraction; it is not possible to multiply or to divide packed BCD numbers. Examples of the use of the decimal adjust instructions DAA and DAS are given in chapter 3.

For ASCII data there are four adjust instructions, one each for addition, subtraction, multiplication and division. Elementary examples of the use the instructions AAA, AAS, AAM and AAD are given in chapter 3 and programs to perform multidigit unpacked arithmetic are explained in detail in chapter 8.

BIT MANIPULATION INSTRUCTIONS

These instructions are further divided into groups which are shown in tabular form in table 4.9.

Table 4.9 Bit manipulation instructions.

	NOT	Invert byte or word
	AND	'AND' byte or word
Logical	OR	'OR' byte or word
	XOR	'Exclusive-OR' byte or word
	TEST	'AND' byte or word to set flags
	SAL/SHL	Shift arithmetic left byte or word
		Shift logical left byte or word
Shift	SAR	Shift arithmetic right byte or word
	SHR	Shift logical right byte or word
	ROL	Rotate left byte or word
	ROR	Rotate right byte or word
Rotate	RCL	Rotate left through carry byte or word
	RCR	Rotate right through carry byte or word

The logical instructions when executed perform logical operations on each individual bit position of their operands which are either bytes or words. Consequently a logical operation can be used to modify a single bit or a selection of bits within a byte or word. The result of the operation is placed in the destination operand. The truth

82 The 8086 and Assembly Language

tables for the logical operations are given in table 4.10.

Table 4.10 Truth tables for logical operations.

Single Operand			Two Operands			
				AND	OR	XOR
X	NOT X	X	Y	X.Y	X+Y	X+Y
0	1	0	0	0	0	0
1	0	0	1	0	1	1
		1	0	0	1	1
		1	1	1	1	0

The AND instruction is used to clear a single bit or a group of bits by 'ANDing' the bits to be cleared with 0 while 'ANDing' the bits to remain unaffected with 1. Hence the instruction AND BX,000FH will cause the clearing of both register AH and the four most significant bits of register AL, leaving the four least significant bits of AL unaltered. The OR instruction is used to set a bit or a group of bits by 'ORing' those particular bits with 1. The instruction OR AX,03FCH will set the two least significant bits of register AH and the six most significant bits of register AL to 1. The XOR instruction is used to invert particular bits by 'exclusive-ORing' those bits with 1. The instruction XOR AX,0F0FH will cause the inversion of the least significant four bits of both registers AH and AL. The NOT instruction causes the inversion of every bit of the operand.

The shift and rotate instructions cause the movement of bits to the left or to the right. A rotate instruction causes the movement of bits in a circular pattern whereas a shift instruction causes a movement of bits in a linear pattern. The effect of these instructions is shown diagrammatically in figure 4.3.

For each of the rotate and shift instructions there are two versions, namely a one-step operation and a multi-step operation. In the multi-step operation the count number is contained in the CL register and this is clearly stated in the instruction, e.g. ROR AX,1, a one-step operation and ROR AX,CL, a multi-step operation.

The rotate instructions can be used to rearrange the bits in the data byte or word. These instructions cause the bit emerging from one end to be rotated round and inserted in the vacant position at the other end. The instructions RCL and RCR allow the carry flag to be a participant in the rotation, in such a way that the emerging bit is inserted in the carry and the bit that was in carry is inserted in the vacant position at the other end.

The shift instructions perform a multiplication by 2 for a left shift and a division by 2 for a right shift. The logical shift instructions cause 0 to be moved into

Instruction Categories **83**

the vacant bit position and so these instructions are used to multiply and divide unsigned numbers by 2. The arithmetic shift instructions maintain the sign of the number while multiplying or dividing by 2. The arithmetic

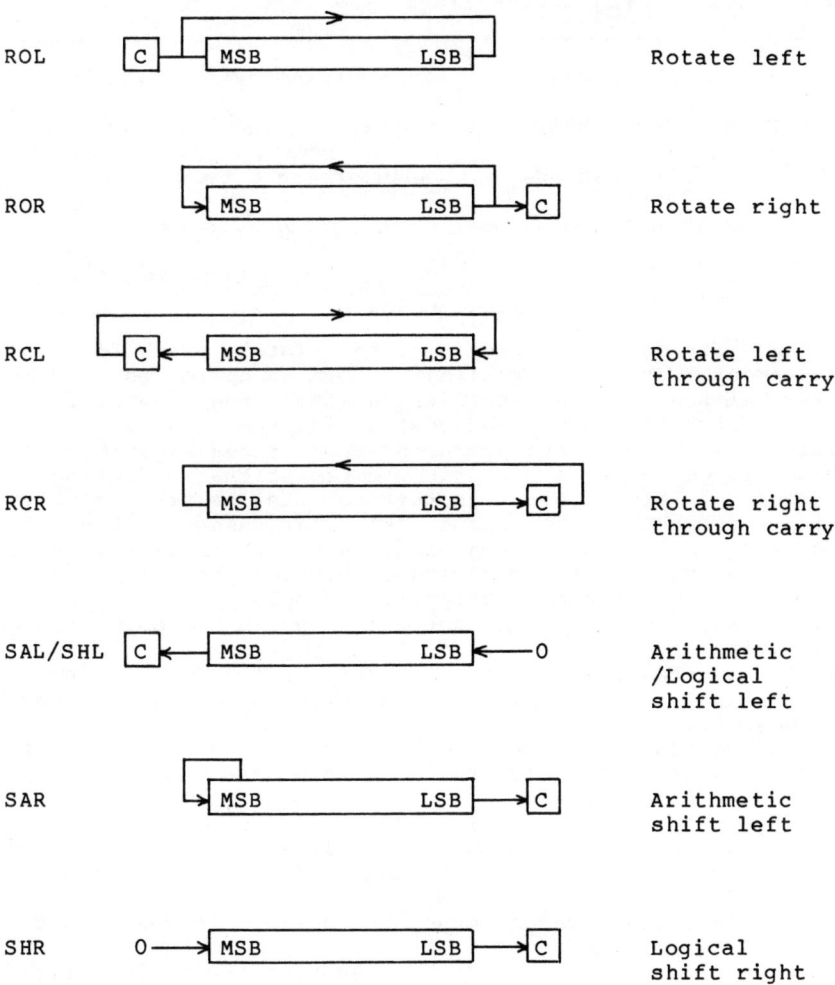

Figure 4.3 Rotate and shift instructions.

shift right instruction causes the MSB to be shifted into itself, so preserving the sign of the number. There is no difference between the arithmetic shift left and the logical shift left, hence they are one and the same instruction.

STRING INSTRUCTIONS

A string is a sequence of data bytes or words. String instructions are those which operate on every string item in turn.

Table 4.11 String instructions.

MOVS (MOVSB/MOVSW)	Move string byte or word
CMPS (CMPSB/CMPSW)	Compare string byte or word
SCAS (SCASB/SCASW)	Scan string byte or word
LODS (LODSB/LODSW)	Load string byte or word
STOS (STOSB/STOSW)	Store string byte or word

These string primitives (the Intel name for the fundamental string operation) perform an operation on an item within the string, using the index registers to access both the source and destination operands, and then autoincrement or autodecrement the index registers. In order to cause the instruction to repeat the operation a number of times the instruction must be prefixed by a single byte REP. The number of iterations within the re-executing loop is contained in the CX register. Hence before using a prefixed string primitive a series of steps must first be carried out; for example, the following steps must be carried out before using the MOVS string primitive:

1) The source index register must be initialised to point to the first item of source data within the data segment.
2) The destination index register must be set to point to the destination location, within the extra segment, of the first item.
3) To ensure either autoincrement or autodecrement the direction flag must be initialised to '0' for autoincrement using CLD and '1' for autodecrement using STD.
4) The loop count value must be placed in register CX.

The flow chart in figure 4.4 shows the action of the string primitive MOVS and the REP prefix in a data move example for which the necessary initialisation has just been discussed.

The repeat prefixes, the conditions under which they operate and the string primitives with which they are used are given in table 4.12.

Instruction Categories **85**

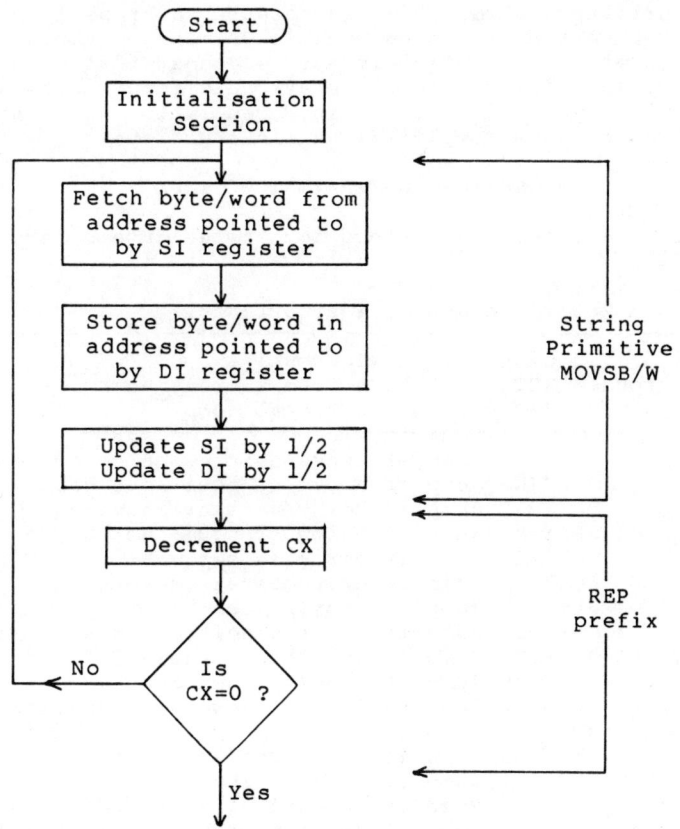

Figure 4.4 Flow chart showing the action of REP MOVS.

Table 4.12 Repeat prefixes used with string instructions.

Prefix	String Primitive	Repeat condition
REP	MOVS STOS	Repeat until CX = 0
REPE/REZ	CMPS SCAS	Repeat until CX = 0 and while string items are equal
REPNE/REPNZ	CMPS SCAS	Repeat until CX = 0 and while string items are unequal

86 The 8086 and Assembly Language

It should be noticed that table 4.12 does not include the string primitive LODS. This is because a repeat prefix used with this instruction would cause the accumulator to be loaded with information in such a manner that each new byte/word would overwrite the previously loaded byte/word. The string primitive LODS is used with other string primitives to form complex string instructions.

PROGRAM TRANSFER INSTRUCTIONS

These instructions are divided into three groups, shown in table 4.13.

Table 4.13 Program transfer instructions.

Unconditional Transfers	CALL RET JMP	Call subroutine Return from subroutine Unconditional jump
Conditional Jumps	JA/JNBE JAE/JNB JB/JNAE JBE/JNA JC JCXZ JE/JZ JG/JNLE JGE/JNL JL/JNGE JLE/JNG JNC JNE/JNZ JNO JNP/JPO JNS JO JP/JPE JS	Jump if above/neither below nor equal Jump if above or equal/not below Jump if below/neither above nor equal Jump if below or equal/not above Jump if carry is set Jump if CX register is zero Jump if equal/zero Jump if greater/neither less nor equal Jump if greater or equal/not less than Jump if less/neither greater nor equal Jump if less or equal/not greater than Jump if no carry Jump if not equal/not zero Jump if no overflow Jump if no parity/parity odd Jump if no sign (jump if positive) Jump if overflow is set Jump if parity is set/even Jump if sign is set
Loop Iteration Controls	LOOP LOOPE/LOOPZ LOOPNE/LOOPNZ	Loop Loop if equal/zero Loop if not equal/not zero

There are two variations of the unconditional jump instruction. The first is an intra-segment jump, i.e. a jump within the current code segment; it is executed by placing the new offset address in the IP. The second is an inter-segment jump, i.e. a jump between segments; this involves placing new values in both IP and CS. A subroutine is a short program subordinate to the main program and is placed in a separate memory area so that it can be easily accessed by the main program. The two instructions for subroutine handling are call (CALL) and return (RET).

Instruction Categories **87**

The conditional jump instruction transfers control to a new area of program provided a particular condition has been satisfied. These instructions use the same second byte displacement to form a relative address as does the unconditional jump instruction. The compare (CMP) and test (TEST) instructions are usually used to determine the conditions for these instructions. The terms 'greater' and 'less' are normally used when signed numbers are compared, whereas 'above' and 'below' are normally used when the comparison is between unsigned numbers. The flag settings on which the conditional jumps depend have been explained in detail in table 4.5.

Table 4.14 shows examples to illustrate the action of the conditional jump instructions. The register contents, immediately prior to the execution of a compare instruction, are stated and the conditional jump instruction directly follows the compare instruction. The question to be answered is whether or not the jump occurs.

Table 4.14 Action of conditional jump instructions.

Register AX contents	Register BX contents	Conditional jump after CMP AX,BX	Jump occurs
0AAAH	0AA9H	JG	YES
9AAAH	0AA9H	JG	NO
0AAAH	0AA9H	JA	YES
9AAAH	0AA9H	JA	YES
0AAAH	0AABH	JL	YES
9AAAH	0AABH	JL	YES
0AAAH	0AABH	JB	YES
9AAAH	0AABH	JB	NO
0AAAH	0ABCH	JPO	?
0AAAH	5987H	JNO	?

These results can be explained by examination of the flags after the comparison instruction has been executed. In the first two examples in table 4.14, the numbers are considered as signed because the term 'greater' is used in the jump instruction. In the first example 0AAAH is positive and greater than 0AA9H so the jump will occur, and in the second example 9AAAH is negative and so less than 0AA9H so the jump will not occur. In the third and fourth examples the numbers are considered as unsigned, because the term 'above' is used in the conditional jump instruction, and so in each case the jump will occur. This

88 The 8086 and Assembly Language

consideration of signed and unsigned numbers does not apply to the final examples involving JPO and JNO.

A loop operation can be organised by placing a count value in the CX register and using the instructions DEC CX followed by JNZ as loop control. However, these two instructions can be replaced by the single instruction LOOP, as shown in the following example:

```
         MOV    CX,COUNT
AGAIN:   -
         -
         LOOP   AGAIN
```

The other loop instructions LOOPZ and LOOPNZ check not only the CX register but also the zero flag, looking for Z = 1 and Z = 0 respectively.

The remaining groups of instructions can be termed system control instructions. However, they are subdivided into the groups shown in tables 4.15, 4.16 and 4.17.

Table 4.15 Flag instructions.

STC	Set the carry flag
CLC	Clear the carry flag
CMC	Complement the carry flag
STD	Set the direction flag
CLD	Clear the direction flag
STI	Set interrupt enable flag
CLI	Clear interrupt enable flag

These are a group of instructions which are used directly with the individual flags. They involve two instructions which are associated with the interrupt flag. These two instructions are not included in table 4.16 which lists only the interrupt instructions.

Table 4.16 Interrupt instructions.

INT	Interrupt
INTO	Interrupt if overflow
IRET	Return from interrupt

Table 4.17 External synchronisation instructions.

HLT	Halt until interrupt or reset
WAIT	Wait for TEST pin to be active
ESC	Escape to external processor
LOCK	Lock bus during next instruction

For an initial appraisal of both the interrupt instructions in table 4.16 and the synchronisation instructions in table 4.17 the reader is referred to chapter 3, and interrupts are examined in detail in chapter 7.

Instruction Categories **89**

Questions

(4.1) Explain in detail the action of the following instructions: AAA, DAA, CWD, PUSH DI and XCHG AX,SI.

(4.2) Consider registers AX and CX to initially contain 08FCH and 04H repectively; state the contents of register AX after execution of the instructions: (a) SHL AX,CL, (b) ROR AX,1 and (c) SAR AX,CL.

(4.3) If the BX and CX registers contain respectively 96A2H and 6F28H, give the state of the flags OF, SF, ZF, and CF after each of the following instructions has executed: (a) CMP BL,CL and (b) CMP BX,CX

(4.4) What will be the contents of the AX, BX, CX and DX registers after each of the following program sections have executed?

```
        (a) MOV  AX,145      (b) MOV  AX,145H
            SUB  AX,59           SUB  AX,59H
            MOV  BX,AX           MOV  BX,AX
            MOV  DX,BX           MOV  DX,BX
            DEC  BX              NEG  BX
            MOV  CX,BX           MOV  CX,BX
            MUL  AX,CX           MUL  CX,AX
            CWD                  CWD
```

(4.5) Trace and explain the purpose of the programs:

```
        (a) CLD              (b) MOV  CX,25
            MOV  DI,20           MOV  SI,20
            MOV  CX,100          MOV  AX,[SI]
            MOV  AL,00      NEX: INC  SI
      REPNZ SCASB                INC  SI
            MOV  BX,DI           CMP  AX,[SI]
            HLT                  JGE  AGAIN
                                 MOV  AX,[SI]
                          AGAIN: LOOP NEX
                                 MOV  BX,AX
                                 HLT
```

(4.6) Write program sections to carry out the following:
(a) Add the contents of the AX, BX, CX and DX registers; saving the result in the SI register.
(b) Exchange the contents of data segment locations 40H and 60H.
(c) Fill the first 100 bytes of the data segment with the value 0.
(d) Determine (1) how many locations in the data segment between addresses 100H and 150H contain FFH and (2) how many contain the ASCII code for '?'.
(e) Reverse the bits in register AX, i.e. B15, B14, B13, B12 etc. becomes B0, B1, B2, B3 etc.

CHAPTER 5
Assembly language

Any student of the 8086/8088, 80186, 80286 and 80386 microprocessors must be familiar with the machine instruction language, i.e. the language directly associated with the architecture of the microprocessor. ASM86 is the assembly language provided by Intel for this series of microprocessors; the assembler is also known as ASM86. MASM is the assembler that is provided for the IBM PC and is frequently used with IBM compatible microcomputers. The two assemblers use languages which are essentially the same. For example, there is a difference in the way in which macros are defined in what can be referred to as the two assemblers' dialects. It is the purpose of this chapter to examine and explain the usage of the instruction statements, data allocation statements and assembler directives of the assembly language ASM86. It is important for the user to understand the procedure by which programs are written and eventually placed in either the read/write memory (RAM) or the read only memory (ROM) of the microprocessor system in which they are designed to operate. So before studying the assembly language in detail the software development procedure is explained.

SOFTWARE DEVELOPMENT PROCEDURE

The Assembler Program

A program written in the assembly language is usually referred to as a 'source' program or file. All such source files written in the assembly language are translated into machine language by the assembler program. This program acts on the source file of assembly language statements to produce an 'object' file and a 'listing' or diagnostic file. It is the object file which contains the machine readable information. This object file is relocatable, which means that it can be operated on to enable it to run in any memory area associated with the microprocessor. The listing file is the file which is used to display both the assembly language, the machine code in hexadecimal

Assembly Language **91**

format and also any errors in the assembly language format, hence the term diagnostic file. Figure 5.1 illustrates the production of the object and listing files by the action of the assembler on the source file.

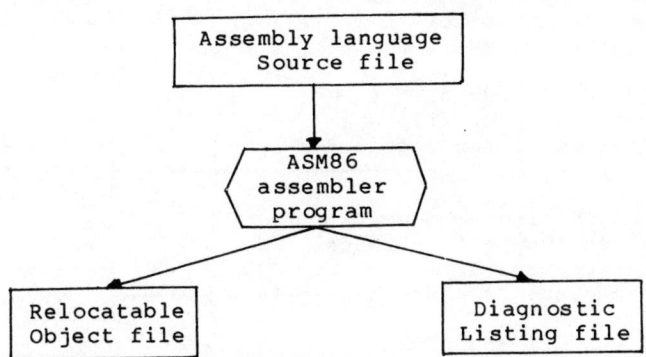

Figure 5.1 Action of assembler program on a source file.

Using a Development System

Any program written in assembly language must be assembled to form relocatable object code, then possibly linked to other relocatable object programs to form a complete object module, and finally located to a definite memory location so that it can be executed in 8086 microprocessor target system. This software development procedure is summarised here and illustrated in figure 5.2. TRIAL is the program name taken to illustrate the procedure.

The editor is the environment used to create and modify the assembly language source program. The source program itself is then automatically saved on some form of mass storage, for example a floppy disk, or hard disk and in this example given the full name TRIAL.A86. The extension to the source program name .A86 is used to indicate that the program is written in the assembly language.

The assembler translates the source file into an object file TRIAL.OBJ which again will be automatically saved in the storage medium. The listing file created TRIAL.LST will also be saved. It is this file which is usually printed and referred to, in order that the assembly language syntatic errors can be corrected. Note that the respective files are recognised by the extensions to the program name. These extensions are automatically given during the assembly process. It is at this stage that the object file can, if required, be combined with other relocatable object files to form a complete relocatable program. The program which is used to perform this combination is known as a linker. In this example

92 The 8086 and Assembly Language

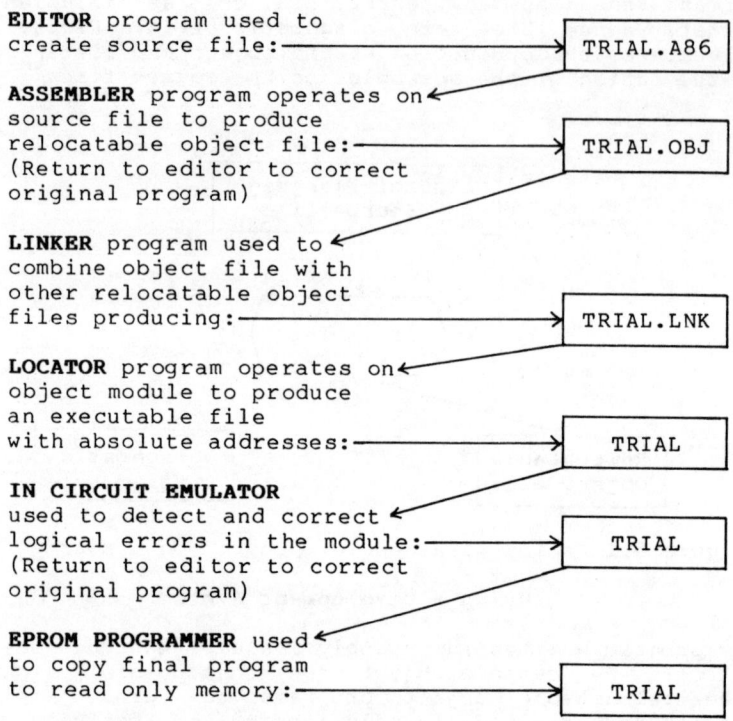

Software Development using a Development System

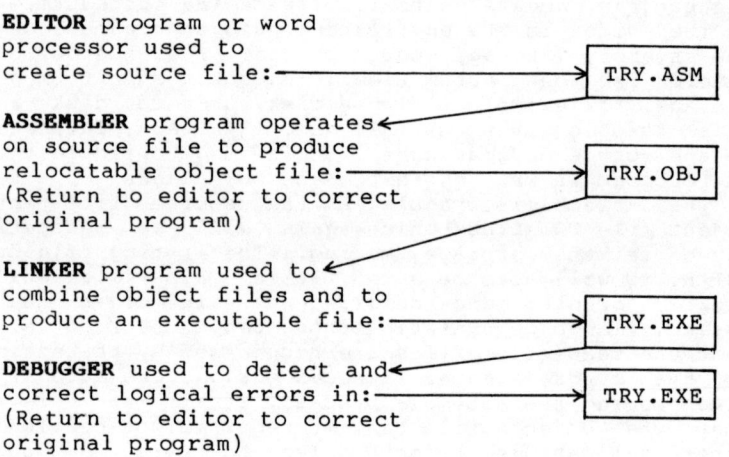

Software Development using a PC

Figure 5.2 Software development procedure.

the resulting combined program has been given the name TRIAL.LNK, the name extension .LNK simply indicating that the linker has been used.

The object file is now loaded/located to a particular memory area, i.e. absolute addresses are given to the code. This is done using a locator program the Intel version of which is LOC86. The resultant program TRIAL which has been allocated absolute addresses (now the name is without an extension) is said to be in executable format. The program TRIAL can be executed and any logical errors in the program can be detected and corrected. This part of the development is known as program debugging. The debugger is the development tool used to detect and remove logical errors from the executable program. The most versatile and most frequently used debuggers are known as 'in circuit emulators'. An in circuit emulator is a device which enables the engineer to debug and test his software in the microprocessor sytem hardware in which it will eventually reside. If the program TRIAL is, for example, a program being developed to operate a microprocessor controller, then it can be tested and debugged with the in circuit emulator plugged into the controller hardware. The final step in the procedure is to copy the debugged program to an EPROM so that it is in a permanent state for use in the microprocessor system.

Using an IBM PC or Compatible PC

The software development procedure is essentially the same. Consider a computer based on either the 8086 or 8088 microprocessors and using, for example, the MS DOS operating system. An editor or a word processing package is the environment used to create an assembly language program and the resident assembler provided is MASM. A resident assembler operates on the assembly language of the microprocessor in the microcomputer running the assembler. In this case consider the example program to be TRY.ASM, it is desirable to use the .ASM extension to the program name. Using the assembler MASM the source program can be assembled to produce an object file TRY.OBJ, and a diagnostic listing file TRY.LST. When several object files need to be combined this is achieved using the the linker program LINK. However the LINK program also produces the executable file, that is, a file with absolute addresses and so needs to be used even with a single file such as TRY.OBJ. When the linker is invoked to act on the object file it will produce TRY.EXE which is an executable file. This executable file can now be run and debugged using the debugging program DEBUG. This system does not allow the engineer to debug the software while embedded in the associated hardware. However a stand alone in circuit emulator can be connected to the computer system producing effectively a development system. If this is done then the in circuit emulator can be used instead of DEBUG to detect and correct errors in the executable file.

94 The 8086 and Assembly Language

SEGMENTATION

The 8086 microprocessor, because it has 20 address lines, can directly address 1 Mbyte of memory. The 20 bit address is formed by adding a displaced 16 bit segment address and a 16 bit offset address. In every case the microprocessor creates its memory address using a segment register. The microprocessor in fact sees the memory as four segments

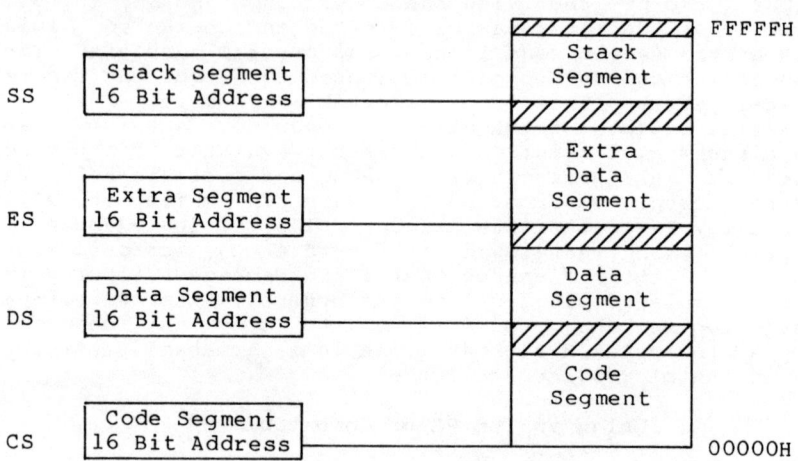

Structure with Four Separate Segments

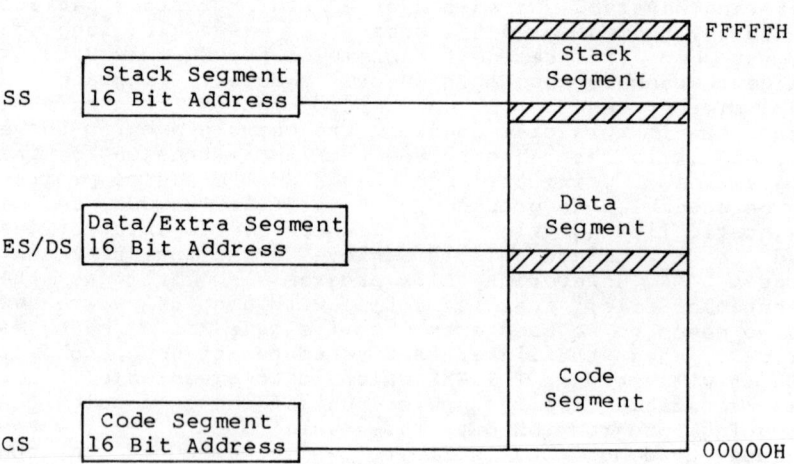

Structure with Overlapping Data Segments

Figure 5.3 Memory segmented structures.

Assembly Language **95**

each defined by a segment register and each of which can occupy 64 Kbytes. Each segment register points to the base of its respective segment. Executable code resides in the code segment, data in the data segment and stack operations relate to information in the stack segment. There is also an extra data segment which can in small systems be overlapped with the data segment creating effectively a three segment system consisting of up to 64 Kbytes of code, 64 Kbytes of data and 64 Kbytes for the stack. The memory segment structures shown in figure 5.3 indicate two arrangements, one with four separate segments, the base address of each segment being held in its corresponding segment register, and a second perhaps more convenient arrangement in which there are effectively only three segments in current use the data segments overlapping to form a single segment. In both arrangements each segment can occupy 64 KBytes.

ASSEMBLY LANGUAGE CONSTITUENTS

The assembly language consists of statements which in turn consist of identifiers, numbers, reserved words, comments, etc. These constituents are now discussed.

Statements
The assembly language can be regarded as having three distinct types of statement:

(a) Instruction statements - those which use mnemonics and operands to specify machine instructions. For example:

```
MOV  DS,AX
XOR  AX,[SI]
```

(b) Data allocation statements - these reserve space in memory for data and can allocate an identifier to the variable data. Examples of which are:

```
DSIN  DB  128
DCOS  DW  4455H
```

(c) Assembler directive statements - those which provide instructions to the assembler and in most cases do not generate code for the microprocessor. Typical examples being:

```
PCODE  SEGMENT
       END
```

Constants
Constants are data containers which are pure numbers without attributes. They can be expressed in binary, octal, decimal, hexadecimal, ASCII or real format. Constants can occur as immediate operands within

instructions and also when defined using the EQU directive.

Variables
Variables are named data containers defined either by data definition statements or by using the LABEL directive. A variable has an address in memory specified by the attributes 'segment' and 'offset', and the storage is specified by the 'type', i.e. byte or word etc. The data contents of a variable can be changed when instructions are executed.

Labels
Labels define offset addresses within a segment, i.e. they provide a name for a particular location. The program can reach this location via either a jump instruction or a call instruction. The attributes of a label are segment, offset and type. The type attribute can be either NEAR or FAR, indicating that the label can be referred to only within a segment (namely the NEAR label) or between segments (the FAR label). For a NEAR label which is defined by using a colon, the assembler need only know the offset address. However, for a FAR label defined by using the LABEL or PROC directives, the assembler must record both the offset and code segments contents because the label can be accessed from all segments.

Identifiers
Identifiers are provided by the programmer to represent constants, variables and labels. Identifiers must be between one and thirty-one characters long, must begin with a letter and can contain letters, numbers, the underscore sign (_) and a question mark (?). The following indentifiers are permissible: FIRST_ONE, NUMB24, P16, DATA?FILL. Assembler mnemonics and directives are classified as reserved words and cannot be used as identifiers.

Comments
Within a program comments should be liberally used and their purpose should be to aid the reader in his understanding of the program. A comment can be recognised as it begins with a semicolon (;) and then continues to the end of the line.

Numbers
Numbers can be expressed in any of the following formats: binary, octal, decimal, and hexadecimal. Examples of which are: 10001011B, 56Q, 23000 and 07ABH. Note that in the case of decimal numbers no identifying letter is required.

SUMMARY OF DIRECTIVES AND OPERATORS

Directives

(1) **SEGMENT/ENDS** - defines segment boundaries.
(2) **ASSUME** - informs assembler of segment names.
(3) **EQU** - equate directive used to specify a constant, an address, a register or an instruction mnemonic.
(4) **DB, DW, DD, DQ** and **DT** data definition directives applying respectively to: a byte, a word, a double word, 8 bytes and 10 bytes.
(5) **PROC/ENDP** - defines the procedure (subroutine) boundaries.
(6) **LABEL** - identifier definition without the allocation of memory storage.
(7) **ORG** - used to originate code at a selected offset address.
(8) **EVEN** - aligns data on an even address.
(9) **PUBLIC** - indicates identifiers that can be used by other modules.
(10) **EXTRN** - indicates identifiers that are external to current module.
(11) **END** - informs assembler of the cessation of processing.
(12) **GROUP** - used to gather named segments under given name.
(13) **NAME** - defines module name.

Operators

(1) **SEG** - returns segment value of variable or label.
(2) **OFFSET** - returns offset address of variable.
(3) **TYPE** - returns value for operand type, e.g. 2 for a word.
(4) **LENGTH** - returns number of data items of array.
(5) **SIZE** - returns number of bytes allotted to a variable.
(6) **PTR** - used to specify type of operand.
(7) **THIS** - used to override the type of a previously defined variable.
(8) **SHORT** - used with short forward jump to save a byte.
(9) **Arithmetic Operators:**
addition and subtraction: +, -
multiplication and division: *, /, MOD, SHR, SHL
relational: EQ, NE, LT, LE, GT, GE
logical: NOT, AND, OR, XOR

Assembler Directives in Detail

Assembler directives are the commands in the language which are used to instruct the assembler, they are also known as 'pseudo ops'. The majority of the directives do not produce object code. The directives which do produce object code are used to define data items. A brief

98 The 8086 and Assembly Language

explanation of each directive in the summary listing will now be given.

SEGMENT/ENDS and ASSUME directives
In the assembly language it is necessary to carefully define logical segments, and then to inform the assembler which segment register is associated with each of the segments defined. A segment is defined using the SEGMENT/ENDS directive combined with the name given to the segment. In the following example the segments PCODE and PDATA are defined.

```
        PCODE   SEGMENT
                  -
                  -
                  -
                  -
        PCODE   ENDS
        PDATA   SEGMENT
                  -
                  -
                  -
        PDATA   ENDS
```

The ASSUME directive informs the assembler which segment is associated with each segment register. This directive does not generate any object code.

```
        ASSUME  CS:PCODE,DS:PDATA
```

The assembler on reading this directive associates the code segment register with the segment PCODE and the data segment register with the segment PDATA. Hence in this program the code segment is called PCODE and the data segment is called PDATA.

Constants and the Directive EQU
Constants are data containers which occur within the program and the value specified cannot be changed. The most obvious occurrence is as an immediate value within an instruction. Consider the example:

```
        MOV  AX,0FFFEH
```

In this case the constant is stipulated as part of the instruction. A much better programming technique is to use an identifier to represent the constant. This has the advantage of being much more readable and need not be defined at the point of usage within the program. The above instruction can be replaced by:

```
        MOV  AX,CONTROL?REG
```

The identifier has been defined using the assembler equate

Assembly Language 99

directive EQU, as shown below. The definition could have been made at the beginning of the code segment.

```
CONTROL?REG   EQU   0FFFEH
```

The directive can be used in other ways besides simply assigning an identifier to a constant. For example it can be used to define a register expression:

```
    VARYA   EQU   [BX + 6]
```

Or it can be used to define a register name:

```
    COUNTER   EQU   CX
```

Variables and Data Definition Directives
A variable is a data item whose value can be changed by the execution of instructions in the program. The assembler directives are used to allocate memory for the variable and allocate a name to the memory address. The use of directives in the definition of variables follows the format:

Identifier DB Expression

The directive DB is used to reserve a byte in memory, whereas DW reserves a word and DD reserves four bytes (doubleword). The use of these directives is clearly shown in the following examples:

(1) Defining a variable and allotting it a value:
```
        INFA   DB   22       ;A byte variable INFA
        VARA   DW   0FF2BH   ;A word variable VARA
```
These variables can now be referred to by instructions in the code segment, typical examples being as follows:
```
            MOV   CL,INFA   ;Loads the value 22 to CL
            MOV   BX,VARA   ;Moves 0FF2BH into BX
```
(2) A variable can be identified without being given an initial value. In this case a question mark is used in place of an expression.
```
        INDIC   DB   ?
        NUMB1   DW   ?
```
Again the variable can be used in the program, the following are typical examples:
```
            MOV   INDIC,CL   ;CL contents copied to INDIC
            MOV   NUMB1,AX   ;AX contents copied to NUMB1
```
(3) These examples show the definition of arrays of data items. An array is a collection of data items of the same type and referred to by a single identifier.
```
        LISTA   DB   10,20,30,40,50,60,70,80
        COLLB   DW   2300,2400,2500,2600
```
Typical references to these data items are as follows:
```
            MOV   CL,LISTA+2   ;Move 30 into CL
            ADD   AX,COLLB     ;Add 2300 to contents of AX
```

(4) A complete data array can be set to a particular value using the duplicate facility as follows:
    BLOCA   DB   25 DUP (0)   ;25 bytes each set to zero
    BLOCB   DW   14 DUP (2FA4H);14 words set to 2FA4H
Equally a data array can be defined but the values of the data items may remain unspecified as shown below:
    BLOCD   DB   88 DUP (?)
(5) Using the DB directive a string of characters up to 255 in length can be defined; the string must be enclosed in single quotation marks. The ASCII code for each character is stored in a byte location.
    LETTERS   DB   'ABCDE'
The variable LETTERS contains the ASCII code for A, i.e. 41H, while LETTERS +1 contains the ASCII code for B, namely 42H.
(6) An address expression can be initialised using either DW or DD. When an identifier is used as the expression in this way, the initialisation is with the offset address of the identifier. For example, if a variable is identified by the name VARD as follows:
    VARD   DB   130
then the address can be initialised using:
    OVARD   DW   VARD
and both offset and segment addresses can be initialised using:
    OSVARD   DD   VARD
Now when OVARD is used within an instruction it is the offset address of VARD which is employed and for OSVARD both offset and segment addresses are employed.

PROC/ENDP Procedure Directives
Procedures or subroutines are named code sequences which are brought into action using a CALL instruction. A procedure must contain at least one RET instruction. The directive PROC is used to define a label marking the entry to a procedure, and the type of procedure, i.e. NEAR or FAR, is indicated in this definition statement. The ENDP directive simply indicates the end of the procedure.

        DEL1   PROC   NEAR
        -
        -
        -
        DEL1   ENDP

When a CALL instruction is used to invoke the procedure the type of procedure must be known by the assembler so that either the long or short form of the instruction is initiated. If the procedure is of the NEAR type then only the IP contents are transferred to the stack for the use of the return instruction RET; if the procedure is a FAR one, i.e. in another segment, then both the CS and the IP contents are transferred to the stack.

LABEL Directive
This directive can be used to define an identifier without allocating memory storage to that identifier, and where the type of identifier can be FAR or NEAR as well as BYTE, WORD, etc. So when a jump to another segment is necessary a FAR label is required. That label must be defined using the LABEL directive and not simply with a colon as in the case of a NEAR label.

In the section dealing with segment register initialisation the stack segment includes the LABEL directive to define STKTOP as a word. This example is also shown here as an indication of the use of the LABEL directive.

```
    PSTAK    SEGMENT
             DW    50   DUP  (?)
    STKTOP   LABEL WORD
    PSTAK    ENDS
```

ORG Directive
This directive can be used to specify a particular offset location within a segment for either code or data. Hence a data list can be placed at a particular offset address within a data segment, as follows:

```
    DATAP    SEGMENT
             ORG   50   DUP  (?)
    DLIST    DB    1,2,3,4,5,6,7,8,9
    DATAP    ENDS
```

EVEN Directive
This directive is used to align the data following on a word boundary. The 8086 fetches a word from an even address in one memory accesss and needs to access memory twice to bring a word at an odd address, this is explained in detail in chapter 6. Hence the use of the even directive may result in a faster operation of the program.

When it becomes necessary to link modules, to form a complete program, it may be that some modules contain variables or procedures that need to be accessed by other modules. The directives which allow this to take place are PUBLIC and EXTRN.

PUBLIC and EXTRN Directives
The PUBLIC directive specifies identifiers that can be used by other modules. Whereas the EXTRN directive specifies identifiers that are external to the current module, but to be accessed they must have been declared as PUBLIC in the other module. Consider as an example two modules MOD1 and MOD2, where procedure TRY in MOD2 is declared as PUBLIC, and as it is declared EXTRN in MOD1 it can be accessed from MOD1.

102 The 8086 and Assembly Language

```
                NAME    MOD1                      NAME    MOD2
                EXTRN   TRY                       PUBLIC  TRY
    ASSUME      CS:PCODE            ASSUME        CS:CODEP
    PCODE       SEGMENT             CODEP         SEGMENT
                -                                 -
                -                   TRY           PROC    FAR
                CALL    TRY                       -
                -                                 -
    PCODE       ENDS                TRY           ENDP
                END                 CODEP         ENDS
                                                  END
```

END Directive
This is the last statement in an assembler module and it is this statement which causes the assembler to stop processing.

NAME directive
This directive is used to define a name for an assembly language module so that modules can be identified and linked together to form a complete program. The example above of the two modules MOD1 and MOD2 illustrate the use of both the END and NAME directives.

GROUP Directive
This is used to arrange segments under a single name, such as grouping together various data segments as in the following example:

```
    DATALL    GROUP   PDAT1,PDAT2
    PDAT1     SEGMENT
              -
              -
    PDAT1     ENDS
    PDAT2     SEGMENT
              -
    PDAT2     ENDS
    ASSUME    DS:DATALL
```

Assembler Operators in Detail

The assembler has built in operators to enable the programmer to return information relating to the variables which have previously been defined within the program. These 'value returning' operators are SEG, OFFSET, TYPE, LENGTH and SIZE.

SEG Operator
This operator causes the segment value of the of the variable concerned to be returned. One use of this operator is to initialise a segment register as follows:

```
    REAL:    MOV   AX, SEG VALA
             MOV   DS,AX
```

OFFSET Operator

This operator causes the offset address of the variable concerned to be returned. It can most usefully be used in the initialisation of registers, such as SI, which are then themselves involved in indirect addressing. A typical example might be as follows:

```
ALLV    DW      1234,2345,3456,4567,5678,6789,7899
        -
        -
        MOV     BX,OFFSET ALLV  ;Offset address of ALLV
                                ;is placed in BX.
```

TYPE operator

This operator causes a value representing the type of operand to be returned. For example, when the operand is defined using DW then 2 is returned; when defined using DD then 4 is returned. It is frequently used in situations where the type of operand is needed to increment a pointer. Such an example follows:

```
ALLV    DW      1234,2345,3456,4567,5678,6789,7899
        -
        -
        MOV     BX,OFFSET ALLV
        MOV     SI,0
        -
        SUB     AX,[BX + SI]    ;Subtract first word of
                                ;array
        -
        ADD     SI,TYPE ALLV    ;2 added to register SI
        ADD     AX,[BX + SI]    ;Add second word of array
```

LENGTH Operator

When a variable has been allocated a number of items as in an array definition, it is useful for the programmer to be able to find out the number of items held. This can be done by employing the LENGTH operator, which returns the number of data items allocated to the variable. An example of its use is in setting a counter for a loop which involves the use of each array item in turn:

```
ALLV    DW      1234,2345,3456,4567,5678,6789,7899
                ;Seven word items
        -
        MOV     CX,LENGTH ALLV  ;Moves 7 into CX
```

SIZE Operator

In this case the operator returns the number of bytes allotted to a variable. So in the following example 14 is moved into BX:

```
ALLV    DW      1234,2345,3456,4567,5678,6789,7899
                ;Seven word items
        -
        MOV     BX,SIZE ALLV;Moves 14 into BX.
```

104 The 8086 and Assembly Language

PTR Operator
This operator is used to specify the type of operand in situations where the assembler may not know the operand type, and in other situations where it is necessary to override the operand type.

```
            INC  WORD PTR [BX];Increment word pointed
                                ;to by BX

INFA        DW   0F00H

            MOV  BYTE PTR INFA ; Move first byte
                                ;of variable INFA to register BL
```

THIS Operator
It is used in conjunction with the EQU directive to redefine for the assembler the type of a variable. Its use is shown in the following example:

```
    NWORD   EQU  THIS WORD
    BYTEA   DB   50H
    BYTEB   DB   51H
```

The contents of the locations identified by BYTEA and BYTEB can be accessed as a word using the identifer NWORD.

SHORT Operator
When the assembler encounters a JMP instruction to a forward referenced label it assumes two bytes for the offset address and so the instruction occupies three bytes. If the label is within +127 bytes, the use of the SHORT operator informs the assembler that a two byte instruction can be used, and so a byte of code can be saved. A typical example is:

```
            JMP  NEW?PLACE ; This is a three byte
                            ;instruction.
            JMP  SHORT NEW?PLACE ; This is a two byte
                                  ;instruction.
```

Arithmetic Operators
The arithmetic operators that can be used are as follows:-
+, -, *, /, MOD. These operators represent addition subtraction multiplication and division respectively. MOD is an operator which produces the remainder after a division. The following statements include some simple examples:

```
        INFO1   EQU  07
        VARA    DW   22

                MOV  VARA+4,AX
                ADD  AX,INFO1/3
                MOV  BX,120 MOD INFO1
```

The relational operators that are valid are as follows:
EQ - equal, NE - not equal, LT - less than or equal,
GT - greater than and GE - greater than or equal.
These relational operators may only be used with numeric
values.

```
NDAT    EQU  55
        MOV  CL,NDAT GE 25 ;Places 0FFH in CL
        MOV  CH,NDAT EQ 50 ;Places 00 in CH
```

The logical operators NOT, AND, OR and XOR may only be
used with absolute numbers. The following examples
illustrate their use:

```
NVAL    EQU  0AAH
        MOV  AX,NVAL AND 0FH ;Masking the
                             ;upper four bits.
        MOV  BX,NVAL OR 0F0H ;Setting the
                             ;upper four bits.
```

MACROS

An assembly language macro processing facility is
essentially a string replacement facility. It allows a
section of code to be named and written in the program
automatically whenever that name is used within the
program. In the assembler ASM86 the function DEFINE is used
to create a macro. The syntax for the definition of a
parameterless macro is as follows:

%* DEFINE(Macro name)(Macro contents)

Consider a very simple macro defined at the beginning of
the program as follows:

```
%*DEFINE(KEEP)(
PUSH    SI
PUSH    DI
)
```

The macro call statement can be used at any position in
the body of the program. Before assembly the call
statement may appear as follows:

```
        MOV  CX,COUNT
        %KEEP         ;Macro call
        CALL SUB1
```

The program listing after assembly will be:

```
        MOV  CX,COUNT
        PUSH SI
        PUSH DI
        CALL SUB1
```

The use of the macro KEEP is exactly the same as writing
PUSH SI and PUSH DI.

It is worth noting that different assemblers define macros in different ways. In the assembler MASM the macro is defined using the syntax:

```
Name MACRO
   -              Macro
   -              Instructions
   ENDM
```

Reverting to ASM86 we can see how parameters can be included in a macro. The syntax used is now:

%*DEFINE (Macro name(Parameter list))(Macro contents)

The following example macro, in which parameters are passed to the macro, is defined at the beginning of the program:

```
%* DEFINE (KEEP(REG1,REG2))(
PUSH   %REG1
PUSH   %REG2
)
```

Within the program the macro call statement can be used at any time such as in the following example:

```
MOV   SI,OFFSET LOT1
MOV   DI,OFFSET LOT2
%KEEP(SI,DI)
MOV   CX,COUNT
LEA   DX,OLDVAL
%KEEP(CX,DX)
```

The macro has been called twice in this program before the assembler has been invoked. After assembly the listing will be:

```
MOV   SI,OFFSET LOT1
MOV   DI,OFFSET LOT2
PUSH  SI
PUSH  DI
MOV   CX,COUNT
LEA   DX,OLDVAL
PUSH  CX
PUSH  DX
```

The parameters can represent registers, addresses of variables, strings, numerical values, etc. A macro when called four times in a program results after assembly in four sequences of code and there is no longer any evidence of the existence of a macro. Note this is not the same with a subroutine, which is a single sequence of code appearing only once in memory. When a subroutine is called the result is a transfer of control to and from the code sequence making up the subroutine.

Segment Register Initialisation

Program machine code instructions are stored in the code segment. Consequently every instruction fetch cycle involves the use of the code segment register. So the code segment register must be initialised before the program begins execution. Usually the code segment register is set at the locate/load stage when an executable file is created. Execution starts at the beginning of the program which resides in the code segment.

There is no immediate instruction associated with a segment register, and so to initialise the segment registers DS, ES and SS the required addresses are moved from another register such as the accumulator. The most convenient operand to use is the segment name itself; this enables the segments to be easily relocated within memory. The values to be placed in the segment registers are alloted at the locating/loading stage of the program development. Frequently the first lines of a program are those which initialise the segment registers to be used within the program. In the following program the segments PCODE, PDATA, PEXTRA and PSTAK are defined using the SEGMENT/ENDS directive and are related to segment registers CS, DS, ES and SS respectively by the ASSUME directive.

In each case the segment name is used as an operand and moved into the corresponding segment register. At the locating/loading stage these operands are given absolute values, and it is these values which become the base addresses of the segments. Using this technique all the segments can be relocated in memory simply by modifying these values at the locate stage, i.e. a program can be located to a different absolute location each time it is used. The initialisation of the stack segment is completed when both the stack segment register and the stack pointer are initialised. The following instruction effectively provides the stack pointer with an offset address well within the stack segment.

```
        MOV   SP,STKTOP
```

The location STKTOP can be seen to be 100 bytes into the stack segment, its offset address is 0050H, this has been achieved by reserving the first fifty words of the stack segment by the DW directive. The stack pointer is set to a location well within the stack segment because as each item of data is placed on the stack, the stack pointer is automatically decremented.

This implies that for the 8086 microprocessor the stack is loaded downwards through memory, the reader is referred to chapter 4 to the detailed section dealing with pushing and popping data off and on the stack.

ASSEMBLER ERRORS

In chapter 8 a series of example programs is given which illustrates the instruction set and the use of the assembly language. The example which follows in this chapter is that of a program designed not to perform a useful task in the usual way, but simply to demonstrate a variety of errors that can occur in assembler programming. The exercise in assembly language programming technique will be achieved if the reader can enter the instruction listing as shown, assemble the program using ASM86 or MASM and obtain a copy of the diagnostic (.LST) file. The object of the exercise is to correct the assembler errors while maintaining the intended nature of each instruction. For those readers who are not immediately able to do this, a copy of the ASM86 diagnostic file printout is given at the end of. this chapter and a corrected version of the listing is given in appendix A.

Program 5.1

```
;
;
;
;
;   Title:    Assembly Language Errors
;   Filename:     ERROR.A86
;   Purpose: This is a list of instructions in
;assembly language each one of which creates an assembly
;error, and in which the intention of the instruction
;is given in the comment field. The student should
;assemble the program, obtain a printout
;of the list file, note the errors and correct them.
;************************************************************
ASSUME   CS:PROGC
;************************************************************
PROGC    SEGMENT
LOOP1    MOV     AL,1234H;Move immediate to accumulator
         MOV     0300,AX :Move AX contents to offset 300H
         MOV     BL,FFH  ;Set each bit in BL to '1'
         MOV     CX,BL   ;Transfer between 16 bit registers
         MOV     OFFFE,BL;Move a byte from BL to memory
LOOP2:   INC     0303H   ;Increment memory location contents
         SBB     0304H   ;Subtract immediate from AX
         CMP     AL,AAH  ;Compare immediate AL with  AAH
         JNZ     LOOP1   ;Conditional jump
         JLE     LOPP2   ;Conditional jump
         DIV     AX,CX   ;Divide by the word stored in CX
PRGC     ENDS
;************************************************************
```

ASM86 ASSEMBLER CONTROLS

When using an assembler there are normally a large number of controls that can be specified to select the options available with the assembly process. It is unnecessary to specify any such controls when invoking the assembler

Assembly Language 109

Table 5.1 A selection of assembler controls for ASM86

DATE(***) Allows the user to include a date in the program listing header. Omission of the date is the default.

ERRORPRINT Directs the assembler to print a list summarising the errors encountered in assembly. The default device is the console.

NOERRORPRINT Directs the assembler not to print a summary of the errors encountered. NOERRORPRINT is the default control.

LIST Directs the assembler to include listing lines.

NOLIST Directs the assembler to suppress printing of listing lines until a LIST control is read. Error messages with the appropriate line numbers and lines are printed.

PAGING The listing file is formatted into numbered pages with headers at each page break. If neither PAGING nor NOPAGING is put on the command line, PAGING is the default.

NOPAGING The listing file does not have formatted pages.

SYMBOLS If SYMBOLS is specified an alphabetical list of symbols appears at the end of the listing.

NOSYMBOLS No symbol table appears at the end of the listing file. NOSYMBOLS is the default control.

XREF Provides a symbol list with a cross reference of the lines where user defined symbols are defined, referenced, and purged. NOXREF is the default. XREF overrides NOSYMBOLS.

NOXREF No cross referencing is placed in the symbol table at the end of the listing file.

---

because all have default values that will occur automatically. A knowledge of these controls can help the programmer to use the assembler in the most efficient manner. The following is an example of invoking the ASM86 assembler and using only the controls that are brought into action by default:

    ASM86 TRIAL.A86

As has been stated at the beginning of this chapter, when a source file is assembled the assembler by default forms an object file having the name extension .OBJ and a listing file with the name extension .LST. With ASM86 there are primary controls which can be used to suppress

110 The 80866 and Assembly Language

the formation of either of these files. At the first assembly of a long program it may be desirable simply to print the errors rather than the complete listing of the file, and perhaps to append to the error list a table of the symbols used within the file. This can be achieved by using the controls as shown in the following example:

ASM86 TRIAL.A86 NOOBJECT NOPRINT SYMBOLS ERRORPRINT

The controls shown above are specified at the invocation of the assembly process. This is not the only place in which ASM86 assembler controls can be specified; in fact, such controls can be imbedded in the source file. Any line within a source file that begins with a dollar sign '$' is an assembler control line. Table 5.1 is a list of some of the assembler controls available with the Intel assembler ASM86.

Questions

(5.1) Write assembler instructions and directives to perform the following:

(a) Define a word variable of initial value AFAFH and identifier INFO.

(b) Set the variable at INFO to the new value 4455H.

(c) Define a byte variable of initial value 55 with identifier DAT1.

(d) Define ARR1 as an array of 20 bytes of undefined value.

(e) Set the third byte of array ARR1 to the value 03H.

(f) Set INDIC1 and INDIC2 as identifiers for word variables having initial values 1234H and 0FF0H respectively, and then perform the logical AND function between these word variables.

(g) Assign a word variable with the value 20 and identifier COUNT and load this into the CX register.

(h) Load the SI register with the offset address of the variable at FIRSTD.

(5.2) What will be the contents of the registers AX, BX, CX, DX and SI after the following instructions have been executed? Consider that the data segment consists only of arrays ARRA and ARRB in that order.

```
        ARRA        DW      0A00H,0A01H,0A02H,0A03H,0A04H,0A05H
        ARRB        DW      2B20H,2B21H,2B22H
                    -
                    MOV     AX,TYPE ARRA
                    MOV     CX,LENGTH ARRB
                    MOV     BX,SIZE ARRB
                    MOV     SI,OFFSET ARRB
                    MOV     DX,SIZE ARRA
```

(5.3) If the data segment and the code segment are located respectively at locations 00810H and 00100H, what will be the contents of AX, BX, CX, DX and DS after the following instructions have been executed.

```
        ASSUME      CS:PCODE,DS:PDATA
        ;*******************************
        PDATA       SEGMENT
                    ORG     50H
        VAR1        DW      2210H
        VAR2        DB      'HAPPY'
        VAR3        DW      ?
        PDATA       ENDS
        ;*******************************
        PCODE       SEGMENT
                    MOV     AX,PDATA
                    MOV     DS,AX
                    MOV     CX,PDATA + OFFSET VAR3
                    MOV     BH,LENGTH VAR2
                    MOV     BL,BYTE PTR VAR1 + 1
                    MOV     DL,BYTE PTR VAR1
                    MOV     DH,SIZE VAR2
                    MOV     AX,OFFSET VAR2
        PCODE       ENDS
        ;*******************************
                    END
```

(5.4) (a) Write a macro to initialise an 8255A port at address 0FFFBH as an input port and to transfer the data at the port to the CL register.

(b) Modify the macro so that parameters can be used to alter both the port address and the register which receives the data.

(5.5) With the aid of examples explain the usage of the following assembly language directives and operators: ASSUME, EQU, DD, EVEN, OFFSET, TYPE, PTR and SHORT.

CHAPTER 6
Memory interfacing

8086 MINIMUM MODE SYSTEM

De-multiplexing the Address/Data Bus

The internal architecture of the 8086 microprocessor is such that the device can be considered as divided into two parts, namely the EU (execution unit) and the BIU (bus interface unit). These two sections of the microprocessor operate independently of each other, as was clearly illustrated in figure 1.9. It is the BIU which performs all external bus operations. When the BIU accesses memory or an IO device the first 16 bits of the address bus must be latched. This is necessary because the address bus and data bus are time division multiplexed.

The 8086 microprocessor generates an address latching signal ALE which is transmitted, typically to 8282 octal latch devices, in order to indicate the presence of the address on the multiplexed bus. The ALE signal of the 8086 is taken to the strobe input STB of the 8282 latches and

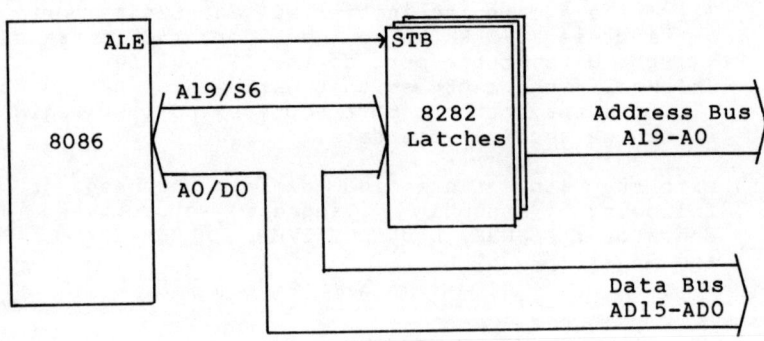

Figure 6.1 Demultiplexing the address/data bus at the microprocessor.

Memory Interfacing 113

latching occurs on the trailing edge of the ALE pulse. The latching of the address enables a stable address to be present for an entire bus cycle because the 8282 devices transmit the address while the ALE signal is high and when ALE goes low the address remains on the outputs of the latches. The process of latching the address bus in this way is sometimes referred to as de-multiplexing the address/data bus; the result is to effectively create separate buses.

The latching of the address information takes place on the trailing edge of the ALE pulse and this occurs at a time when the address information is present on the multiplexed bus. The relationship between the timing of the ALE pulse and the address information is clearly illustrated in the bus cycle shown in figure 6.2. The M/$\overline{\text{IO}}$ signal is the output selecting either memory or I/O device.

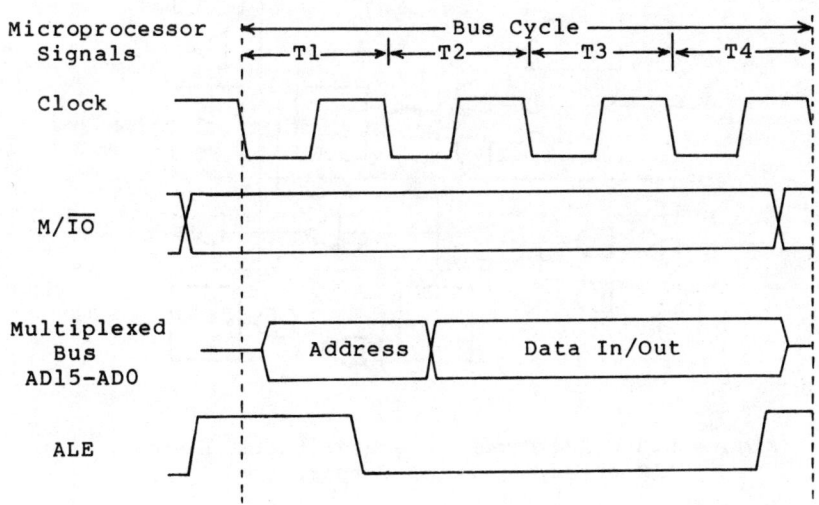

Figure 6-2 8086 Bus cycle

Examination of the basic bus cycle shown in figure 6.2 reveals that the microprocessor generates signals to control system operation, the most obvious of these being the generation of ALE to ensure latching of address information. The timing of these signals relates to the clock signal, provided in this case by the 8284A clock generator device. This device is used with the 8086 microprocessor because the 8086 microprocessor does not have an on board clock generator. The timing of the 8086 bus signals is examined in detail at the end of this chapter. The complete timing diagrams are given in Appendix D.

8284A Clock Generator

The 8284A device is used to generate clock signals for microprocessors such as the 8086 and the 8088. It is also used to provide clock signals for the 8087 and the 8089 coprocessors. The clock signal which it provides determines the speed at which the microprocessor system operates, e.g. the standard rate being 5 MHz. Figure 6.3 is a block diagram of the clock generator. The device contains a crystal controlled oscillator and a divide-by-three counter. When a 15 MHz crystal is connected to the X1 and X2 inputs this fundamental clock frequency is divided by three to a produce a 5 MHz clock signal available at output CLK.

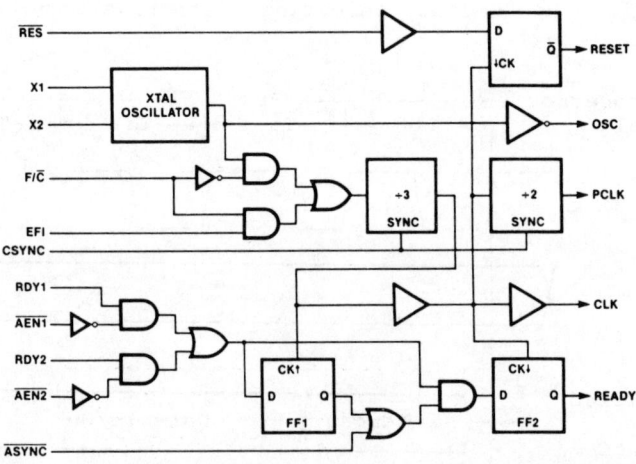

Figure 6.3 8284 Clock generator block diagram. (Courtesy of Intel Corporation)

There are three clock outputs from the 8284 device: CLK, PCLK and OSC. Figure 6.4 shows the basic connection of the 8284 device to the 8086 microprocessor in which the CLK output is the one providing the microprocessor with its clock. The other two output clock signals are the peripheral clock PCLK, whose frequency is one half the value of CLK, which is used to drive peripheral devices, and the oscillator clock OSC which is at the fundamental clock frequency and can be used to source the external frequency of other 8284 devices in the system.

Input F/$\overline{C}$ allows clock source selection of either a crystal or an external frequency source. This 8284 device is also used to provide the microprocessor with synchronised READY and RESET signals, both of which are taken to the microprocessor via the clock generator in order to achieve synchronisation with the CLK signal. The

Memory Interfacing 115

READY signal is used to allow the microprocessor to communicate successfully with slower external devices. This is achieved by increasing the bus cycle by either one or more clock cycles known as wait states. The RESET signal is used to initialise the microprocessor system.

Data Bus Buffering

Data bus buffering is employed to ensure first, that satisfactory drive requirements for the rest of the system can be provided and second, that the microprocessor can overcome any capacitive loading effects on the data bus. As the data bus is bidirectional the buffers used must be bidirectional. Two 8286 octal data bus transceivers are used for this purpose. These devices have tristate output buffers that will provide a 32 mA current on the system side of the bus and a 10 mA current on the microprocessor side of the bus. These values will satisfy most drive requirements. Also these tranceivers can switch capacitive loads of 300 pF and 100 pF respectively on system and microprocessor sides in 30 ns, so overcoming capacitive loading problems.

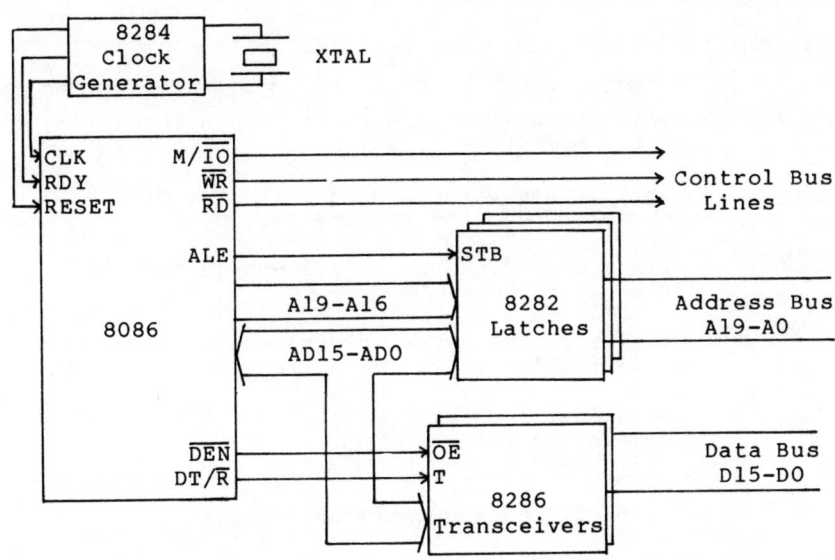

Figure 6.4 8086 Minimum mode configuration.

The 8086 microprocessor provides two control signals specifically for use with such buffer transceivers. These are the data enable signal $\overline{DEN}$ used, as the name suggests, to enable the transceivers, and the data direction signal

116 The 8086 and Assembly Language

DT/R̄ which controls the direction in which the transceiver will allow data to pass.

8086 Minimum Mode Operation

The 8086 microprocessor combined with the 8284 clock generator, the 8282 latches and the 8286 transceivers forms the basis of the minimum mode system. This arrangement is illustrated in figure 6.4. So far, then, a system has been built up in which there are effectively separate address, data and control buses. The addition of memory and I/O peripheral devices to this arrangement produces a complete 8086 minimum mode system

We have seen that in a simple system employing the 8086 microprocessor latches are used to produce a de-multiplexed address/data bus and tranceivers are used to achieve data bus buffering, with the result that viewed from the memory or I/O devices there are separate identifiable address, data and control buses. The control signals that are employed in a read or write bus cycle are clearly shown in figure 6.4, and they are M/ĪO, D̄ĒN, DT/R̄, R̄D or W̄R and ALE. To emphasise the importance of these control signals they are listed in table 6.1 along with a description of their purpose.

Table 6.1 8086 Minimum mode control signals.

M/ĪO	Indicates whether memory or I/O is involved in the bus cycle.
DT/R̄	Controls the direction in which the data passes through the transceiver.
D̄ĒN	Signal providing the output enable for the transceiver.
R̄D,W̄R	Enables either a read or write data transfer respectively to or from either memory or I/O.
ALE	The signal causing the latching of the address information.

8086 Read and Write Bus Cycles

The timing of these control signals during read and write bus cycles is examined relative to the microprocessor clock periods or T states in figures 6.5 and 6.6. The minimum length of a bus cycle is four T states. During the state T1 the 20 bit address is placed on the address bus and the ALE signal causes latching of this address on its trailing edge. Also M/ĪO will go to logic '1' for a memory read/write and to logic '0' for an I/O read/write.

Memory Interfacing 117

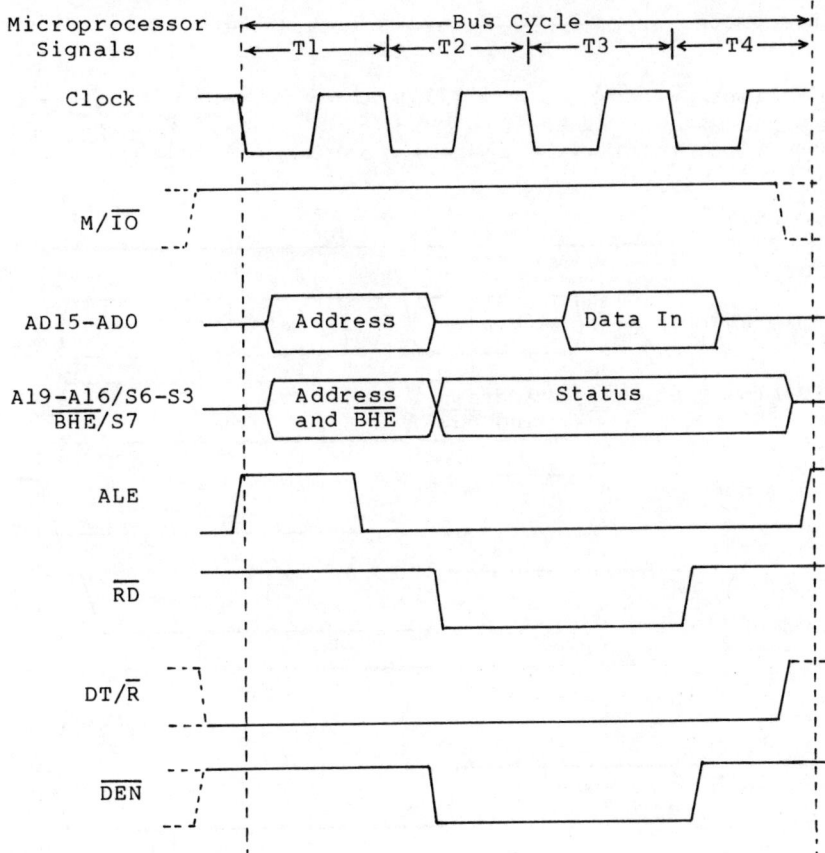

Figure 6.5 8086 Memory read bus cycle.

During the second clock cycle state T2, status information S3, S4, S5, and S6 is transmitted on the four uppermost multiplexed address lines. This information remains for the rest of the bus cycle. Also in this T state in a read cycle the data bus lines are floated, while in a write bus cycle valid data is transmitted by the microprocessor. The $\overline{RD}$ signal or the $\overline{WR}$ signal becomes active during state T2 by going to logic '0' and also the data bus transceiver signal $\overline{DEN}$ goes to logic '0'. During T3 the microprocessor continues to transmit data in the write bus cycle. In a read bus cycle the microprocessor samples the data at the end of the T3 state. During T4 the control signals cease to be active and hence the external memory or I/O devices are disconnected from the bus system.

118 The 8086 and Assembly Language

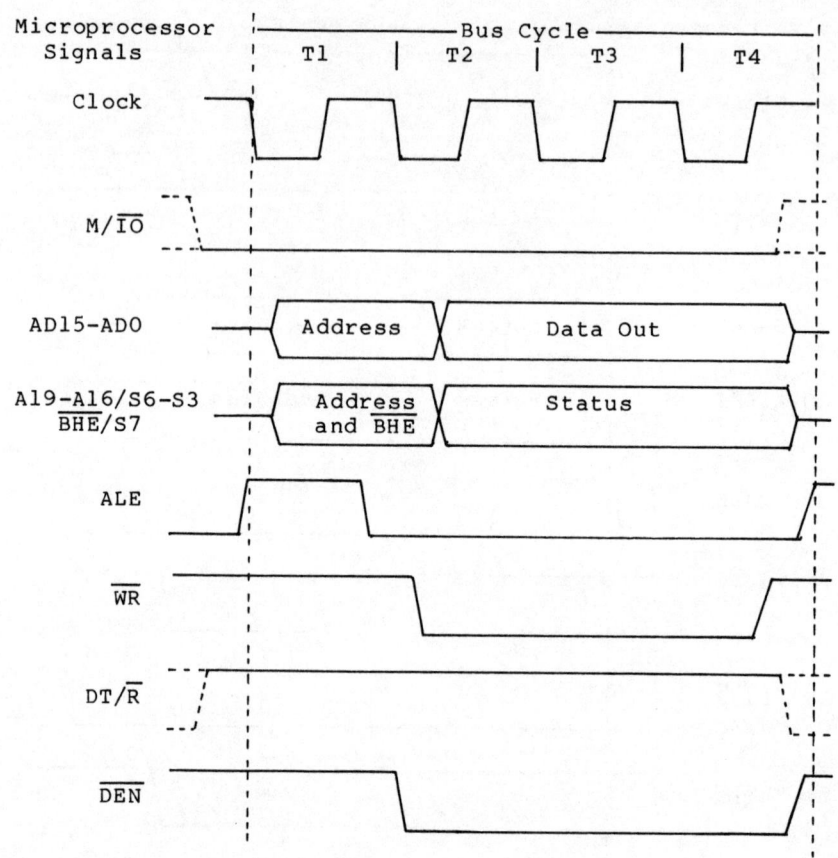

Figure 6.6 8086 I/O write bus cycle.

The 8086 microprocessor does not continuously perform bus cycles. In some situations, such as when the queue is full and the EU is not requesting memory access, the bus is idle. During this condition the only valid information is the status information of the previous bus cycle, which remains on the upper four address/status lines.

Minimum System Operating in Minimum Mode

Now that the control signals for memory and I/O devices, as well as for latches and buffers, have been considered, a minimum system including these devices can be drawn; figure 6.7 is a diagrammatic representation of such a fundamental system.

Memory Interfacing 119

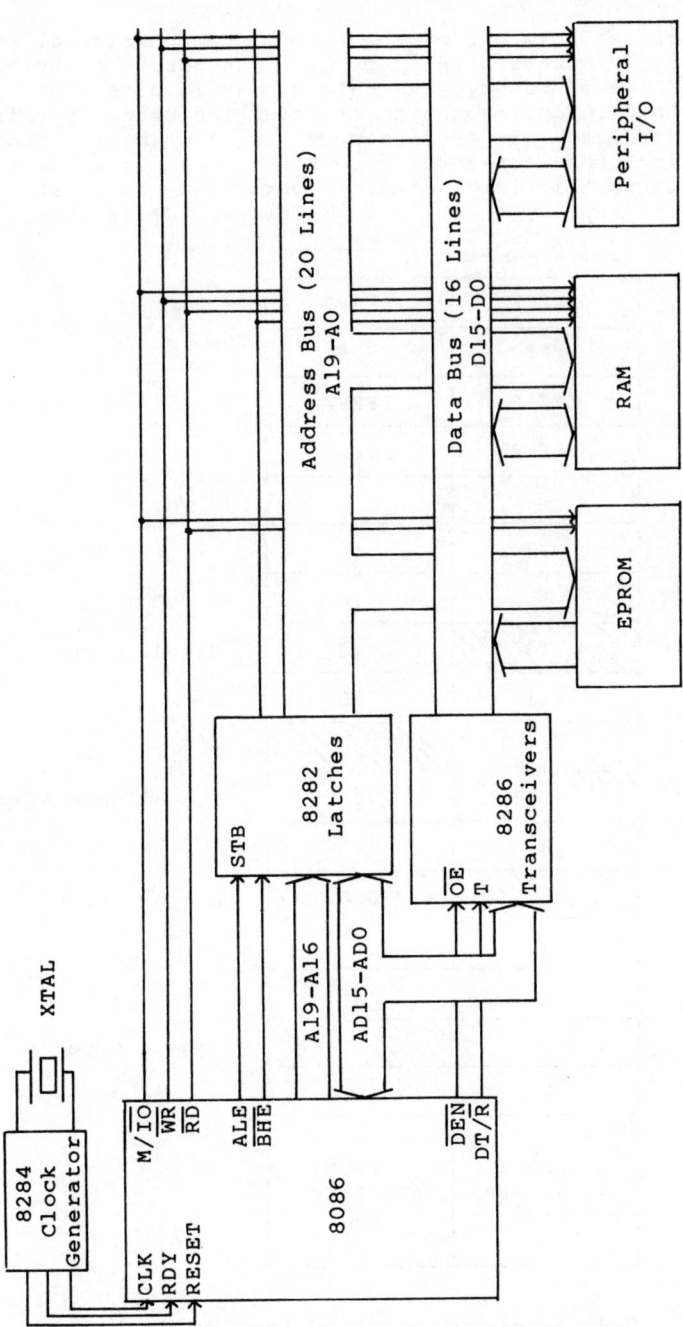

Figure 6.7 8086 Minimum mode system in the minimum mode configuration.

120 The 8086 and Assembly Language

8086 MEMORY ORGANIZATION

The 20 bit address bus of the 8086 microprocessor allows it to directly access a total of 2^{20} consecutive bytes, i.e. 1 Mbyte of memory. The data bus is 16 bits wide, so allowing the microprocessor to transfer two bytes (forming a 16 bit word) to or from memory in a single memory access. Any two consecutive bytes can form a word, and there is no restriction on the microprocessor in that it can access any byte or word address. Hence the

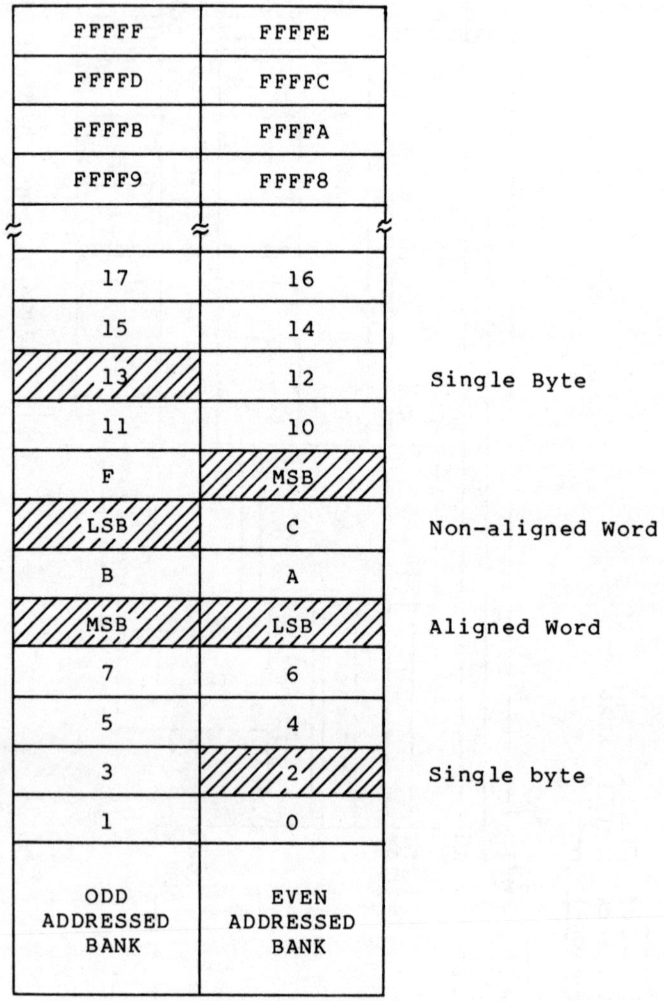

ODD	EVEN
FFFFF	FFFFE
FFFFD	FFFFC
FFFFB	FFFFA
FFFF9	FFFF8
≈	≈
17	16
15	14
13	12
11	10
F	MSB
LSB	C
B	A
MSB	LSB
7	6
5	4
3	2
1	0
ODD ADDRESSED BANK	EVEN ADDRESSED BANK

- Single Byte (13, 12)
- Non-aligned Word (F, MSB / LSB, C)
- Aligned Word (MSB, LSB)
- Single byte (2)

Figure 6.8 8086 Memory organised into two banks.

Memory Interfacing **121**

microprocessor can access 512 Kwords. To achieve the connection to the 16 bit data bus the memory address space is physically divided into two 8 bit banks, each capable of holding 512 Kbytes. One bank is connected to the lower half of the data bus and the other bank to the upper half of the data bus. The lower bank contains even addressed bytes and the upper bank odd addressed bytes. Figure 6.8 shows the two banks, one for all the even addresses and the other for all the odd addresses. The shaded areas indicate:

(1) Single bytes at addresses 00002H and 00013H.
(2) An aligned word at address 00008H, i.e. an even addressed word.
(3) A non-aligned word at address 0000DH, i.e. an odd addressed word.

The microprocessor can access an aligned word in a single bus cycle, whereas the access of a non-aligned word requires two bus cycles. Address lines A1 to A19 are used to access a memory location in both banks. However, the even and odd memory banks themselves are selected by the lines A0 and $\overline{BHE}$ respectively. Reference to the microprocessor pin definitions shown in figure 1.12 indicates that $\overline{BHE}$ is a signal multiplexed with a status line. The $\overline{BHE}$ signal timing is similar to that of the multiplexed address lines, and therefore this line must be latched in the same way as the address lines, so providing a signal for the whole of the bus cycle. When A0 is at

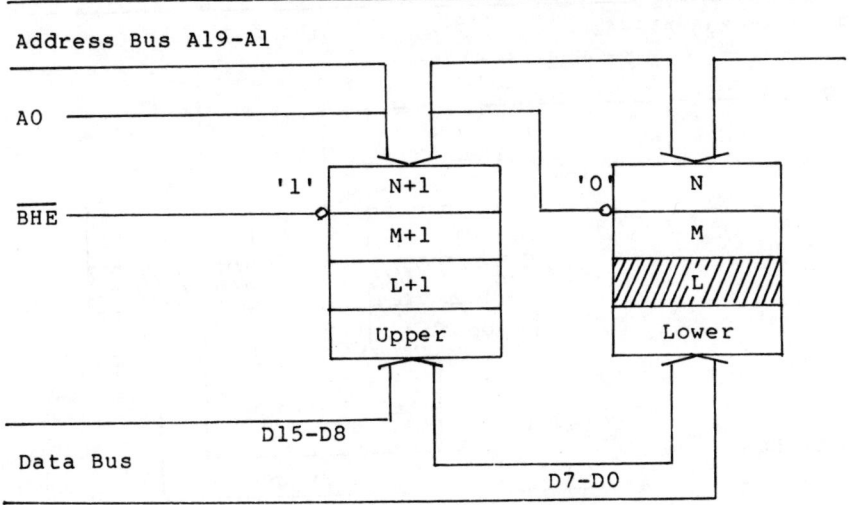

Figure 6.9 Even addressed byte transfer between lower memory bank and microprocessor (single bus cycle).

122 The 8086 and Assembly Language

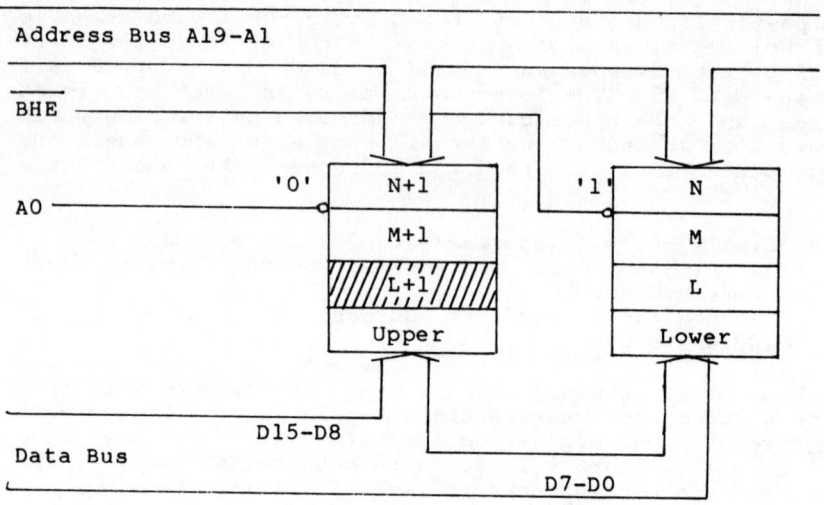

Figure 6.10 Odd addressed byte transfer between upper memory bank and microprocessor (single bus cycle).

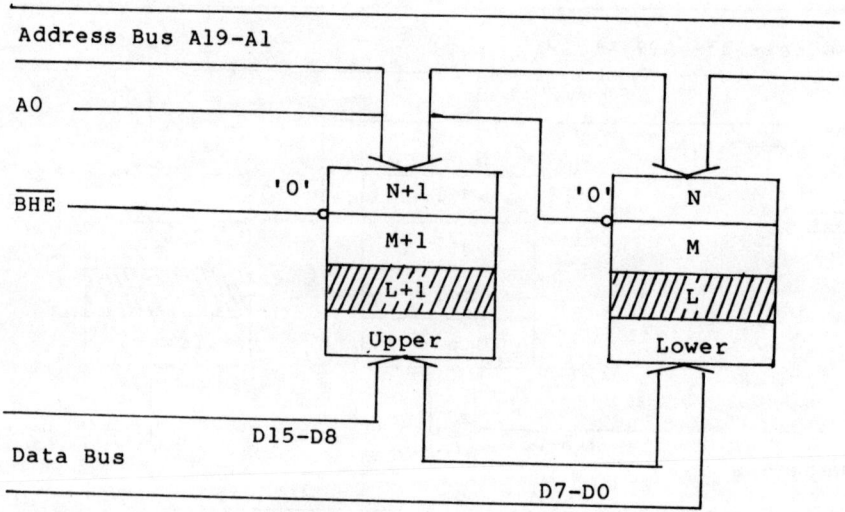

Figure 6.11 Even addressed word transfer between both memory banks and microprocessor (single bus cycle).

Memory Interfacing **123**

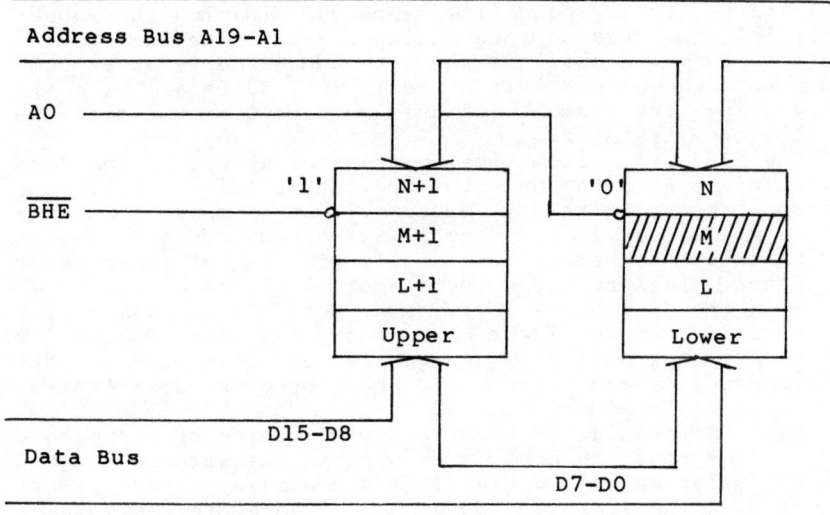

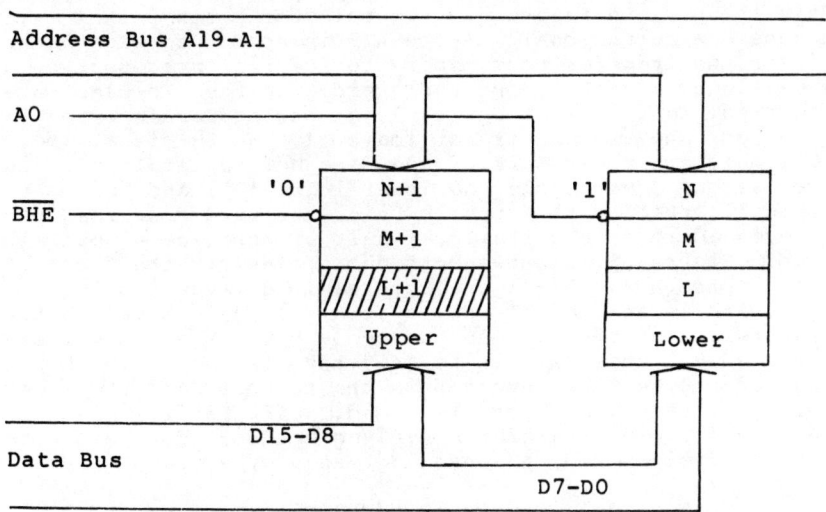

Figure 6.12 Odd addressed word transfer between both memory banks and microprocessor (two bus cycles).

logic '0' the lower memory bank is connected to the data bus and when BHE is at logic '0' the upper memory bank is connected to the data bus. When accessing a byte in memory these enable signals are of opposite logic level.

If the byte addressed is at an even address A0 is at logic '0' and $\overline{BHE}$ is at logic '1', hence $\overline{BHE}$ disables the upper half of the data bus preventing its participation in the data transfer. Equally if the byte addressed is at an odd address then while $\overline{BHE}$ is at logic '0', A0 is at logic '1' preventing involvement of the lower half of the data bus in the byte transfer.

The 8086 will automatically transfer a byte from one side of the data bus to the other side within the microprocessor if this is necessary. An example of such a case would be when a byte at an odd address is being transferred to the lower half of a microprocessor register. The transfer from memory would be on the upper half of the data bus and yet the byte would reach its destination in the lower half of the register. Figure 6.9 shows byte transfer from an even address in memory to the microprocessor and figure 6.10 shows byte transfer from an odd address in memory.

When accesssing a word in memory the number of memory bus cycles required depends on whether the word is aligned (that is, at an even address) or non-aligned (that is, at an odd address). In the case of an even addressed word, a single memory accesss is required and both A0 and $\overline{BHE}$ are low, so activating both memory banks; with the result that the whole of the data bus is employed in the bus cycle. This is shown in figure 6.11 where bytes L and L + 1 are accessed simultaneously, A1 to A19 is common to each bank.

For the transfer from memory to the microprocessor of a non-aligned odd addressed word two bus cycles are required. In the first bus cycle an odd addressed byte is invovled and so A0 is at logic '1' and $\overline{BHE}$ is at logic '0'; only the upper half of the data bus is employed. In the second bus cycle A0 is at logic '0', and $\overline{BHE}$ is at logic '1' because the upper byte of the word concerned has an even address; and the lower half of the data bus is used. Figure 6.12 shows both bus cycles, in the first of which bytes L and L + 1 are accessed. However, only the high bank is enabled so only byte L + 1 is involved in the transfer. In the second bus cycle bytes M and M + 1 are accessed but this time it is only the low bank which is enabled. Byte M is involved in the transfer and the lower half of the data bus is used. Effectively, an odd addressed word transfer involves an odd addressed byte transfer followed by an even addressed byte transfer.

Read Only Memory (ROM/EPROM) Interface

When the microprocessor performs a read operation a word is transferred from memory if both odd and even memory banks are enabled. If a word is required then this is suitable for the microprocessor, but if only a byte is required this is also satisfactory as the microprocessor will ignore the byte that it does not require. Therefore read only memory bank devices require only a single memory

Memory Interfacing **125**

bank selection signal. Separate memory bank signals A0 and $\overline{BHE}$ are only really necessary for read/write devices.

The address lines connected to these read only memory devices are from A1 through to the largest value address line the individual device can accept, e.g. a 2732 device accepts 12 address lines A1 to A12. The remaining address lines are decoded to produce the chip select signals for these memory devices, and the output enable for both banks of these ROM/EPROM devices is simply $\overline{RD}$. The arrangement shown in figure 6.13 illustrates these points with relation to chip selection and to chip output enable for the EPROM's 2732.

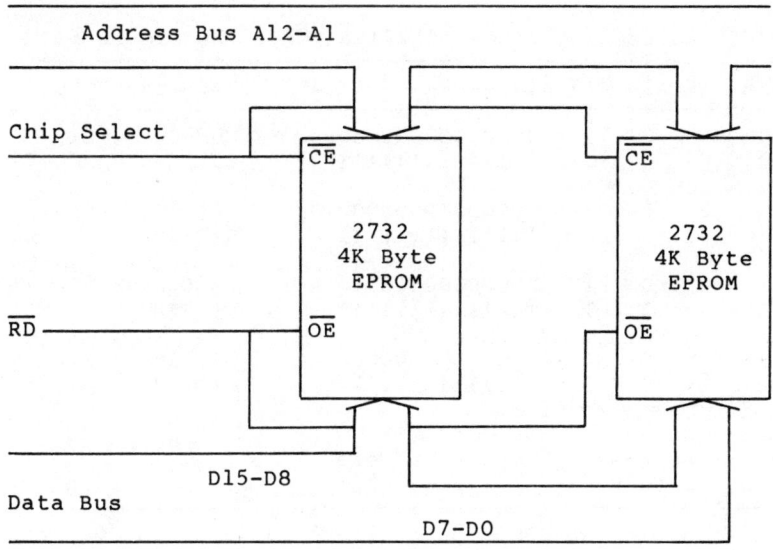

Figure 6.13 8086 EPROM interface using two 2732 devices.

A more detailed circuit arrangement of an EPROM interface is shown in figure 6.14. The EPROMs employed are type 27128 which each provide 2 bytes of memory, i.e. 16 Kbytes, so with four such devices the memory space occupied is 64 Kbytes (32 Kwords). Address lines A1 to A14 are directly connected to the address input pins of the EPROMs. Address lines A15, A16 and A17 are connected to the address inputs of the 1 out of 8 binary decoder device type 8205 and it is these lines which select the output of the decoder. Address lines A18 and A19 must both be at logic '1' to enable the 8205 decoder.

126 The 8086 and Assembly Language

Table 6.2 8205 address select.

A2	A1	A0	Active Output
0	0	0	0
0	0	1	1
0	1	0	2
0	1	1	3
1	0	0	4
	etc.		

By reference to the table 6.2 and considering that A18 and A19 must both be at logic '1' to enable the decoder then the addressing ranges in table 6.3 apply to the EPROMs of figure 6.14.

Table 6.3 Addressing range of 27128 EPROMs in figure 6.14.

A19	A18	A17	A16	A15	A14----------A1	A0	Hex Address	EPROM
1	1	0	0	0	00000000000000	1	C0000H	L1
1	1	0	0	0	11111111111111	1	C7FFEH	
1	1	0	0	0	00000000000000	1	C0001H	H1
1	1	0	0	0	11111111111111	1	CFFFEH	
1	1	0	0	1	00000000000000	1	C8000H	L2
1	1	0	0	1	11111111111111	1	CFFFEH	
1	1	0	0	1	00000000000000	1	C8001H	H2
1	1	0	0	1	11111111111111	1	CFFFFH	

Decoder enable | Decoder address select | Device address lines

The chip enable for EPROM pair H1 and L1 is output 0 from the decoder, whereas output 1 from the decoder provides chip enable for EPROM pair H2 and L2. The output enable for all the EPROMs is provided by the read signal RD.

As an example of the EPROM interface operation consider a read bus cycle in which an instruction word is transferred from EPROM to the microprocessor; a 20 bit physical address is generated by the combination of CS and IP register contents and placed on the address bus A19 to A0. This address is latched along with $\overline{BHE}$, although $\overline{BHE}$ is not used in this EPROM interface. Because this is a memory read bus cycle, M/$\overline{IO}$ will be at logic '1', and if A19 and A18 are also at logic '1' then the 8205 decoder will be enabled. A17, A16 and A15 will decide which decoder output is active, e.g. 001 will select output 1 which provides the chip select for EPROM pair H2,L2. Address lines A14 to A1 are connected to the EPROMs and these values select the instruction word to be transferred. The outputs of the EPROMs are enabled when the read signal $\overline{RD}$ goes to logic '0' and the selected word is placed on the data bus.

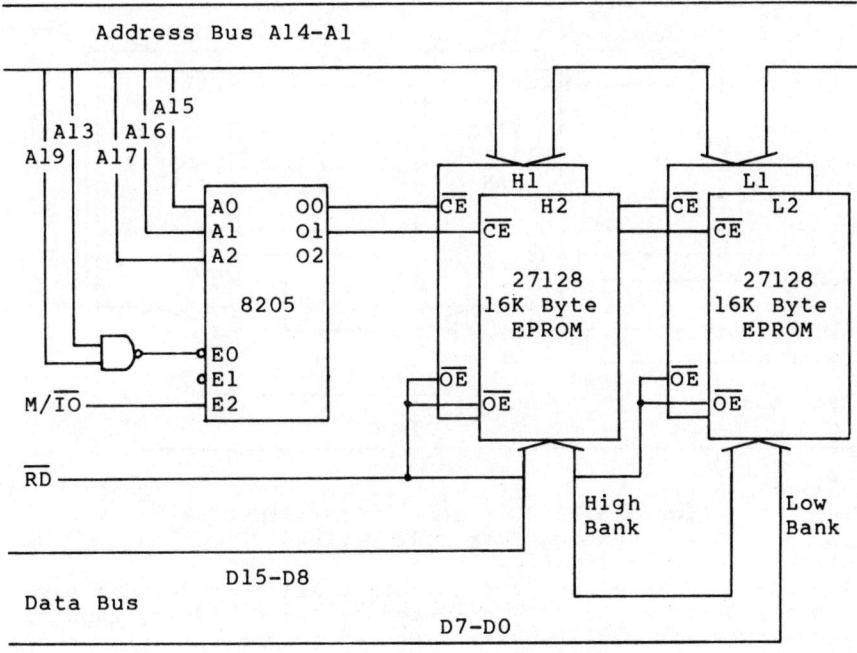

Figure 6.14 8086 EPROM interface using four type 27128 devices.

Read/Write Memory (RAM) Interface

In many applications data will be stored in read/write memory and for applications where the memory space required is small, i.e. less than 16 Kword, static RAM will be used. This is because dynamic RAM memory devices are often organised as 16K * 1 or 64K * 1 and also require refresh circuitry. The small system example of a read/write memory interface shown in figure 6.15 involves the use of static RAM chips type 2142. However, in the larger read/write memory interface of figure 6.16 the use of type 2186 dynamic RAM devices provides static RAM characteristics because the chips contain integrated refresh operation.

The memory interface shown in figure 6.15 employs 2142 static RAMs. These devices are organised in a 1K by 4 bit arrangement and so four such devices are needed to form a 1 Kword memory configuration. The high memory bank marked H consists of two 2142 devices, and the two devices

128 The 8086 and Assembly Language

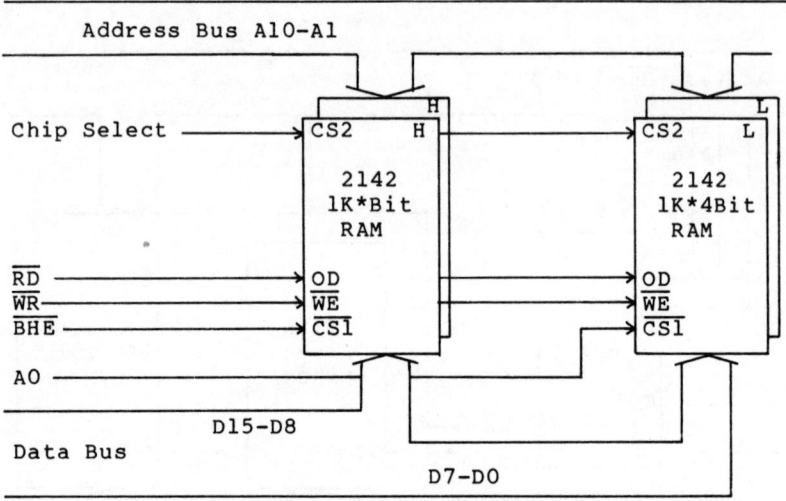

Figure 6.15 8086 Static RAM interface using four 2142 devices

labelled L make up the low bank. All four devices have address lines A1 to A10 connected to their address inputs. The higher address lines are decoded to provide the chip select input to CS2, so selecting the complete memory bank.

Type 2142 devices have two chip enable inputs. The $\overline{CS1}$ chip select select input is used in the differentiation between the two banks of memory. $\overline{BHE}$ is used to select the high bank, while A0 is used to select the low bank. This requirement to distinguish between the two banks arises from the need to write a single byte to memory, in which situation it is imperative that only one bank be enabled. When a byte is to be written to an even address $\overline{BHE}$ is high, so disabling the high bank, and A0 is low, so enabling the low bank to store the byte of information. The banks are again selected separately for a byte read bus cycle. For even addressed word operations, both $\overline{BHE}$ and A0 are at logic '0' and both memory banks are selected.

It has been pointed out in the last section that for a read only memory interface the two banks of memory do not need to be separately selected. This is because when a byte is to be read the microprocessor will select the byte required from the word on the data bus. The 8086 write signal $\overline{WR}$ is connected to the write enable input $\overline{WE}$ on all the 2142 devices. When $\overline{WR}$ is active i.e. at logic '0' valid data on the data bus will be written to the selected

Memory Interfacing **129**

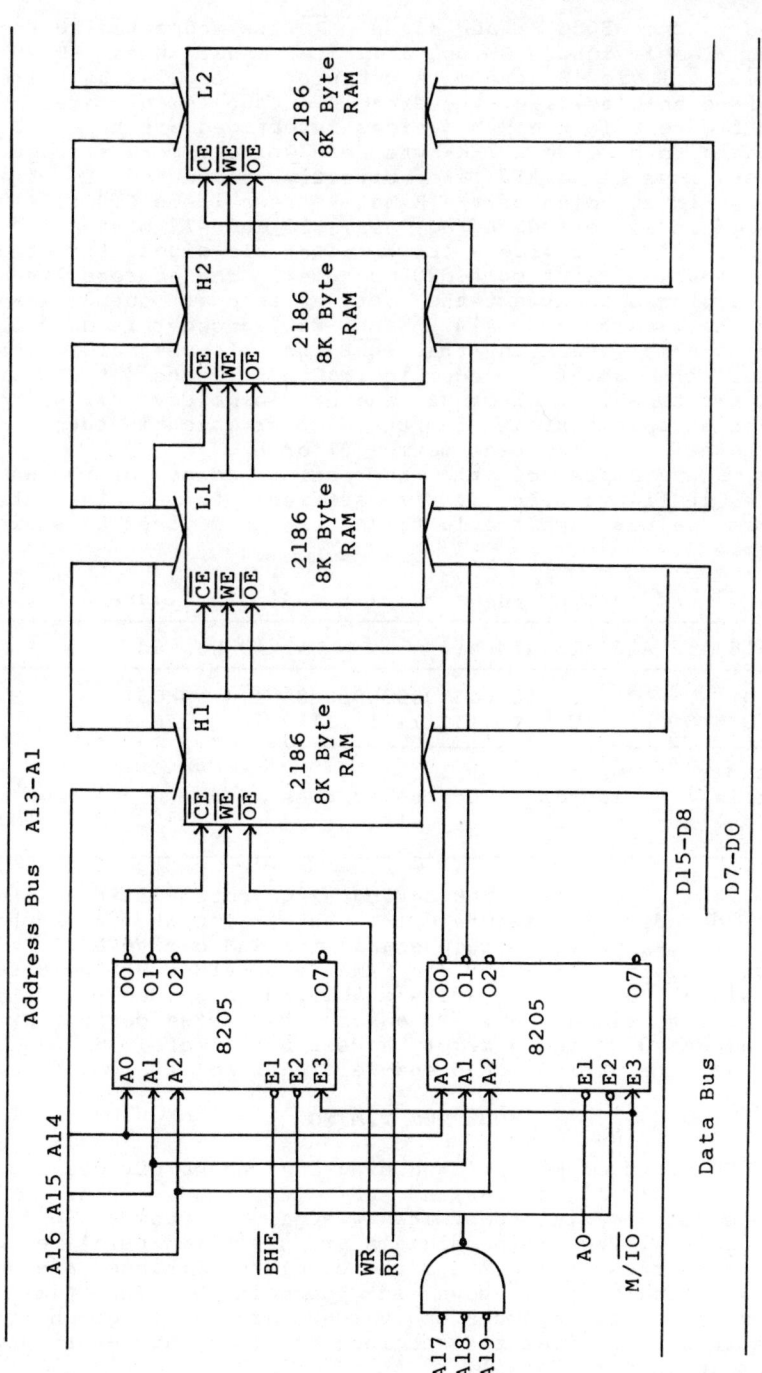

Figure 6.16 8086 RAM interface using type 2186 RAM devices.

130 The 8086 and Assembly Language

address. The 8086 read signal $\overline{RD}$ is connected to the output disable inputs OD on all the RAMs. When $\overline{RD}$ is active at logic '0' the data outputs of the 2142 RAMs are therefore enabled, i.e. the disable output is inactive.

In figure 6.16 the RAM devices interfaced are type 2186 combining to provide a 32K-byte read/write memory storage. Address lines A1 to A13 are directly connected to the address input pins of the RAMs. Address lines A14 to A19 are used in address decoding; A19, A18 and A17 must all be at logic '0' to provide a logic '0' enable signal for the input enable E2 of both 8205 decoders. The address lines which are used to select the active decoder output are lines A16, A15 and A14. Each 8205 decoder is used to select a memory bank in that $\overline{BHE}$ is the signal which enables the upper decoder in figure 6.16 the outputs of which are to select H1 or H2, the high bank devices. A0 is used as an enable signal for the decoder which in turn is used to select a low bank device L1 or L2.

As an example of the addressing range of the RAM devices in figure 6.16 it is suffient to examine the address values applicable to one of the devices as shown in table 6.4.

Table 6.4 Addressing range of 2186 RAM'S in figure 6.16.

A19 A18 A17	A16 A15 A14	A13---------A1	A0	Hex address	RAM
0 0 0	0 0 1	0000000000000	1	04001H	H2
0 0 0	0 0 1	1111111111111	1	07FFFH	
Decoder enable	Decoder address select	Device address lines			

The chip enable for RAM device H2 is output 1 from the upper decoder in figure 6.16, whereas output 1 from the lower decoder provides chip enable for RAM device L2. The output enable for all the RAMs is provided by the 8086 read signal $\overline{RD}$, and the write enable is provided by the 8086 write signal $\overline{WR}$. To ensure that these devices are only accessed during a memory access bus cycle, $M/\overline{IO}$ is used as the third chip enable signal for the decoders.

8086 BUS TIMING

The 8086 minimum mode timing diagrams can be divided into six sections: (1) address and ALE, (2) read cycle, (3) write cycle, (4) interrupt acknowledge, (5) ready, and (6) bus control. The timing signals are specified relative to the microprocessor clock and the complete minimum system timing signals are shown in Appendix D. The timing parameters, their symbols and values are also given in Appendix D. The first two sections mentioned above are now discussed in some detail.

Address and ALE Timing

The 8086 address bus is time division multiplexed with its data bus and the signal ALE is used to ensure latching of address information. The state of the address lines at the end of the trailing edge of the ALE signal is important because it is at this point in time that, for example, the 8282 device latches the address. Consider an 8086 microprocessor operating at a clock rate of 5 MHz, the parameter TAVAL = TCLCH - 60ns guarantees that the addresses are valid 58ns before the trailing edge of ALE; (TCLCH is the clock low time, the minimum value of which is 118ns). The addresses are guaranteed to remain valid beyond the termination of ALE by the parameter TLLAX = TCHCL - 10ns, the value of which in this case is 59ns; (TCHCL is the clock high time, the minimum value of which is 69ns). TLLAX applies to the whole of the address bus. As the 8282 is a flow through latch it does not provide a valid address on the bus until ALE is active. So the two delay times which compete to decide the worst case delay to a valid address appearing on the address bus, are the maximum delay time before the occurance of a valid address TCLAVmax, and TCLLHmax the maximum possible delay before the rising edge of ALE occurs. As TCLAVmax = 110ns and TCLLHmax = 80ns, it is TCLAVmax which decides the worst case delay time. The address and ALE timing parameters are shown in the timing diagram of figure 6.17

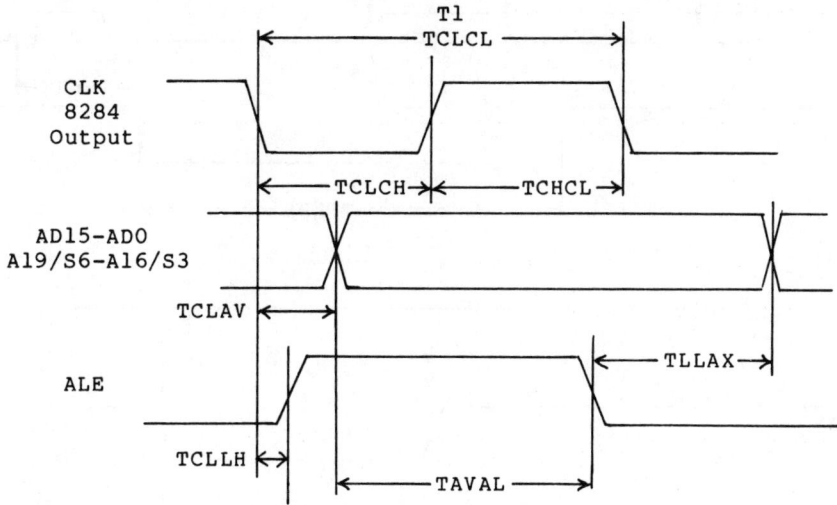

Figure 6.17 Address and ALE timing.

132 The 8086 and Assembly Language

Read Cycle Timing

The microprocessor control signals involved in the read timing are the data direction control signal DT/$\overline{\text{R}}$, the read signal $\overline{\text{RD}}$ and the data tranceiver enable signal $\overline{\text{DEN}}$. Figure 6.18 shows the timing parameters and signals relating to the read cycle. The DT/$\overline{\text{R}}$ is low from early in the bus cycle. The data transceiver enable signal $\overline{\text{DEN}}$ must be such as to allow the transceivers to transmit data to the microprocessor for the required data in setup time TDVCL, and to present data at the microprocessor for the required hold time for data in TCLDX. The turn on delay for the $\overline{\text{DEN}}$ signal allows TCLCL + TCHCLmin - TCVCTVmax - TDVCL = 27ns transceiver enable time before valid data is required by the microprocessor; (TCLCL is the clock period, TCHCL is the clock high time, TCVCTV is the control active delay and TDVCL is the data in setup time).

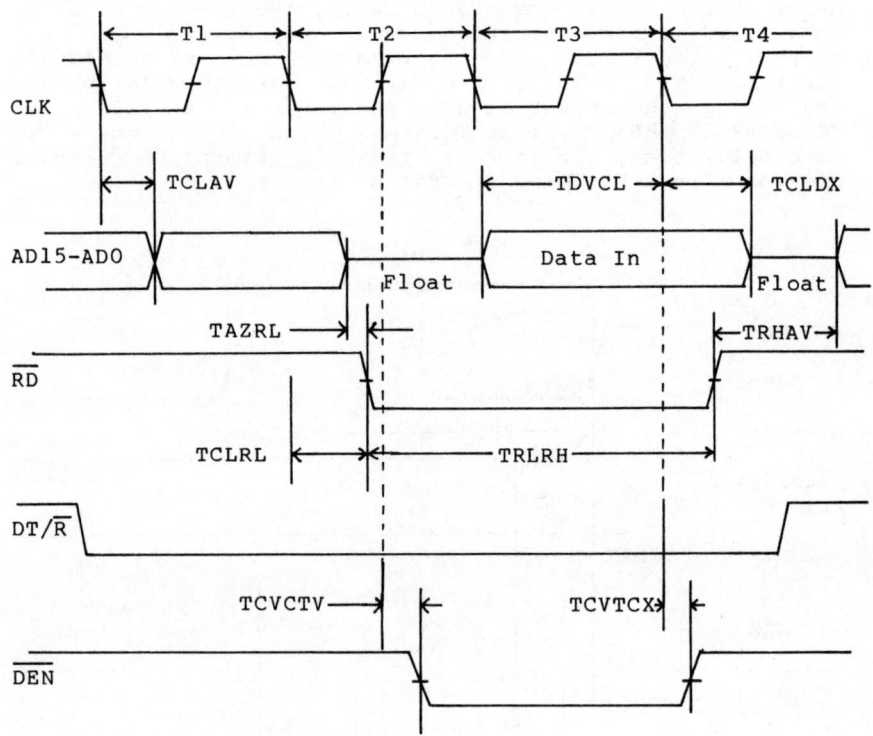

Figure 6.18 Read cycle timing.

The microprocessor data hold time TCLDXmin is 10ns and the minimum $\overline{\text{DEN}}$ turnoff delay time TCVCTXmin is also 10ns relative to the same clock edge, so the data hold is

Memory Interfacing 133

guaranteed. The $\overline{DEN}$ signal is also required to disable the transceivers before the microprocessor drives the bus with the next address. This is achieved because the maximum delay time before $\overline{DEN}$ turns off is TCVCTXmax relative to edge of T3 and is 110ns. This is much less than the minimum time relative to the same edge before which addresses from the microprocessor can occur TCLCL + TCLAVmin = 200 + 10. So the transceivers are disabled 100ns before the microprocessor places the address on the bus.

To decide whether or not a memory device will operate successfully with the microprocessor the timing parameters for each device must be compared. The following section deals with 8086 timing parameters shown in figure 6.18 and the parameters of EPROM type 2732 shown in figure 6.19.

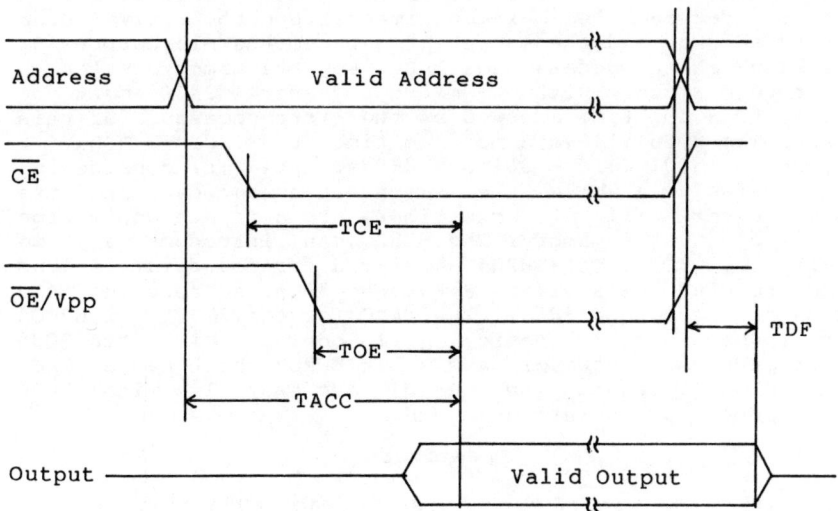

Figure 6.19 Timing diagram for the 2732A EPROM.

TAZRL is the 8086 parameter which, for memory devices connected directly to the multiplexed address bus and the data bus, guarantees that the bus will be floated before the read signal is activated, that is before allowing the memory device to drive the bus. At the end of the 8086 bus cycle the memory device which is deselected at the rising edge of $\overline{RD}$ must satisfy the parameter TRHAV = TCLCL − 45ns = 155ns. That is, within this time the memory device must stop driving the bus. This is to avoid bus contention when the microprocessor supplies the address for the next bus cycle. Note that avoiding bus contention means avoiding a

134 The 8086 and Assembly Language

situation where more than one device is connected to the bus at one time. For the 2732 device TDF has a maximum time of 60ns, and as this is less than 155ns bus contention will be avoided.

For the 8086 the maximum time available after the read signal is active and before which the data must be presented at the microprocessor is 2TCLCL - TCLRL - TDVCL = 205ns, (TCLCL is the clock period, TCLRL is the time taken before the read is guaranteed to be active, and TDVCL is the setup time for data in, i.e. the time the data must be present to guarantee that it is read). Now for the 2732 device the maximum delay time between the arrival of the output enable signal and data output from the device is TOE = 70ns. As this is less than 205ns the 2732 will provide the data to the microprocessor within the time allotted by the microprocessor. For the 8086 microprocessor TRLRH is the read signal pulse width and has a minimum value given by 2TCLCL - 75ns = 325ns. For a memory device the maximum time between the arrival of a valid address and the output of data to the microprocessor is known as the access time TACC. For the memory device to operate correctly with the microprocessor, TACC must be less than the time allowed by the microprocessor for this task. The 8086 allows a maximum time of 3TCLCL - TCLAV - TDVCL = (600 - 110 - 30)ns = 460ns. However, considering the system as a whole, the latch, the decoder and the transceiver will all contribute to a reduction in time available to the memory. The 8282 can introduce a time delay of 30ns, the 8205 decoder a further delay of 18ns and the 8286 transceiver a further 30ns, so reducing the time from 460ns to 382ns. The TACC for the 2732A - 2 EPROM is 200ns so this device will operate with the 8086 microprocessor. However, a similar EPROM which has a TACC of 450ns cannot be used successfully with 8086 microprocessor operating at 5MHz.

Questions

(6.1) With the aid of a diagram of an 8086 minimum mode system explain:
 (a) Demultiplexing of the address data bus
 (b) Buffering of the data bus
 (c) Interfacing static RAM, including chip selection

(6.2) State two advantages of using memory segmentation and draw a diagram of a typical 8086 memory segmented structure. With the aid of diagrams explain the organisation of memory into banks, and the difference beween even and odd addressed data transfer.

(6.3) Draw timing diagrams for both an EPROM and the 8086 microprocessor. Use the diagrams to show the suitablity of the EPROM for use in an 8086 minimum mode system.

(6.4) Draw a detailed circuit diagram of an 8086 minimum mode system having a 128 Kbyte memory facility consisting of both RAM and EPROM.

CHAPTER 7
Input/output interfacing

Data transfer between the microprocessor and external peripherals uses the multiplexed address/data bus connected to programmable I/O interface controller devices. Such devices as parallel interface controllers, serial interface controllers, interrupt controllers, CRT controllers, floppy disk controllers, etc. can all be used to interface the microprocessor to external peripherals. For the 8086 in the minimum mode operation, the control signals necessary for the operation of the programmable peripheral interface which links the microprocessor to the I/O devices are produced by the microprocessor in the same way as in the memory interface. Control signals such as M/$\overline{\text{IO}}$, $\overline{\text{RD}}$, $\overline{\text{WR}}$ are shown connected to the peripheral interface in figure 6.7.

In the maximum mode configuration control signals are produced not by the microprocessor, but by the bus controller device type 8288. In this mode co-processors are employed, the complexity of which can be similar to that of the 8086 CPU itself. For example, the numeric data processor 8087 adds eight 80 bit floating point registers to the 8086 register set and provides accuracy and speed of operation resulting in a powerful arithmetic processing capability. The 8089 input/output co-processor enables the handling of fast input/output streams independently of the 8086 CPU. However, in this introductory text the maximum mode of operation is not considered in any detail.

The I/O instructions IN and OUT cause the transfer of data between the accumulator and an I/O port address. This address is placed by the microprocessor on the bus lines AD0 to AD15, i.e. the microprocessor can address an I/O space of 64 Kbyte. During the IN or OUT bus cycle the M/$\overline{\text{IO}}$ control line is at logic '0', indicating to the external circuitry that the address on the bus is for an I/O device. The I/O addressing range is 0000H to FFFFH, but eight addresses 00F8H to 00FFH are reserved by Intel. Either bytes or words can be transmitted in an I/O operation; however, word ports should be given an even address to ensure that word transfer takes place in a single bus cycle. Each register within an 8 bit I/O device will be addressed by either all even addresses or all odd addresses. The method of operating input/output in its own address space is called 'accumulator I/O' as all data transfers involve the accumulator.

Memory mapping of I/O can be used in an 8086 microprocessor system. In this type of input/output operation the 8086 microprocessor treats an I/O port as a memory location. So the transfer of data is performed by MOV instructions rather than IN and OUT instructions. The major disadvantages of memory mapping of I/O ports are (1) that memory space is lost and (2) that memory reference instructions take place more slowly than the IN and OUT instructions. The advantage of using memory mapping is that many more instructions can be used directly with the I/O data, e.g. the logical operations can be performed directly on the data by instructions such as AND BX,[SI] where SI indicates an I/O address in the memory space. Memory mapped I/O devices can be at any location in the memory space because the whole 20 bit address can be used for addressing the device.

The major circuit difference between the two methods of I/O operation is that in the accumulator I/O method the microproceesor signal $M/\overline{IO}$ is used as an I/O enable - for example, to the I/O decoder - whereas in the memory mapping method address bits are used as enable signals and $M/\overline{IO}$ remains constantly at logic '1'.

8255A PROGRAMMABLE PERIPHERAL INTERFACE PPI

This device is a programmable parallel interface controller used to implement parallel communication between the microprocessor and the I/O device. It is extremely flexible in that it can be programmed to allow up to 24 bit input/output parallel connection arranged in various configurations of bits at any specific time, e.g. 4 bit, 8 bit, 12 bit, 16 bit and 24 bit words as well as single line communication can all be implemented and the device can operate in one of three modes, namely: mode 0 - straightforward input/output, mode 1 - strobed input/output and mode 2 - bidirectional bus. The 8255A is an LSI device in a 40 pin dual in-line package, the pin configuration of which is shown in figure 7.1(a). The block diagram of the PPI is shown in figure 7.1(b).

Referring to the block diagram, the left hand side can be considered to be the interface to the microprocessor which includes the data bus buffer and control blocks. When a register within the device is addressed during an input or output bus cycle, data is transferred via the data bus buffer at pins D0 to D7. As with memory bus cycles, shown in figures 6.5 and 6.6, the timing of the data transfer is controlled at the $\overline{RD}$ and $\overline{WR}$ signal inputs.

Input/Output Interfacing **137**

```
PA3  □ 1        40 □ PA4
PA2  □ 2        39 □ PA5
PA1  □ 3        38 □ PA6
PA0  □ 4        37 □ PA7
RD   □ 5        36 □ WR
CS   □ 6        35 □ RESET
GND  □ 7        34 □ D0
A1   □ 8        33 □ D1
A0   □ 9        32 □ D2
PC7  □ 10 8255A 31 □ D3
PC6  □ 11       30 □ D4
PC5  □ 12       29 □ D5
PC4  □ 13       28 □ D6
PC0  □ 14       27 □ D7
PC1  □ 15       26 □ Vcc
PC2  □ 16       25 □ PB7
PC3  □ 17       24 □ PB6
PB0  □ 18       23 □ PB5
PB1  □ 19       22 □ PB4
PB2  □ 20       21 □ PB3
```

Figure 7.1(a) 8255A Pin configuration

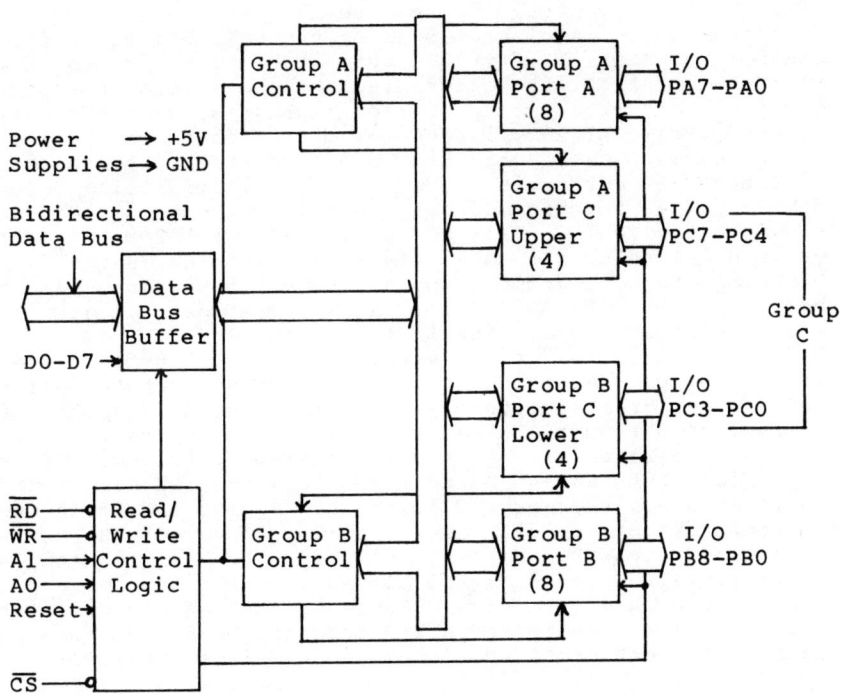

Figure 7.1(b) 8255A Block diagram.

138 The 8086 and Assembly Language

The ports/register within the 8255A are selected by a 2 bit code at inputs A0 and A1; address lines are usually connected to these inputs to select the port/register. Table 7.1 indicates the port select codes.

Table 7.1 Port select codes for the 8255A PPI.

A1	A0	Port/register
0	0	Port A
0	1	Port B
1	0	Port C
1	1	Control register

The 8255A is enabled by the input to the $\overline{CS}$ pin being kept at logic '0'. The RESET input, taken to logic '1' at power switch-on, allows the device to be initialised with all three ports in the input mode and the control register cleared.

Each port is programmable and is initialised as a result of a control byte being written by the microprocessor into the 8 bit control register. This control register is divided into two sections in the right-hand half of the block diagram; one section for port group A and the other for port group B. When the port select code is A1 A0 = 11 and the microprocessor operates a write bus cycle to the 8255A device, the control register contents are modified, so initialising the device. The function of each bit in the control word is shown in figure 7.2. Bits D0, D1 and D2 relate to port group B, D2 being the mode select bit. Bits D3, D4, D5 and D6 relate to port group A, D5 and D6 being the mode select bits. D7 is the mode set flag and must be at logic '1' when the mode of operation is to be changed.

Mode 0 is the straightforward uncomplicated input/output mode of operation, in which each of the ports can be programmed either as a level sensitive input or a latched output port. To set this mode of operation the control register bits must be allocated as follows: D7 to logic '1', both D6 and D5 to logic '0', and D2 to logic '0'. Each of the ports C lower, B, C upper and A can now be configured to operate as either input or output ports determined by the setting of bits D0, D1, D3 and D4 respectively. A and B are 8 bit ports while C upper and C lower are both 4 bit ports. Consider the address of an 8255A control register in I/O space to be 80FFH; then an example of port configuration in mode 0 is as follows:

```
MOV  AL,91H    ;8255A Control word in AX
MOV  DX,80FFH  ;Control register address in Dx.
OUT  DX,AL     ;Control word to control register.
```

Input/Output Interfacing **139**

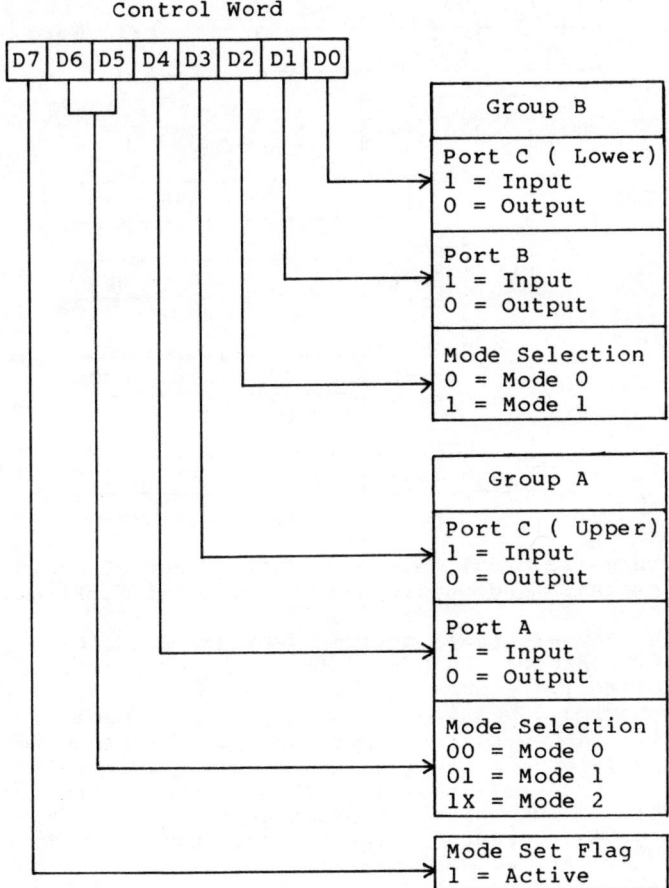

Figure 7.2 8255A Control word bit definitions.

Figure 7.3 shows the control register contents and port configuration which result from the execution of the above instructions. In figure 7.3, because D0 and D4 are at logic '1', port C lower and port A respectively are input ports; and because D1 and D3 are at logic '0', ports B and C upper respectively are output ports.

Mode 1 is the strobed (or handshaking) input/output mode of operation. The ports are divided into two groups, each consisting of an 8 bit port for input or output data transfer and a 4 bit port which acts as a control port. Port A and port C upper form group A, while port B and port C lower form group B.

140 The 8086 and Assembly Language

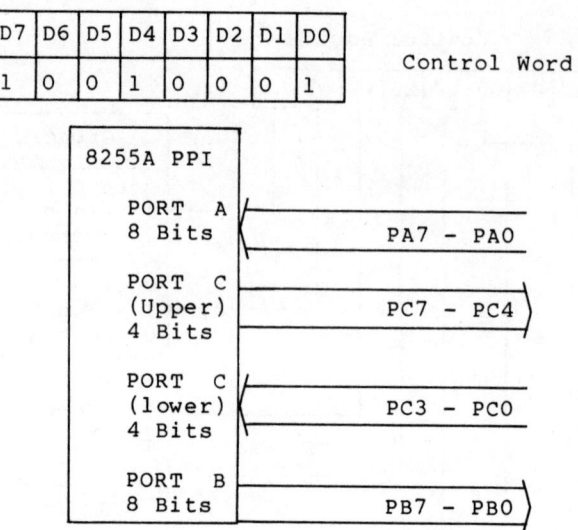

Figure 7.3 8255A Mode 0 operation control register contents and corresponding port configuration.

When an external device provides a strobe signal by taking the strobe pin STB of the control port to logic '0', incoming data can be transferred via the corresponding 8 bit input port. Consider mode 1 to be selected, and port A and port C upper to be configured as input ports by initialising the control register with the control word 10111XXX. In this case PC4 is the $\overline{STB}$ input and logic '0' on this input strobes data into the input latch on PA7 to PA0. PC5 is the input buffer full (or IBF) output signal which goes to logic '1', indicating to external circuitry that input data has been latched. IBF is set to logic '1' when $\overline{STB}$ is taken to logic '0' and IBF is restored to logic '0' by the $\overline{RD}$ input signal.

The third control signal is the interrupt request (or INTR) on PC3. This output acts as an external interrupt to the 8086 microprocessor. INTR is used to inform the microprocessor that newly latched data from the interrupting device is available at the input port. Interrupt enable INTE can be programmed to logic '0' or to logic '1' using the bit set/reset feature of the 8255A; it is logically ANDED with IBF to produce the INTR output. Hence when both INTE and IBF are at logic '1', INTR will be at logic '1' requesting an interrupt service routine to input data from the input port. The control word and control signals relating to port A are shown in figure 7.4.

When port A is configured for output operation, PC7

Input/Output Interfacing 141

is the output buffer full ($\overline{OBF}$) signal. OBF goes to logic '0' when the microprocessor writes data to the output port, and this is used to signal to external devices that data is ready at the output port. PC7 is the control line $\overline{ACK}$ which an external device can take to logic '0' to indicate that data has been accepted. Again the interrupt request output signal INTR is at PC3, and in this case it can be used to interrupt the microprocessor for the service routine which follows the acceptance of data by the external device. The control word and the control signals relating to port A as an output port are shown in figure 7.4.

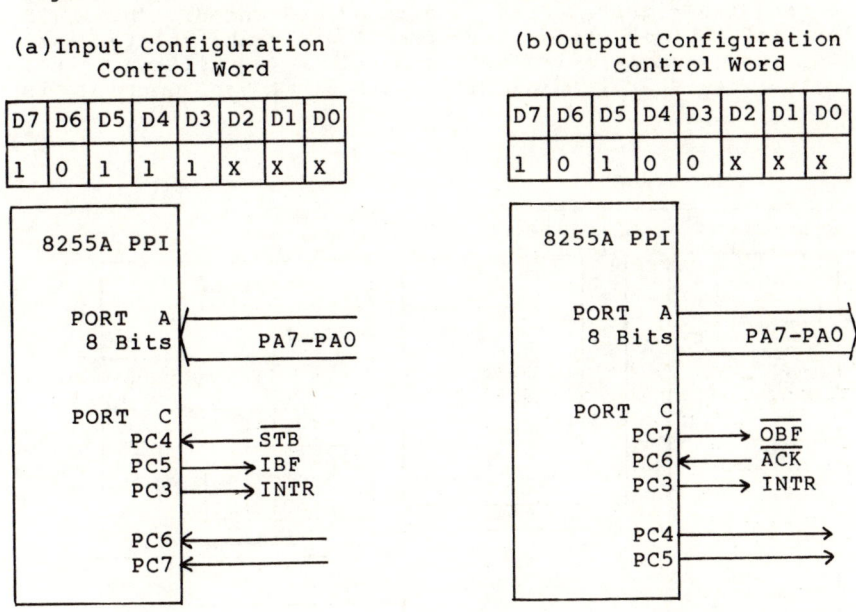

Figure 7.4 8255A Mode 1 operation – port A and corresponding port C control signals.

Table 7.2 8255A Mode 2 control signals and port action.

Control Signal		Port bit	Direction w.r.t 8255	Bidirectional Port A
Interrupt request	INTR	PC3	Out	Input/Output
Output buffer full	$\overline{OBF}$	PC7	Out	Output
Data Acknowledge	$\overline{ACK}$	PC6	In	Output
Stobe input data	$\overline{STB}$	PC4	In	Input
Input buffer full	IBF	PC5	Out	Input

Mode 2 is the strobed bidirectional I/O mode in which port A alone can both receive and transmit data, and control signals for both operations are provided by port C. The control signals, similar to those of mode 1, and the bit of port C at which they are active are given in table 7.2

In mode 1 the bit set/reset feature is used to program the interrupt enable INTE. It can also be used to program individual control bits of port C. The bit set/reset format is shown in figure 7.5. In programming the bits of port C, the data written to control register must have D7 = 0, and the selection of the port C bit is achieved by writing the required code to bits D3, D2 and D1. The logic level of the selected bit is the logic value written into D0. For example, if the control word written to the control register is 0XXX1011 then PC5 bit 5 of port C is set to 1.

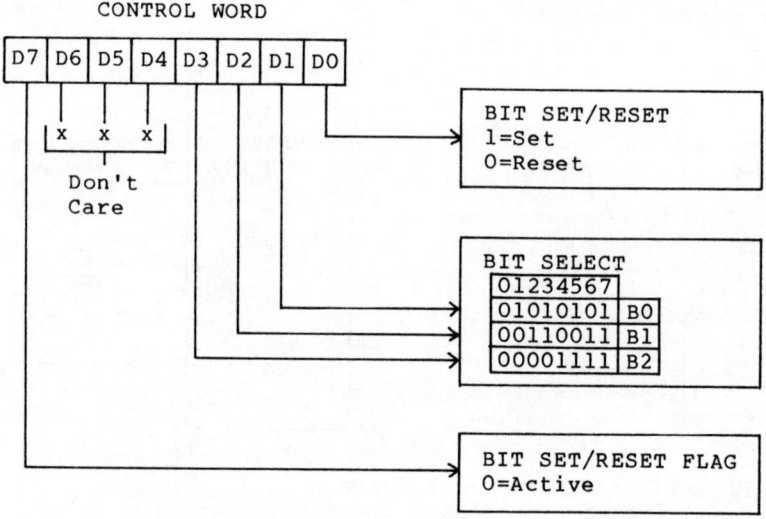

Figure 7.5 8255A Bit set/reset format.

I/O Interface using four 8255A Devices

An example of four programmable I/O devices providing twelve 8 bit parallel ports for a minimum mode 8086 system is given in figure 7.6. As 8205 address decoders are employed the system can be extended so that 8 peripheral devices can be enabled by each decoder. For byte operations the 8086 maintains either A0 or $\overline{BHE}$ at logic '1' so, as both are used as active low enable signals to a decoder, only one of the decoders will be enabled during a byte operation.

The lower decoder enables PPI devices (0) and (2) which

Input/Output Interfacing **143**

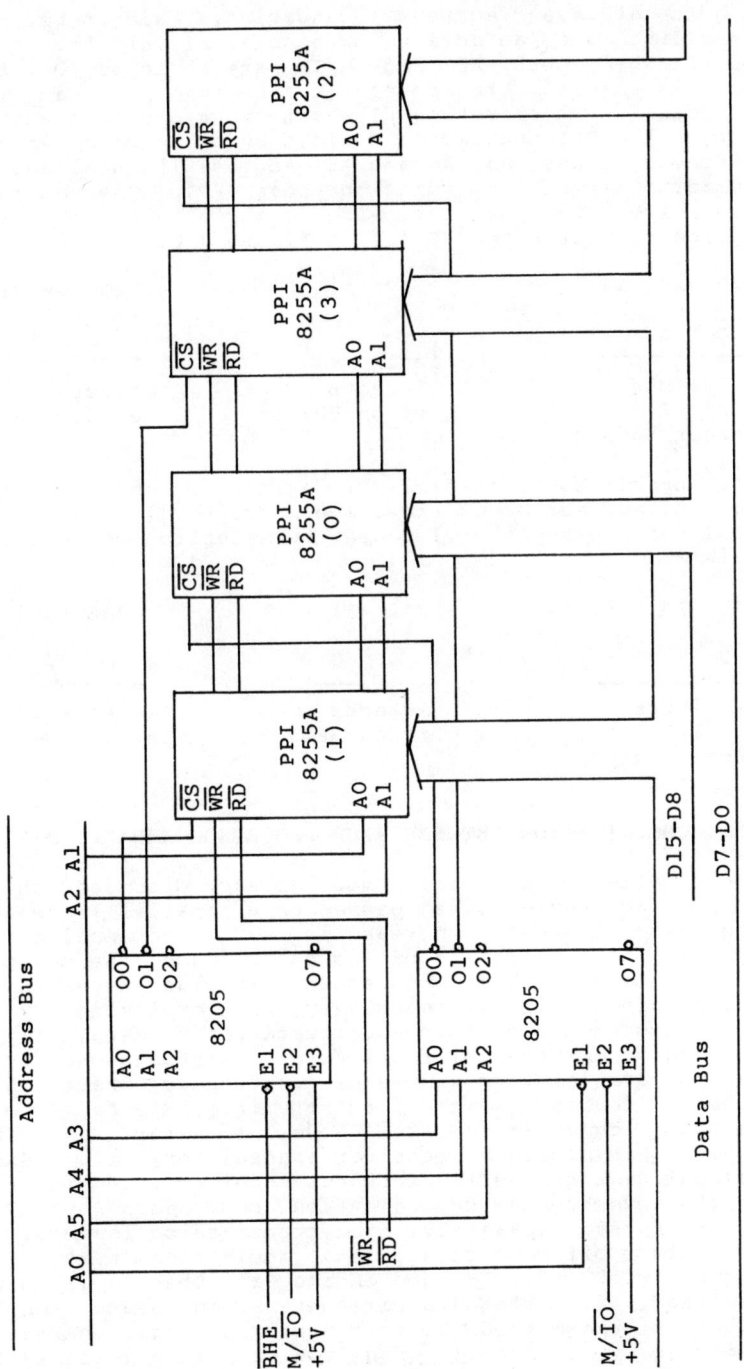

Figure 7.6 8255A I/O ports at even and odd boundaries.

144 The 8086 and Assembly Language

are both at even address boundaries. This is because address line A0 is an active low enable signal for this decoder. When both A0 and M/$\overline{\text{IO}}$ are at logic '0', the decoder is enabled, the address must be even and an I/O bus cycle is in operation. The active chip select output and hence the PPI enabled is decided by the logic values on address lines A5, A4 and A3. Address lines A2 and A1 are used to select the port on that PPI. The address values given in the following example will cause the selection of port B in PPI (2) in figure 7.6.

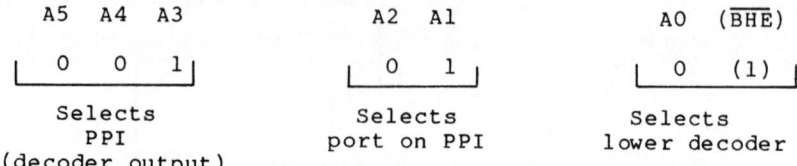

The upper decoder enables PPI devices (1) and (3) which are on odd address boundaries. The address values given in the following example will cause the selection of port A in PPI (3).

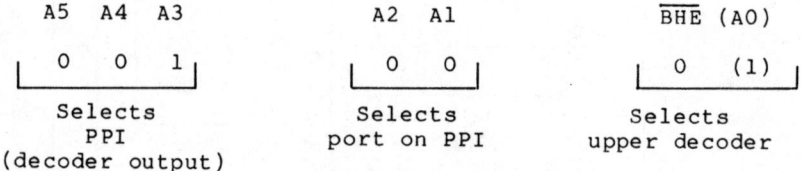

SERIAL COMMUNICATION BETWEEN MICROPROCESSOR AND I/O DEVICE

In the parallel communication mode already discussed the 8 bits of each byte were passed on 8 parallel lines and latched simultaneously, whereas in serial communication every bit of the byte is passed on the same line one bit at a time. Because microprocessors organise data in a parallel manner it is necessary, when employing serial communication methods, to convert data from parallel to serial form at the microprocessor output and back from serial to parallel form at the microprocessor input. LSI peripheral devices which form the interface to perform these data conversions are known as eiter a UART (universal asynchronous receiver/transmitter) or a USART (universal synchronous/asynchronous receiver/transmitter).

In the asynchronous communication mode each byte of data is passed separately. When transmission is about to begin a start bit or bits are sent indicating that data beginning with the LSB and ending with the MSB is to be transmitted. After the data bits have been sent then a stop bit is transmitted. So to transmit a single character 10 bits must be sent; when the data is a 7 bit ASCII

Input/Output Interfacing **145**

code the eighth bit can be an error detecting parity bit. The asynchronous transmission of the ASCII character 'J' is shown in figure 7.7.

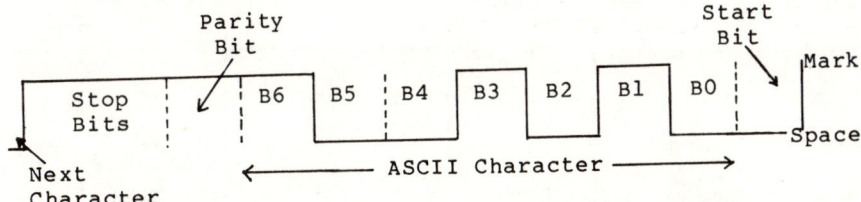

Figure 7.7 7 bit ASCII character 'J' with even parity and 2 stop bits (J = 4AH = 1001010B).

The rate at which the bit stream is transmitted is called the 'baud rate'. This is the number of bits transmitted per second. So a data transfer rate of 300 baud (300 bits/sec), when there are 11 bits for a character, allows the transmission of approximately 27 characters per second. Typical baud rates are 300, 1200, 4800 and 9600.

For asynchronous transmission the lines 'Receive Data', 'Transmit Data' and 'Common' are all that are fundamentally required. For synchronous transmission a 'Clock' line must be included to synchronise data transmission and reception. Asynchronous links can be 'simplex' (transmission in one direction only) as in the case of a microprocessor transmitting information to a printer; they can be 'half - duplex' (transmission in both directions but in only one direction at a time) as in the case of a microprocessor communicating with a CRT and keyboard, and they can be 'full - duplex' (transmission in both directions simultaneously).

RS-232C Interface
For asynchronous serial data communication, compatibility between equipment produced by a wide range of manufacturers is ensured by the use of a standard interface known as the RS-232C interface. This interface defines a 25 pin arrangement in which each pin has a specific function (a list of the pins and associated functions are given in Appendix B). The signals most commonly used in an asynchronous link are at pins 2, 3, 4, 5 and 7; these are respectively transmit data, receive data, request to send $\overline{RTS}$, clear to send $\overline{CTS}$, and common. An asynchronous communication link between a microcomputer and an external device is shown in figure 7.8

In the synchronous communication mode the transmitting and receiving devices are synchronised by the transmission of clock synchronising characters; thereafter it is possible to transmit a long stream of characters. The signal sequence by which two systems indicate to each

146 The 8086 and Assembly Language

other that they are ready to communicate is called the communication protocol.

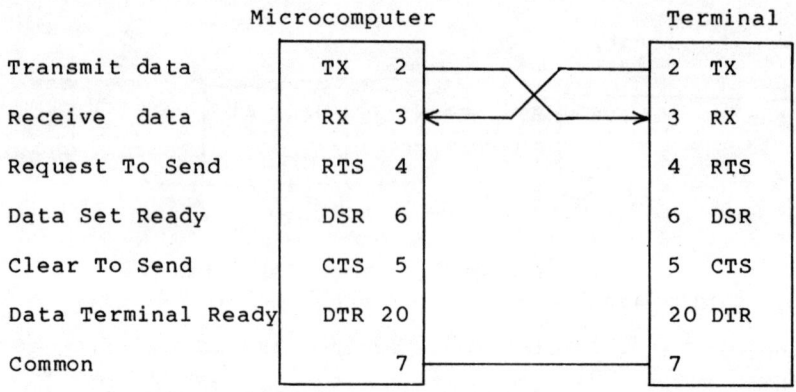

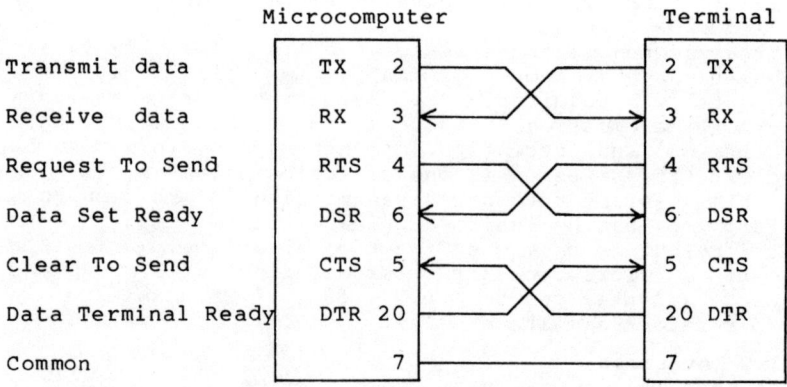

Figure 7.8 RS-232 Links

8251A PROGRAMMABLE COMMUNICATION INTERFACE

The 8251A device is a universal synchronous/asynchronous receiver/transmitter or USART and is used as a serial communication interface between the microprocessor and external peripherals. The microprocessor can be used to program the device by setting control registers which determine, for example: the mode of operation as either synchronous or asynchronous, the baud rate, the character length, the number of stop bits and the parity type used. The 8251A is an LSI device in a 28 pin dual-in-line

Input/Output Interfacing **147**

package, the pin configuration and block diagram are shown in figures 7.9(a) and figure 7.9(b) respectively.

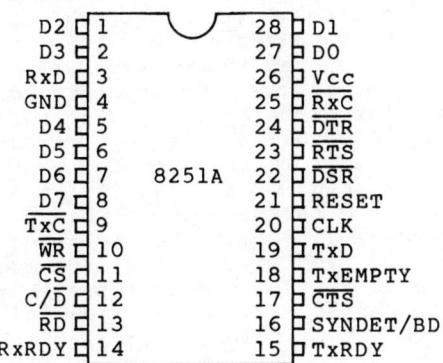

Figure 7.9(a) 8251A Pin configuration.

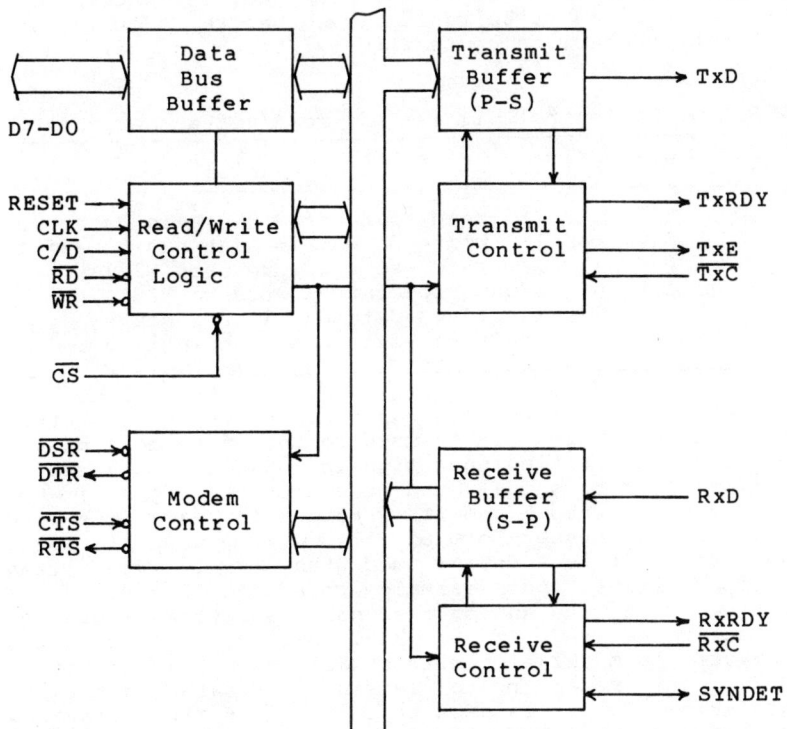

Figure 7.9(b) 8251A Block diagram.

148 The 8086 and Assembly Language

The left-hand side of the block diagram consists of two sections, namely the modem control block and the interface to the microprocessor which itself contains the data bus buffer and the control logic block. The bidirectional data bus buffer which is connected to the microproceesor at pins D0 to D7 is used to receive data and control words from the microprocessor and to transmit data and status words to the microprocessor. Signals to the control logic block inputs $\overline{RD}$ and $\overline{WR}$ come directly from the microprocessor and control the timing of the information transfer, i.e. when $\overline{RD}$ is at logic '0' the microprocessor can read data from the device and when $\overline{WR}$ is at logic '0' the microprocessor can write data to the device. The input to the $C/\overline{D}$ pin is used to inform the device that the incoming data from the microprocessor is either a control word or a data character. The 8251A device is enabled by an active low chip select signal to the control block input $\overline{CS}$.

Table 7.3 shows that the data bus is enabled when $\overline{CS}$ is low. The enable signal will usually originate from an address value via the decoder within the system. When the RESET input is taken to logic '1' the device enters an idle mode and has to be reprogrammed before it can again be used. The operations controlled by these signals are summarised in table 7.3

Table 7.3 8251A Control signals and read/write operations.

$\overline{CS}$	$C/\overline{D}$	$\overline{RD}$	$\overline{WR}$	Operation
0	0	0	1	I/O read -data from 8251A to data bus
0	0	1	0	I/O write-data from data bus to 8251A
0	1	0	1	I/O read -status word from 8251A
0	1	1	0	I/O write-control word to 8251A
0	x	1	1	Inactive -data bus in tri-state
1	x	x	x	Inactive -data bus in tri-state

The modem control section has a set of input and output control signals which can be used to interface to a modem. These consist of two input signals, $\overline{DSR}$ (data set ready) and $\overline{CTS}$ (clear to send), and two output signals, $\overline{DTR}$ (data terminal ready) and $\overline{RTS}$ (request to send). The word 'modem' is a shortened form of the words modulator and demodulator, it is a device used when data is transmitted over long lines, for example telephone lines. On a telephone line the analogue signal transmitted is in the frequency range 300 Hz to 3400 Hz. Digital data is transmitted by modulating this signal and a demodulator is used at the receiver to regain the data. In two way transmission a modem is used at each end of the telephone link, because modulation and demodulation is required at each end of the link.

Both the transmit and receive sections are on the right-hand side of the block diagram. The transmit buffer takes parallel data from the data bus and converts the data to serial form, inserting the start bit, the required number of stop bits and the requested parity bit. The completed serial information is stored in the transmit data buffer. When the transmitter is enabled, i.e. $\overline{\text{CTS}}$ taken to logic '0', the serial data stream is transmitted on the TxD line, each bit of data being transmitted on the trailing edge of the transmit clock $\overline{\text{TxC}}$.

In the synchronous mode the baud rate is equal to the transmit clock frequency, but in the asynchronous mode it can also be a fraction of this frequency, e.g. 1 or 1/16 or 1/64. When the transmit buffer is empty the TxRDY output is taken to logic '1'. This signal can be used as an interrupt input to the microprocessor and so inform it that another character can be transferred to the transmit section of the 8251A. When data transfer is complete TxRDY is automatically returned to logic '0'. TxEMPTY is also taken to logic '1' when the transmit buffer is empty and returned to logic '0' when the transmit buffer is full. It is used to indicate the end of transmission in the half-duplex mode of operation.

Serial data is received on the RxD pin. It is clocked in on the rising edge of $\overline{\text{RxC}}$, the receiver clock pulse, and converted in the receiver buffer to parallel form. In the asynchronous mode of operation RxD is normally at logic '1', and initially a valid start pulse at logic '0' must be detected. When this is the case a bit counter causes RxD to be sampled at the centre of every bit time and a character is said to be assembled. The stop bit signals the end of the character. The RxRDY output is taken to logic '1' when the receiver buffer contains a character. This signal can be used as an interrupt input to the microprocessor and so inform it that a character is available in the buffer to be read.

When the microprocessor reads the buffer, RxRDY returns to logic '0'. The receiver clock $\overline{\text{RxC}}$ input controls the reception baud rate. In the synchronous mode the baud rate equals the frequency of the receive clock, but in the asynchronous mode it can also be a fraction of this frequency in a similar way to the transmit situation. In many applications the USART is handling both transmission and reception of data, so one external baud rate generator is used and is connected to both $\overline{\text{TxC}}$ and $\overline{\text{RxC}}$. Finally the pin labelled SYNDET can be used in the synchronous mode as a SYNC detector output, and in the asynchronous mode as a BREAK detector output.

The use of the USART device 8251A in both asynchronous and synchronous operation is illustrated in a general manner in figure 7.10.

Programming the 8251A PCI USART

The operation of the device is governed by the setting of three control registers: the mode control register, the command register and the status register, in that order.

150 The 8086 and Assembly Language

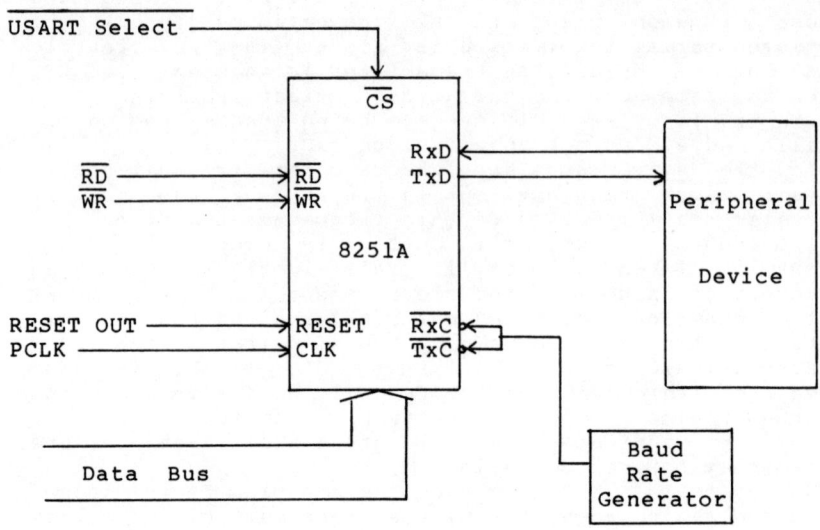

(a) Use of the 8251A as an Asynchronous Serial Interface

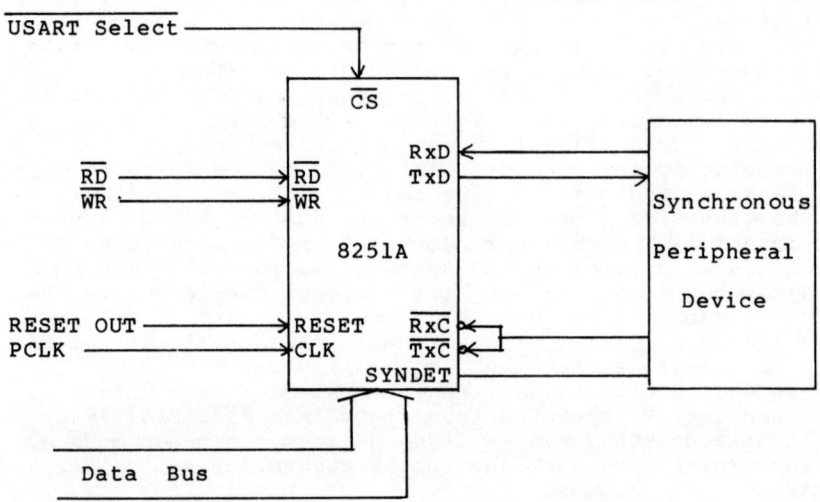

(b) Use of the 8251A as an Synchronous Serial Interface

Figure 7.10 8251A as a serial interface

When power is switched on to the microprocessor system the connections are usually such that a hardware reset is sent to the 8251A interface. This is necessary as before the device can be programmed it must be reset.

Input/Output Interfacing **151**

Programming the mode control register involves the selection of: (1) synchronous or asynchronous operation, (2) the value by which the external baud rate will be divided internally within the 8251A, (3) whether or not parity is to be used, (4) if parity is used whether it is odd or even, and (5) if in the asynchronous mode the number of stop bits.

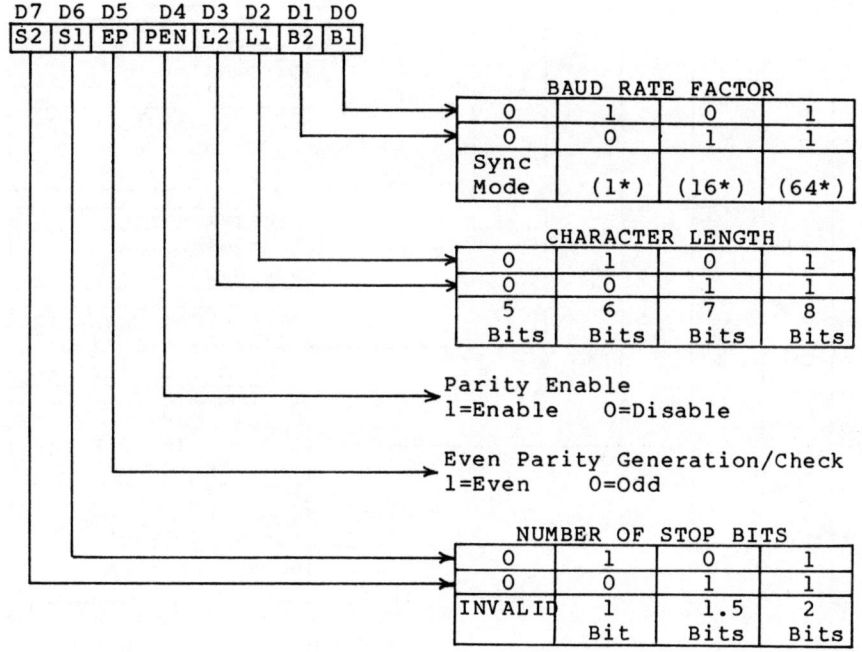

Only effects TX; RX never requires more than one stop bit

Figure 7.11 8251A Mode instruction format asynchronous mode.

The mode instruction format is shown in figure 7.11. In the following asynchronous mode example, if the mode control register is loaded with 0CFH the mode setting is:

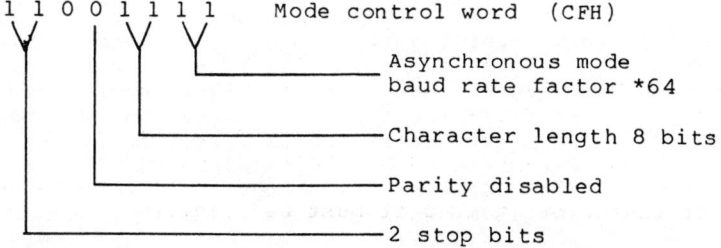

152 The 8086 and Assembly Language

When the asynchronous mode has been selected by programming the mode control register, programming the command register will allow control of the serial interface.

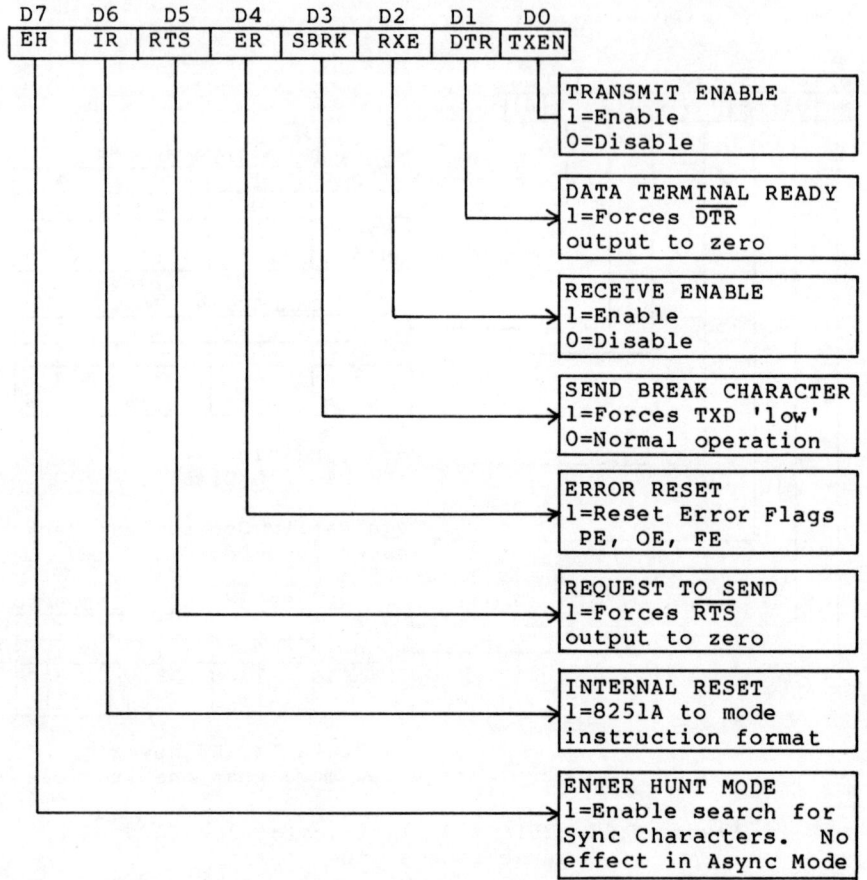

Figure 7.12 8251A Command instruction format.

Programming the command register involves enabling or disabling the transmit and receive sections by setting to logic '1' or resetting to logic '0' bits 0 and 2 respectively. Disabling these sections means only that they no longer signal the microprocessor that they are ready to operate. For example, when the transmit section is disabled and the transmit buffer becomes empty, the 8251A does not inform the microprocessor, i.e. TxRDY output will not be taken to logic '1'. The command register format is shown in figure 7.12. The command word

Input/Output Interfacing 153

is also used to set the error reset bit ER to logic '1' and so clear the error flags PE, OE and FE in the status register. To allow software initialisation of the 8251A the internal reset bit IR can be set to logic '1'.

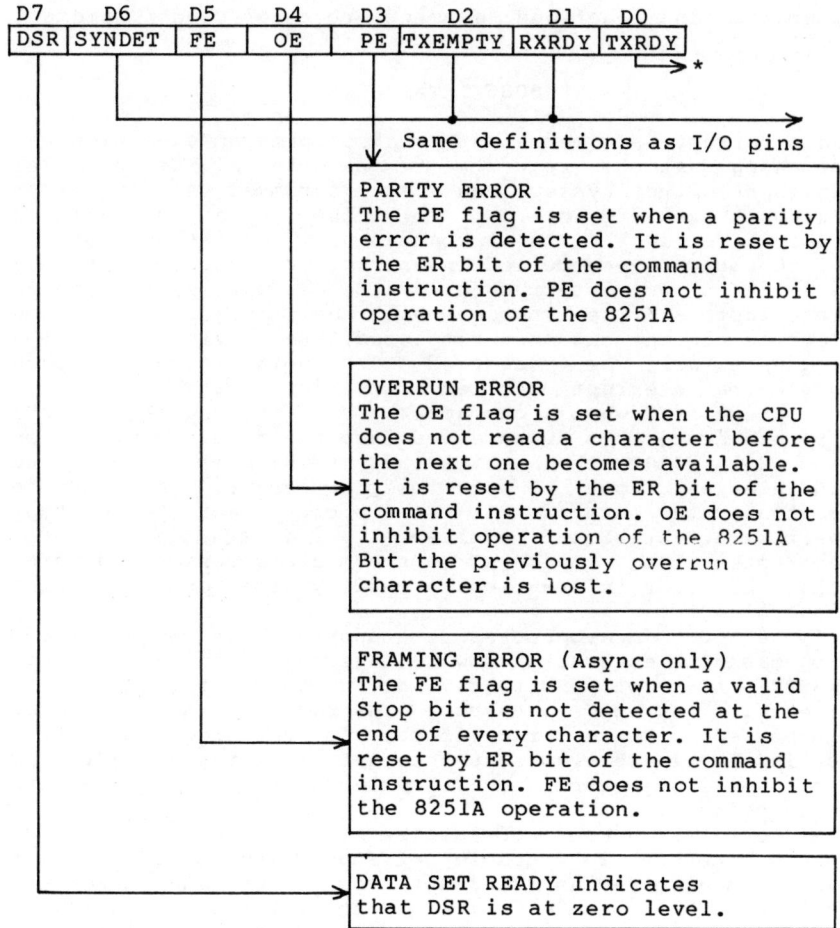

*TXRDY Status bit is not conditioned by CTS and TXEN.

Figure 7.13 8251A Status register format.

The status register, the format of which is shown in figure 7.13, should be examined before data is received or transmitted by the microprocessor. If on examination of the register the error flags indicate either parity, overrun or framing error in, say, the incoming data, then a routine should be entered to cause the error flags to be reset and the data character to be retransmitted.

Program 8.11 is an example of a program in which an 8251A is used for the simplest of asynchronous serial communication between a microprocessor and a printer.

8086 INTERRUPTS

An interrupt is a mechanism by which program execution can be changed at the request of an external device. For instance, the system can be programmed to expect an external hardware interrupt to occur at an unspecified time during the continuous operation of a microprocessor-controlled industrial process. The process will then be interrupted by the hardware signal and an interrupt service routine will be invoked. When the service routine has been completed, the previous execution sequence will be restarted at the point in the sequence where the interrupt occurred. For example, the process may be interrupted when a character, from a transducer in the process system, is transferred into the receiver buffer of an 8251A USART, the RxRDY output of which is connected to an interrupt input of the microprocessor. The service routine now entered will be a program dedicated to that particular interrupt requirement, i.e. transferring the character from the USART to the microprocessor and using that character information to modify the process being controlled.

The 8086 microprocessor supports both maskable and non-maskable external hardware interrupts and a hardware RESET interrupt. Software interrupts initiated by the execution of the interrupt instruction INT are also supported. These are effectively vectored subroutine calls. There are also four internal interrupts dedicated to: divide error, overflow error, single step and breakpoint.

The total number of different interrupts the 8086 microprocessor is capable of supporting is 256, each of which is allotted an interrupt type number. An interrupt vector table (table 7.4) links the interrupt number with the address of the corresponding service routine. The service routine address consists of two words: the higher addressed word defines the base address of the code segment, and the lower addressed word defines the offset address of the first instruction of the routine. So the interrupt vector address is four bytes long; the first two bytes are loaded into the IP and the next two bytes into CS. The interrupt vector address table occupies the first 1 Kbyte of memory, the range of addresses being 00000H to 003FEH. Of the first five vectors, four are dedicated to the 8086's internal interrupts. Types 0, 1, 3 and 4 are respectively used for divide error, single step, breakpoint and overflow; the type 2 is used for the NMI

Input/Output Interfacing **155**

Table 7.4 8086 Interrupt vectors.

	Interrupt Vector Type Number		Memory Address
↑	Type 255	CS(255)	
		IP(255)	003FC
	Type 254	CS(254)	
224 Vectors Available for User		IP(254)	003F8
	Type 34	CS(34)	
		IP(34)	00088
	Type 33	CS(33)	
		IP(33)	00084
	Type 32	CS(32)	
↓		IP(32)	00080
↑	Type 31	CS(31)	
27 Reserved Vectors		IP(31)	0007C
↓	Type 5	CS(5)	
		IP(5)	00014
↑	Overflow Type 4	CS(4)	
		IP(4)	00010
	Breakpoint Type 3	CS(3)	
5 Dedicated Vectors		IP(3)	0000C
	NMI Type 2	CS(2)	
		IP(2)	00008
	Single Step Type 1	CS(1)	
		IP(1)	00004
↓	Divide Error Type 0	CS(0)	
		IP(0)	00000

156 The 8086 and Assembly Language

service routine. The next 27 interrupt types are reserved by Intel so that the user can have compatibility with future products. Consequently it is advisable not to use these interrupts. The remaining interrupt types 32 to 255 are available to the user for the storage of interrupt vector addresses.

The 8086 calculates the vector table storage address by multiplying the interrupt type number by four. As an example, consider that the type number of the interrupt to be serviced is 33; then the vector table address for this interrupt is given by the decimal number 132 because 4 * 33 = 132. The hexadecimal equivalent of this is 84H and so the vector table address is 84H. The two words stored in addresses 84H to 87H are those necessary to form the interrupt vector address. When interrupt 33 is executed, the word at address 84H is moved to IP and the word at 86H is moved to the CS, and so the corresponding interrupt service routine is initiated. If at 84H the word stored is 0446H and at 86H the word is 0100H, then the physical address of the interrupt service routine is 01000H + 0446H = 01446H. This process is illustrated in figure 7.14.

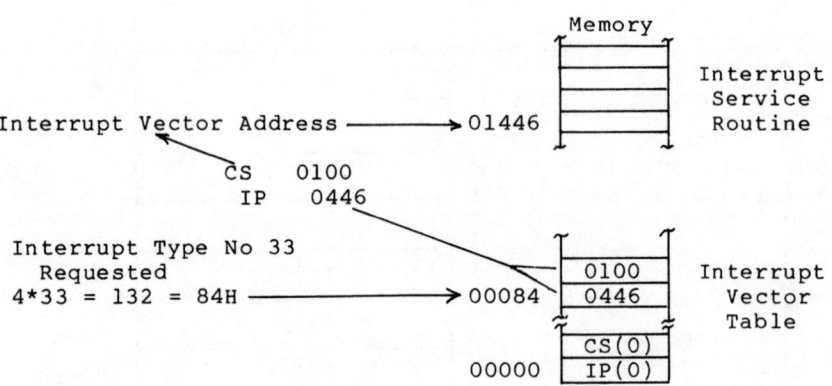

Figure 7.14 Interrupt process.

Software Interrupts

These are interrupts initiated by the instruction INT N, where N represents the interrupt type number. So execution of the instruction INT 34 causes the program control to pass to the interrupt service routine whose starting address is calculated from the instruction pointer address IP(34) stored at 00088H, and the code segment address CS(34) stored at 0008AH. The organisation of a software interrupt and corresponding service routine is demonstrated in program 8.13.

Input/Output Interfacing **157**

Internal Interrupts

These four interrupts are predefined in that, as shown in the interrupt vector table (table 7.4), they have assigned vector type numbers. The corresponding vector addresses for IP and CS must be provided by the programmer, as must the vector service routine. These interrupts cannot be masked out with the interrupt enable flag, so they have the highest priority except, that is, for the single step interrupt. Because external interrupts via INTR can be disabled they have the lowest priority. The interrupt priorities are, from highest to lowest: predefined internal interrupts, non maskasble interrupt NMI and external interrupts using INTR.

Type 0 – divide error
If in the execution of a division instruction the quotient is larger than the specified destination, e.g. if the microprocessor is instructed to divide by zero, then a type 0 interrupt is automatically initiated by the microprocessor. The service routine should be such that the system recovers from such a division error; for example, the service routine can halt the program and also provide an error message indicating 'divide by zero'.

Type 1 – single step
This interrupt is used to allow program execution one instruction at a time. When the TF (trap flag) is set a type 1 interrupt is initiated by the microprocessor after each program instruction is executed. Note that when an interrupt is acknowledged the flag register is pushed onto the stack and then the TF is reset. This avoids the single step interrupt service routine itself being interrupted by a type 1 interrupt. The return from interrupt instruction IRET, which should end the service routine, pops the flag register off the stack and so TF is again set. Consequently another type 1 interrupt can occur when the next instruction is executed. The service routine can provide various debugging capabilities, such as displaying the microprocessor register contents, which allows an evaluation of the effect of executing the instruction. The process is known as single stepping.

Type 3 – breakpoint
This interrupt is initiated by executing the single byte INT 3 instruction and is used to set a breakpoint in the program execution. The breakpoint facility is used in program debugging so that the program can be executed to a strategic point at which a service routine can be entered and, for example, register contents can be displayed, allowing an evaluation of the program up to this point. Because it is a single byte instruction it can be used within a debugging program to substitute for any instruction in the program being debugged. The use of breakpoints is a common software debugging technique.

158 The 8086 and Assembly Language

Type 4 - overflow error
An overflow can occur when any arithmetic instruction is executed and as a result the overflow flag will be set. If the arithmetic instruction on execution sets the overflow flag and if it is followed by the interrupt instruction INTO, then a type 4 interrupt is initiated. The associated service routine can either be used to halt the program or to substitute the signed maximum value. Whenever an arithmetic instruction is used with signed numbers it should be followed by the INTO interrupt on overflow instruction.

Interrupt Masking
The interrupt enable flag IF, shown in the flag register word of figure 1.5, affects the hardware interrupts and not the software interrupts. When the flag is set using the instruction STI the interrupt at INTR is enabled, and if the flag is reset by the instruction CLI then the interrupt at INTR is masked. In the interrupt acknowledge sequence the 8086 clears IF automatically, masking further hardware interrupts at INTR.

External Hardware Interrupts

These consist of maskable interrupts at the INTR pin, a non-maskable interrupt at the NMI pin and a reset interrupt. The arrangement is shown in figure 7.15 and includes an interrupt control unit as an interface between the interrupting sources and the INTR input to the 8086 microprocessor.

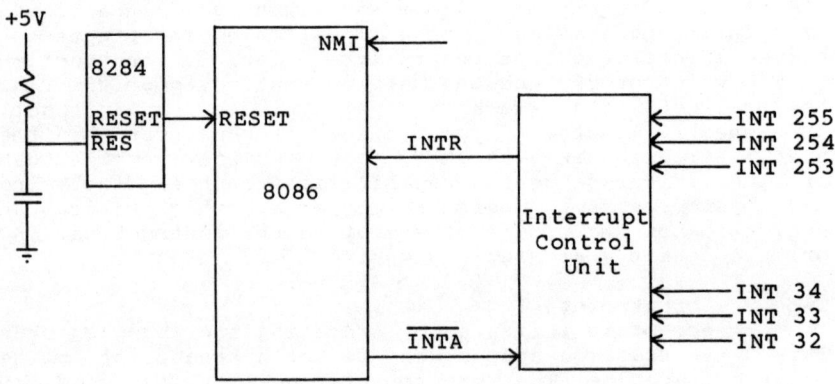

Figure 7.15 8086 External hardware interrupt interface.

System Reset Interrupt
The 8284 clock generator device provides a system hardware reset function. When power is switched on the RES input of the 8284 device is taken to ground via the capacitor of the RC circuit, shown in figure 7.15. This input is to an

internal Schmitt trigger circuit which causes the RESET output to switch to logic '1'. The reset signal to the microprocessor must be kept at logic '1' for a period of four clock cycles in order to be recognised by the microprocessor. The RC value at the 8284 RES input provides this period. At reset the 8086 terminates activities, placing bus lines in the high impedance state and control lines in their inactive state. When the reset signal returns to logic '0' the 8086 initialises the flags and registers IP, DS, SS and ES to 0000H and the CS register to FFFFH, and empties the queue. As the CS is taken to FFFFH and IP to 0 the 8086 executes the instruction at FFFF0H. Usually this location contains a jump instruction to the start-up routine of the system.

Non-Maskable Interrupt NMI
This is a positive edge triggered interrupt, the interrupting signal being latched within the 8086 microprocessor. The NMI has a dedicated type 2 vector; the address of the interrupt service routine is obtained from words stored in locations 0008H and 000AH, as shown in table 7.4. When the NMI interrupt is acknowledged the current flag register contents are placed on the stack; then the interrupt enable flag and the trap flag are both cleared, so disabling maskable and single step interrupts. The NMI interrupt is usually used to detect catastrophic events such as a power failure.

Maskable External Hardware Interrupts
The signal lines INTR (interrupt request) and INTA (interrupt acknowledge) are used with these interrupts. When the input INTR is taken to logic '1' this represents an interrupt request. The microprocessor samples the INTR input during the last clock period of each instruction. If the interrupt flag has been set, so enabling the interrupts, the interrupt request is recognised by the microprocessor which sends a signal on the INTA output line. The external device must then place an 8 bit type number on the data bus. The 8086 reads this number to identify the interrupt. An interrupt interface circuit such as the 8259A is necessary to handle these signals and to allow the microprocessor to deal with more than one interrupting device at the INTR input.

External Hardware Interrupt Acknowledge Sequence
So that the response of the microprocessor to an interrupt can be made as clear as possible, the operations when an external interrupt is activated are described as follows in note form. Figure 7.15 illustrates the connections between the interrupt controller and the microprocessor operating in minimum mode.

160 The 8086 and Assembly Language

(1) An external device requests service by taking one of the interrupt lines, e.g. INT 32, to logic '1'.
(2) The interrupt controller decides on the priority of the request, and if, for example, there is not already an active interrupt, then it requests service of the 8086 microprocessor.
(3) The INTR input is taken to logic '1' by the controller.
(4) The 8086 samples INTR during the last clock cycle of each instruction.
(5) Provided the IF is set the 8086 executes two interrupt acknowledge bus cycles. During each of these cycles INTA is taken to logic '0' for about two clock periods.
(6) In response to the second $\overline{\text{INTA}}$ low the interrupt controller places the interrupt number on the data bus, and as DT/$\overline{\text{R}}$ and $\overline{\text{DEN}}$ are active this byte is read by the microprocessor.
(7) The controller removes the logic '1' at INTR.
(8) The interrupt number is multiplied by 4, producing the vector table storage address.
(9) The 8086 pushes the contents of the flag register onto the stack and then resets both the trap flag TF and the interrupt flag IF.
(10) The CS and IP contents are pushed onto the stack. The storage on the stack has involved three write cycles.
(11) Two read cycles are executed to load the CS and IP registers from the interrupt vector table. No segment register is used when referencing the vector table.
(12) Program control is transferred to the service routine which is executed.
(13) The service routine ends with the instruction IRET which returns the register contents of IP, CS and the flags, in that order, from the stack.

8259A PROGRAMMABLE INTERRUPT CONTROLLER PIC

This is a programmable interrupt control unit used as an interface between the interrupting devices and the microprocessor, as shown in figure 7.15. The PIC is used to interface the microprocessor to eight external interrupts. These interrupts are given a priority rating by the controller. The 8259A interrupt controller is an LSI device in a 28 pin dual-in-line package. Figure 7.16 shows the pin configuration and the device block diagram.

The left-hand side of the block diagram shows the interface to the controlling microprocessor. This consists of the bidirectional data bus buffer which is connected to the microprocessor data bus at lines D0 to D7. The read/write logic block organises the data transfers through the buffer using the control lines $\overline{\text{RD}}$ and $\overline{\text{WR}}$. When $\overline{\text{RD}}$ is at logic '0' the microprocessor is able to read data from the controller and when $\overline{\text{WR}}$ is at logic '0' to write data to the controller. The device is enabled by a logic '0' applied to the chip select $\overline{\text{CS}}$. The input to pin A0 is

Input/Output Interfacing **161**

```
      ___
      CS  ┤1        28├ Vcc
      ___
      WR  ┤2        27├ A0
      ___              ____
      RD  ┤3        26├ INTA
      D7  ┤4        25├ IR7
      D6  ┤5        24├ IR6
      D5  ┤6   8259A 23├ IR5
      D4  ┤7        22├ IR4
      D3  ┤8        21├ IR3
      D2  ┤9        20├ IR2
      D1  ┤10       19├ IR1
      D0  ┤11       18├ IR0
    CAS 0 ┤12       17├ INT
                        _____
    CAS 1 ┤13       16├ SP/EN
      GND ┤14       15├ CAS 2
```

Figure 7.16(a) 8259A Pin configuration.

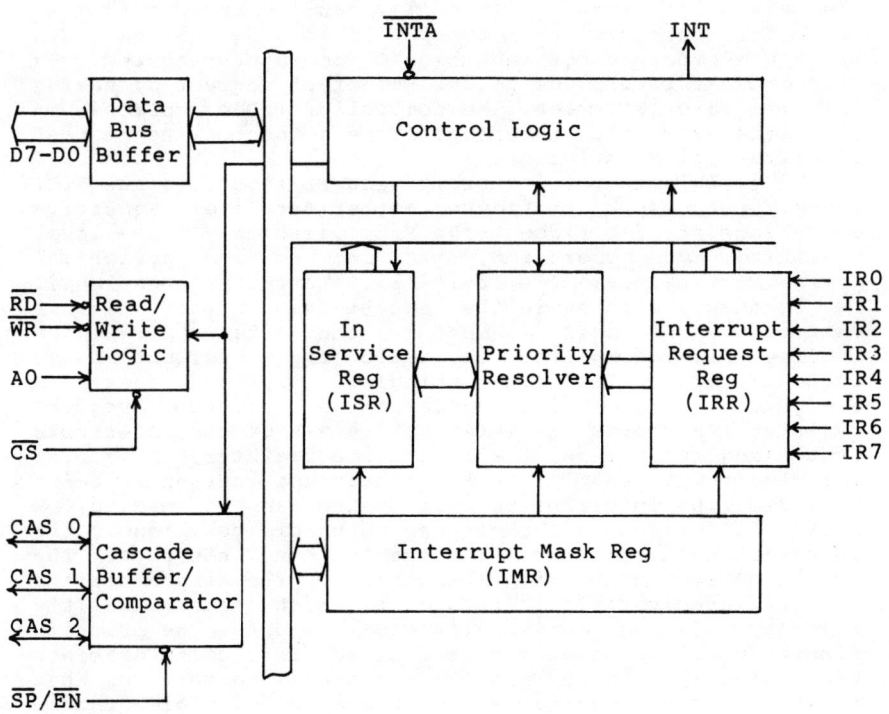

Figure 7.16(b) 8259A Block diagram

usually the A1 address line of the 8086 microprocessor and the input signal is used to distinguish between the command words accessed by the microprocessor.

The 8259A PIC can be programmed to act as a single controller handling eight interrupting sources or to act with other 8259A devices to cope with a larger number of interrupting sources. When several 8259A devices are used in a system, one device acts as a master and the others act as slaves. This is called the cascade mode. The interface for this master/slave arrangement is provided by the cascade buffer comparator. The cascade lines CAS0, CAS1 and CAS2 are used as outputs from the master 8259A and as inputs to the slave 8259As, effectively providing a bus between the devices. In the cascade mode the pin connection $\overline{SP}/\overline{EN}$ is used as an input to select the device as master or slave, whereas in the single mode this pin provides an output enable signal which can be used with transceivers on the data bus.

The interrupt control interface is provided by INT and $\overline{INTA}$, that is they are used to provide communication controls between the microprocessor and the interrupt controller. INT is the interrupt request output of the 8259A and this is connected to the INTR input of the 8086 microprocessor. When the 8259A receives a valid interrupt then INT is taken to logic '1', causing an interrupt at the microprocessor. The interrupt acknowledge lines $\overline{INTA}$ of the microprocessor and the PIC are interconnected. The microprocessor responds to the interrupt request by taking $\overline{INTA}$ to logic '0' twice. The controller then places on the data bus the interrupt type number of the highest priority active interrupt.

IR0 to IR7 are the interrupt request inputs to the PIC. These inputs can be configured either for level sensitive operation or for edge triggered operation. In the level sensitive type operation, the interrupting peripheral device must maintain the logic '1' interrupt request until it is answered to avoid the request being missed. Also it must remove the logic '1' before the interrupt service routine is completed to avoid the interrupt being requested again. The edge triggered type of operation overcomes these difficulties. The interrupt request register IRR stores the interrupt levels of the interrupts requesting service and the in-service register ISR stores the interrupt level of the interrupt currently being serviced. The interrupt request inputs can be masked, a logic '1' placed in the corresponding bit position in the interrupt mask register will disable the interrupt. The final block on the right-hand side of the diagram is the priority resolver. It is this unit which determines the priority of the active interrupt inputs. The priority scheme applied is software controlled. This unit examines the interrupt inputs and the interrupts in service. When an interrupt requesting service has a priority higher than the interrupt presently being serviced an interrupt request is sent to the microprocessor, so allowing the higher priority interrupt to be serviced.

Input/Output Interfacing **163**

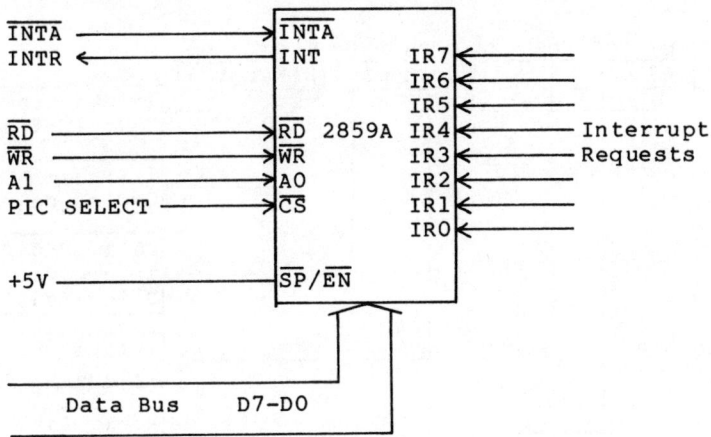

Figure 7.17 8259A Interrupt interface.

The connection of an 8259A programmable interrupt controller as an 8086 minimum mode interrupt interface is shown in figure 7.17.

Programming the 8259A PIC

Before the device can be used, it must first be intialised and this is accomplished by loading the control registers with initialisation command words. The initialisation command words are ICW1, ICW2, ICW3 and ICW4. The first initialisation command word ICW1 involves the selection of: (1) single or cascade mode, (2) edge triggered or level triggered interrupt input, and (3) whether or not ICW4 is to be used. The second initialisation command word ICW2 is used to decide the interrupt vector type number. The third ICW3 is used in the cascade mode only. Finally ICW4 is used to select the device for use with either the 8085, an 8 bit microprocessor, or the 8086 microprocessor. If the 8259A is to be used with the 8086 microprocessor then ICW4 further selects either the buffered mode employing an 8288 bus controller or the non buffered mode for the small 8086 system. The format of these initialisation command words is shown in figure 7.18.

The operation of the 8259A device may entail the use of further command words known as operation command words. These are OCW1, OCW2 and OCW3, and can be issued at any time after initialisation. Modifications to the operation may be achieved by loading the internal control registers with these operation command words. The first operation command word OCW1 is used to access the contents of the interrupt mask register IRR. By writing a command word to IRR selected interrupt inputs can be masked, and by reading the IRR the present interrupt mask status can be

164 The 8086 and Assembly Language

ICW1

A0	D7	D6	D5	D4	D3	D2	D1	D0
0	A7	A6	A5	1	LTIM	ADI	SNGL	IC4

- 1=ICW4 needed
- 0=No ICW4 needed

- 1=Single
- 0=Cascade mode

- Call addr interval
- 1=interval of 4
- 0=interval of 8

- 1=level triggered
- 0=edge triggered

- A7-A5 Int Vector (8085 mode only)

ICW2

A0	D7	D6	D5	D4	D3	D2	D1	D0
1	A15/T7	A14/T6	A13/T5	A12/T4	A11/T3	A10	A9	A8

- A15-A8 Int Vector (8085 mode only)
- T7-T3 Int Vector Address (8086 mode)

ICW3 (Master)

A0	D7	D6	D5	D4	D3	D2	D1	D0
1	S7	S6	S5	S4	S3	S2	S1	S0

- 1=IR Input has a slave
- 0=IR Input does not have a slave

ICW3 (Slave)

A0	D7	D6	D5	D4	D3	D2	D1	D0
1	0	0	0	0	0	ID2	ID1	ID0

Slave ID							
0	1	2	3	4	5	6	7
0	1	0	1	0	1	0	1
0	0	1	1	0	0	1	1
0	0	0	0	1	1	1	1

Slave ID = corresponding Master IR input

Figure 7.18 8259A Initialisation command word format.

Input/Output Interfacing **165**

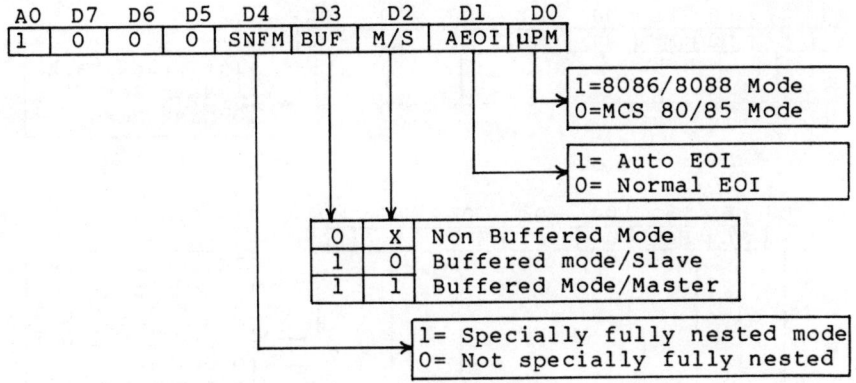

Figure 7.18 Con't
8259A Initialisation command word format.

determined. The priority scheme to be used is selected by the second operation command word OCW2. The third operation command word OCW3 facilitates reading of the ISR and IRR registers. Figure 7.19 shows the format of these operation command words.

An example of the command words used when the 8259A is in the single non-buffered mode with an 8086 microprocessor is given. The initialisation command words are written to the the 8259A device in the sequence ICW1, ICW2 and ICW4 (note that ICW3 is not required), and that the interrupt mask is set using the operation command word OCW1. The values given to the command words are appropriate to the system in question and are explained below. In this example the first command word is used to specify single mode operation, a requirement for ICW4 and edge triggered interrupts.

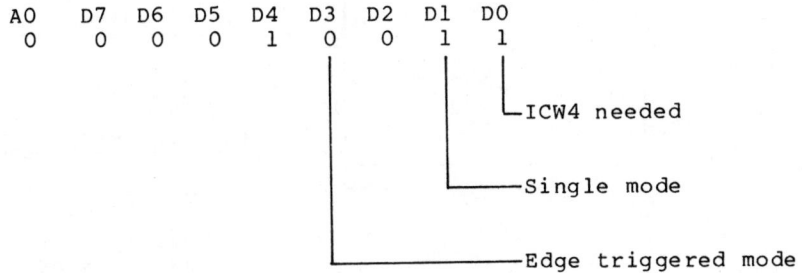

166 The 8086 and Assembly Language

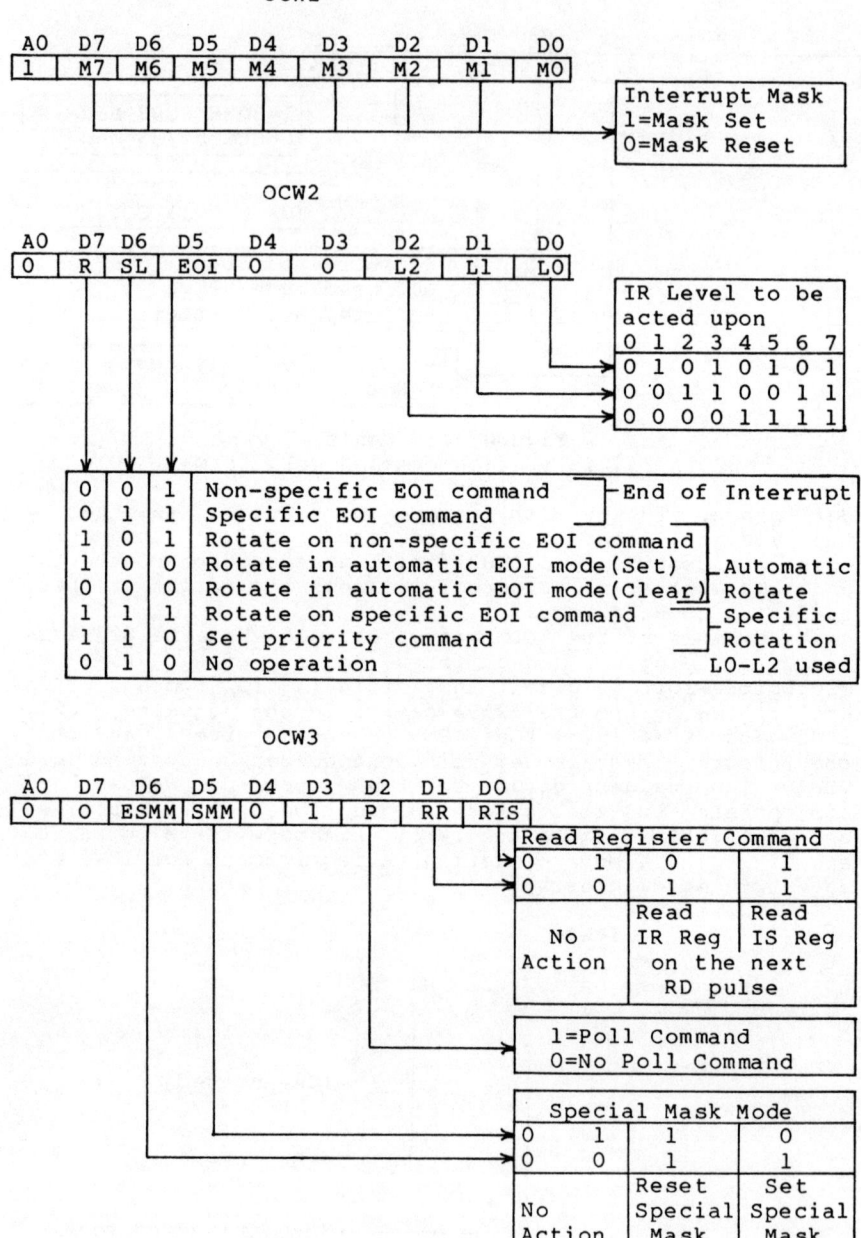

Figure 7.19 8259A Operation command word format.

Input/Output Interfacing **167**

The second command word is used to select the interrupt type number.

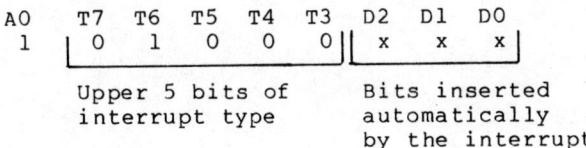

For interrupt type 64 to 71 (40H to 47H) the command word ICW2 would be as shown above and the 3 least significant bits required to make up the interrupt type number are provided by the interrupt input as shown below.

```
T7  T6  T5  T4  T3  T2  T1  T0
 0   1   0   0   0   0   0   0    IR0
 0   1   0   0   0   0   0   1    IR1
 0   1   0   0   0   0   1   0    IR2
 0   1   0   0   0   0   1   1    IR3
 0   1   0   0   0   1   0   0    IR4
 0   1   0   0   0   1   0   1    IR5
 0   1   0   0   0   1   1   0    IR6
 0   1   0   0   0   1   1   1    IR7
```

The third command word used in this case is ICW4 and specifies that the 8259A device is to be used with the 8086 microprocessor, that 'end of interrupt' is either automatic or normal and that buffered or non-buffered mode is employed.

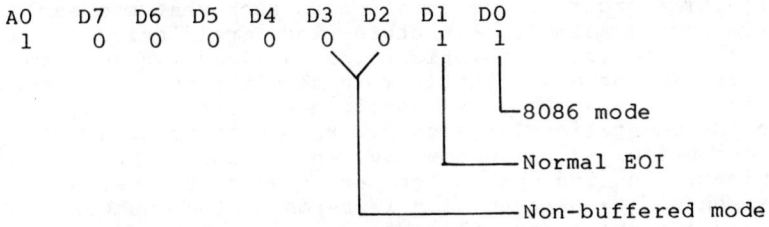

The operation command word OCW1 can be used to mask out selected interrupt inputs. A bit set to 1 causes the corresponding interrupt to be masked so in this example interrupts IR7 to IR3 are masked.

```
         OCW1
A0  M7  M6  M5  M4  M3  M2  M1  M0
 1   1   1   1   1   1   0   0   0
```

CHAPTER 8
8086 Assembly language programs

The purpose of this chapter is to provide a series of programs in assembly language that can be used :

(1) to illustrate the instruction set of the language.
(2) to demonstrate assembly language program structure.
(3) to provide programming techniques that can be adopted by the less experienced programmer.
(4) to provide subroutines which can be used and adapted for inclusion in longer programs.
(5) to give program examples which depend on simple interfacing devices and use elementary peripherals such as: banks of switches and light emitting diodes (LEDs), digital to analogue convertors (DACs), analogue to digital convertors (ADCs) and stepper motors.

The programs are intended as an aid to those who want to familiarise themselves with the assembly language as quickly as possible and who, by running and modifying the routines presented, can immediately gain a grasp of the language. The order of presentation is such that the early programs have a simple structure and are included to illustrate the use of various instructions, whereas the later programs have a slightly more complicated structure involving, for example, the use of subroutines.

The documentation for each program consists of a title for the routine, a filename by which the routine is recognised, an indication of the registers used, an indication of the program size in terms of the number of bytes and a section describing the purpose of the routine. A potential user of any of these subroutines should be aware of two factors, namely (a) how to use the routine, and (b) the side effects of using the routine. By providing program size in bytes and naming the registers used within the routine the attention of the user is drawn to the storage occupied and to the microprocessor registers affected by running the routine. One other important aspect of using such a routine is the execution time of the routine, this is not discussed. However in some applications it is the execution time of the routine which is of overriding importance.

The programmer who has to modify his own earlier programs or those of another programmer will appreciate the careful use of comments within the program. These comments should, if well chosen, explain the operation of the program to the first-time user and be of use to the person who may wish to modify the program for his own purpose at a later date.

The software development procedure outlined in chapter 5 indicates that when the software has been developed, tested and debugged a final version can be transferred to an EPROM and this inserted in the microprocesssor target system. In all the examples in this section the target system in which the programs have operated is the Intel 8086 microcomputer system design kit SDK-86.

Program 8.1 Movement of a Block of Data within Memory

The program contains two segments, a code segment for the executable statements and a data segment to store the required data. The name PDATA is allotted to the data segment and PCODE to the code segment in the ASSUME directive. The assembler directive DB is used to assign the data to memory, the variable identifiers used are SECO and ORIG. This program is included to emphasize the power of the string instruction MOVS. In both versions of this program registers SI and DI are used as memory location pointers and CX is used as a loop count value register. The string instruction MOVS with prefix REP is fundamentally all that is needed to carry out the task and this is used in the data movement section of program version two. CLD is the instruction which ensures autoincrement of the location pointers used by the instruction MOVS. The data movement section of version one uses the instructions which are the equivalent of REP MOVSW. Version one is included simply to show this equivalence.

Program 8.2 Sinusoidal Voltage Waveform Generator using a Digital to Analogue Convertor (DAC)

The EQU directive is used to assign names to the constants used within the program. The address identifier for the data variable list is DSIN. There are two loops in the program. Within the inner loop each of the 36 data values is first transferred to the accumulator using a MOV instruction, the SI register being the address pointer, and second transferred to the port using an OUT instruction. The loop control is provided by the instruction LOOP which decrements the CX register and, providing CX is not ZERO, causes a jump to take place. The outer loop provides repeated operation.

Program 8.1 (Version 1)

```
;           Title:   Data Block Movement Version One
;           Filename: SHIFT1.A86
;           Registers used: AX,CX,SI,DI
;           Size:    Program 28 Bytes
;                    Data variable
;           Purpose:The program moves a block of data in
;memory from the offset address given by the identifer
;ORIG to the offset address denoted by the identifier SECO
;***********************************************************
ASSUME  CS:PCODE,DS:PDATA
;***********************************************************
PDATA   SEGMENT
ORIG    DB      15 DUP (22H)
SECO    DB      ?
PDATA   ENDS
;***********************************************************
PCODE   SEGMENT
        ;Register initialisation section
        MOV     AX,PDATA
        MOV     DS,AX
        MOV     ES,AX
        MOV     SI, OFFSET ORIG
        MOV     DI, OFFSET SECO
        MOV     CX, LENGTH ORIG
        ;Data movement section
AGAIN:  MOV     AX,[SI]
        MOV     [DI],AX
        INC     SI
        INC     SI
        INC     DI
        INC     DI
        DEC     CX
        JNZ     AGAIN
        HLT
PCODE   ENDS
;***********************************************************
        END
```

Program 8.1 (Version 2)

```
;       Title:   Data Block Movement Version Two
;       Filename: SHIFT2.A86
;       Registers used: AX,CX,SI,DI
;       Size    Program 20 Bytes
;               Data variable
;       Purpose:The program moves a block of data in
;memory from the offset address given by the identifier
;ORIG to the offset address denoted by the identifier SECO
;***********************************************************
ASSUME  CS:PCODE,DS:PDATA
;***********************************************************
PDATA   SEGMENT
ORIG    DB      15 DUP (22H)
SECO    DB      ?
PDATA   ENDS
;***********************************************************
PCODE   SEGMENT
        ;Register initialisation section
        MOV     AX,PDATA
        MOV     DS,AX
        MOV     ES,AX
        MOV     SI, OFFSET ORIG
        MOV     DI, OFFSET SECO
        MOV     CX, LENGTH ORIG
        ;Data movement section
        CLD
REP     MOVSW
        HLT
PCODE   ENDS
;***********************************************************
        END
```

172 The 8086 and Assembly Language

Program 8.2

```
;       Title:   Sinusoidal Waveform Generator
;       Filename:NSINE.A86
;       Registers used:AX,CX,DX,SI
;       Size:    Program 38 Bytes
;                Data 39 Bytes
;       Purpose:This is a program to generate a sinusoidal
;voltage waveform at the output of a digital to analogue
;convertor of offset binary type, connected to an output
;port of an 8255A PPI. To obtain a continuous sinewave a
;dummy instruction ADD  (VAL1+02),0 is used to compensate
;for the time which elapses in returning to the beginning
;of the data output sequence via instruction JMP SINE.
;************************************************************
        ASSUME  CS:PCODE,DS:PDATA
;************************************************************
        PDATA   SEGMENT
        P1A     EQU     0FFF9H
        P1B     EQU     0FFFBH
        CREG    EQU     0FFFFH
        CDAT    EQU     82H     ;Port initialisation data
        DSIN    DB      128,150,171,192,210,225,238,247,253,255
                DB      253,247,238,225,210,192,171,150,128,106
                DB      85,65,46,31,18,9,3,0,3,9
                DB      18,31,46,65,85,106
        VAL1    DB      0,0,0
        PDATA   ENDS
;************************************************************
        PCODE   SEGMENT
                MOV     AX,PDATA
                MOV     DS,AX
                MOV     DX,CREG
                MOV     AL,CDAT
                OUT     DX,AL   ;8255A port initialisation complete
                MOV     DX,P1A
SINE:           MOV     SI,OFFSET DSIN   ;Clock periods          4
                MOV     CX,36            ;Clock periods          4
AGAIN:          MOV     AL,[SI]
                OUT     DX,AL
                INC     SI
                CMP     CX,1
                JZ      NEXT             ;Clock periods    4     16
                ADD     (VAL1+02),0      ;Clock periods    23(Dummy)
NEXT:           LOOP    AGAIN            ;Clock periods    17    5
                JMP     SINE             ;Clock periods          15
        PCODE   ENDS
;Alternate number of clock periods inner loop = 44
;Alternate number of clock periods when traversing
;the outer loop = 44
;************************************************************
        END
```

The following four programs involve the subtraction of numbers. They are shown not in the source program format but in the list program format. The reason for this is to show the data and the program machine code as stored in memory.

Program 8.3(A) Subtraction of Signed Numbers (BYTES)

The data in program 8.3(A) is written into memory in hexadecimal format with the least significant byte of each number being entered first. It should be noted that assembler directives such as ASSUME and SEGMENT/ENDS do not generate machine code in memory.

In line 23 two bytes of machine code are missing and following the code is the letter R. This implies that the data is set on locating the program, i.e. the value PDATA is relocatable, hence of course the data segment is relocatable. This segment is placed in a particular location in memory only when the object code is located. The software development stages are explained in figure 5.2.

The registers BX, DI and SI are used as address pointers and as such are loaded with their respective addresses using the assembler operator OFFSET. The object code for each of the instructions involving the OFFSET operator has as second and third bytes an offset address. The instruction 'SBB', subtract with borrow, is used so that multiple byte numbers can be subtracted without error. CLC is used to ensure that the carry flag is cleared before the least significant bytes of each number are subtracted. The example data shown in program 8.3(A) involves the negative number FFFFDH which represents -3.

Program 8.3(B) Subtraction of Signed Numbers (WORDS)

The data is again entered in hexadecimal format but in this case the data is in word form. The assembler causes the least significant byte to be entered first in memory, so 8125H is stored in consecutive locations as 25H and 81H. The data is separated in memory by using the address identifiers FIL1, FIL2, and FIL3 for variables which each occupy six bytes. Because the data transfer instructions involve words each of the pointers must be incremented twice so as to point to a new word location.

Program 8.3(A)

```
LOC     OBJ         LINE    SOURCE
                    1       ;       Title:   Subtraction of Signed Numbers
                    2       ;       Name:    SUBHEX.A86
                    3       ;       Registers used  :AX,BX,CX,SI,DI
                    4       ;       Size:    Program 30 Bytes
                    5       ;                Data 9 Bytes
                    6       ;       Purpose:This program performs subtraction
                    7       ;of signed numbers. The numbers and the resultant
                    8       ;difference are in hexadecimal format. In this
                    9       ;example the NUM2 FFFFFDH is subtracted from NUM1
                    10      ; 721425H and the result is stored as variable
                    11      ;DIFF of value 721428H. These numbers are
                    12      ;stored as an array of bytes and the program
                    13      ;operates on bytes.
                    14      ;**************************************************
                    15              ASSUME   CS:PCODE,DS:PDATA
                    16      ;**************************************************
----                17              PDATA    SEGMENT
0000 25             18              NUM1     DB       25H,14H,72H
0001 14
0002 72
0003 FD             19              NUM2     DB       0FDH,0FFH,0FFH
0004 FF
0005 FF
0006 ??             20              DIFF     DB       ?
----                21              PDATA    ENDS
                    22      ;**************************************************
----                23              PCODE    SEGMENT
0000 B8---- R       24              MOV      AX,PDATA
0003 8ED8           25              MOV      DS,AX
0005 BB0000         26              MOV      BX,OFFSET NUM1
0008 BF0300         27              MOV      DI,OFFSET NUM2
000B BE0600         28              MOV      SI,OFFSET DIFF
000E B90300         29              MOV      CX,LENGTH NUM1;Pointers/Counter
                    30                                      ;initialised
0011 F8             31              CLC
0012 8A07           32      BEGIN:  MOV      AL,[BX]
0014 1A05           33              SBB      AL,[DI]
0016 8804           34              MOV      [SI],AL  ;Difference stored
0018 43             35              INC      BX
0019 46             36              INC      SI
001A 47             37              INC      DI       ;Pointers updated
001B E2F5           38              LOOP     BEGIN    ;Repeat the subtraction
001D F4             39              HLT
----                40              PCODE    ENDS
                    41      ;**************************************************
                    42              END
```

Program 8.3(B)

```
LOC     OBJ      LINE    SOURCE

                 1       ;        Title:Subtraction of Signed Numbers (WORDS)
                 2       ;        Filename:      SBHEXW.A86
                 3       ;        Registers used :AX,BX,CX,SI,DI
                 4       ;        Size:   Program 33 Bytes
                 5       ;                Data 28 Bytes
                 6       ;        Purpose:This program performs subtraction
                 7       ;of signed numbers in hexadecimal format. These
                 8       ;numbers are stored as an array of words and the
                 9       ;program operates in words. In this example
                 10      ;00F6AAFDH is subtracted from 03148125H and the
                 11      ;result 021DD628H is stored again in word form.
                 12      ;***********************************************
                 13      ASSUME  CS:PCODE,DS:PDATA
                 14      ;***********************************************
----             15      PDATA   SEGMENT
0000 2581        16      NUM1    DW      8125H,0314H
0002 1403
0004 FDAA        17      NUM2    DW      0AAFDH,00F6H
0006 F600
0008 ????        18      DIFF    DW      ?
----             19      PDATA ENDS
                 20      ;FIL1, FIL2, and FIL3 separate data arrays
                 21      ;***********************************************
----             22      PCODE   SEGMENT
0000 B8---- R    23              MOV     AX,PDATA
0003 8ED8        24              MOV     DS,AX
0005 BB0000      25              MOV     BX,OFFSET NUM1
0008 BF0400      26              MOV     DI,OFFSET NUM2
000B BE0800      27              MOV     SI,OFFSET DIFF
000E B90200      28              MOV     CX,LENGTH NUM1
0011 F8          29              CLC
0012 8B07        30      BEGIN:  MOV     AX,[BX]
0014 1B05        31              SBB     AX,[DI]
0016 8904        32              MOV     [SI],AX
0018 43          33              INC     BX
0019 43          34              INC     BX
001A 46          35              INC     SI
001B 46          36              INC     SI
001C 47          37              INC     DI
001D 47          38              INC     DI        ;Pointers updated
001E E2F2        39              LOOP    BEGIN
0020 F4          40              HLT
----             41      PCODE   ENDS
                 42      ;***********************************************
                 43              END
```

Program 8.4 (A)
Subtraction of ASCII numbers (Unpacked BCD)

This program relates to the ASCII number format which is a form of unpacked BCD, where each byte represents a single digit. The unpacked and packed BCD formats are shown in table 4.8. In this case the data is entered directly into the data segment as part of the program as shown.

String instructions LODSB and STOSB are used respectively to load and to store data to and from the accumulator. The CX register, which holds the count value for these string instructions is loaded, with the number of digits, using the LENGTH operator. CLD is the instruction used to clear the direction flag so as to allow autoincrement of the pointers SI and DI when the string instructions are executed. As the string instructions refer to different segments, LODS to the data segment and STOS to the extra segment, these two segments are overlapped by setting ES, as well as DS, equal to the value PDATA. The value of PDATA is established during the LOCATE stage of the software development.

The ASCII adjust instruction AAS is used after the subtract instruction to ensure that the result is in BCD format. Each digit of the result is transformed to the ASCII format by setting the upper hexadecimal digit to 3. In line 41 the byte pointer operator BYTE PTR is used. This is because if it were omitted and the instruction simply read OR [SI],30H then the assembler would have no indication from the instruction as to whether the location pointed to by SI was that of a byte or a word and would indicate an error.

Program 8.4(B)
Subtraction of Binary Coded Decimal Numbers (Packed BCD)

This version of the subtraction of decimal numbers relates to the packed binary coded decimal format, where each byte represents two BCD digits. The data in memory is assumed to be in this form and not to be in hexadecimal format. There are two main differences between this version of BCD subtraction and the ASCII version, first the instruction used to correct the result after subtraction is now DAS decimal adjust after subtraction; and second there is now no need to convert the result to any other form as it is already in packed BCD format.

Program Examples **177**

Program 8.4(A)

```
LOC    OBJ       LINE    SOURCE
                  1      ;          Title: Subtraction of Unpacked BCD
                  2      ;                 Numbers (ASCII format)
                  3      ;          Filename: SUBBCD.A86
                  4      ;          Registers used: AX,BX,CX,SI,DI
                  5      ;          Purpose:In this program the subtraction
                  6      ;is of data in the ASCII format, so decimal values
                  7      ;can be subtracted. For the example shown
                  8      ;NUM2 (6455) is subtracted from NUM1 (8793)
                  9      ;and the result in unpacked BCD format is
                 10      ;converted to ASCII format. This program
                 11      ;operates with bytes of information.
                 12      ;************************************************
                 13      ASSUME   CS:PCODE,DS:PDATA
                 14      ;************************************************
----             15      PDATA    SEGMENT
                 16      ;Data input in ASCII format - enclosed in quotes
0000 33          17      NUM1     DB     '3','9','7','8';Decimal value 8793
0001 39
0002 37
0003 38
0004 35          18      NUM2     DB     '5','5','4','6';Decimal value 6455
0005 35
0006 34
0007 36
0008 ??          19      RESLT    DB     ?
----             20      PDATA    ENDS
                 21      ;************************************************
----             22      PCODE    SEGMENT
0000 B8---- R    23               MOV    AX,PDATA
0003 8ED8        24               MOV    DS,AX
0005 8EC0        25               MOV    ES,AX
0007 B90400      26               MOV    CX,LENGTH NUM1
000A FC          27               CLD
000B F8          28               CLC
000C BE0000      29               MOV    SI, OFFSET NUM1
000F BB0400      30               MOV    BX, OFFSET NUM2
0012 BF0800      31               MOV    DI, OFFSET RESLT
0015 AC          32      LOAD:    LODSB
0016 1A07        33               SBB    AL,[BX]
0018 3F          34               AAS
0019 AA          35               STOSB  ;Difference stored at RESLT.
001A 43          36               INC    BX
001B E2F8        37               LOOP   LOAD
                 38      ;Convert the result to the ASCII format
001D B90400      39               MOV    CX,LENGTH NUM1
0020 BE0800      40               MOV    SI,OFFSET RESLT
0023 800C30      41      ASET:    OR     BYTE PTR [SI],30H
0026 46          42               INC    SI
0027 E2FA        43               LOOP   ASET
0029 F4          44               HLT
----             45      PCODE    ENDS
                 46      ;************************************************
                 47               END
```

178 The 8086 and Assembly Language

Program 8.4(B)

```
LOC     OBJ      LINE    SOURCE
                 1       ;       Title: Subtraction of Packed BCD Numbers
                 2       ;       Name:   SBPBCD.A86
                 3       ;       Registers used: AX,BX,SI,DI
                 4       ;       Purpose:In this program the subtraction
                 5       ;is of data in the packed BCD format i.e a single
                 6       ;byte represents two digits. For the example shown
                 7       ;the decimal number 0862 (NUM2) is subtracted
                 8       ;from the decimal number 9361 (NUM1). The result
                 9       ;is in packed BCD format and stored in byte form.
                 10      ;***********************************************
                 11      ASSUME  CS:PCODE,DS:PDATA
                 12      ;***********************************************
----             13      PDATA   SEGMENT
                 14      ;Consider that the data in memory has been received
                 15      ;in the packed BCD format, for example this data
                 16      ;could have been presented to an input port in
                 17      ;binary coded decimal (BCD).
0000 ??          18      NUM1    DB   ?,?; Input the byte values 61 and 93
0001 ??
0002 ??          19      NUM2    DB   ?,?; Input the byte values 62 and 08
0003 ??
0004 ??          20      RESLT   DB   ?
----             21      PDATA   ENDS
                 22      ;***********************************************
----             23      PCODE   SEGMENT
0000 B8----R     24              MOV     AX,PDATA
0003 8ED8        25              MOV     DS,AX
0005 8EC0        26              MOV     ES,AX
0007 B90200      27              MOV     CX,LENGTH NUM1
000A FC          28              CLD
000B F8          29              CLC
000C BE0000      30              MOV     SI, OFFSET NUM1
000F BB0200      31              MOV     BX, OFFSET NUM2
0012 BF0400      32              MOV     DI, OFFSET RESLT
0015 AC          33      LOAD:   LODSB
0016 1A07        34              SBB     AL,[BX]
0018 2F          35              DAS     ;Decimal adjust after subtraction.
0019 AA          36              STOSB   ;Difference stored at RESLT.
001A 43          37              INC     BX
001B E2F8        38              LOOP    LOAD
001D F4          39              HLT
----             40      PCODE   ENDS
                 41      ;***********************************************
                 42              END
```

Program 8.5 Insertion of a New Element in a List

This program involves both data and extra data segments but they are overlapped forming effectively a single segment dealing with one data list. This is necessary because the instruction SCAS relates to data in the extra segment, while the usual data variable instructions relate to the data segment. The data is given in decimal form each item occupying a word, while the new data item is given as a hexadecimal number, simply to indicate that they need not be in the same form. A comparison of the new data item with each item already present in the data list is performed by the SCAS instruction, prefix REPNE causes the comparison to continue until either the compared items are equal or the count in CX reaches zero. If the comparison ends because the count value in CX is zero then the new data item is not already present in the list and so must be added to the list, this is ensured by using the instruction JCXZ to jump to location INSERT. To find the address for the insertion of the new item at the end of the list, the number of bytes at present in the list is added to the offset address of the first item, i.e. BYTNUM is added to OFFSET WRDLST.

Program 8.6 Conversion of Data Elements to their Equivalent Positive Values

Two segments are used in which to store data. The data segment is used to hold the initial list in which some of the items may be negative in value, and the extra segment is used to store the revised list. The practice of setting the segment registers to hold the segment names PDATA and PEXTRA is employed, and these values are allotted at the LOCATE stage. The index registers SI and DI are used as pointers to the data locations. The data is loaded to the accumulator from the data segment using the instruction LODS, with this instruction SI is used as the pointer. A copy of the data in the BX register is rotated left by one place, so shifting the most significant bit into the carry register. If this is '1' then the data is negative in sign and therefore the original data in the accumulator is converted to its equivalent positive value using NEG AX. The string instruction STOS uses the DI register as a pointer to locations in the extra segment.

180 The 8086 and Assembly Language

Program 8.5

```
;       Title:  Inserting Element in List
;       Filename: INSERT.A86
;       Registers used: AX,CX,SI,DI
;       Size:   Program 47 Bytes
;               Data - Variable number of Bytes
;       Purpose: This program will check a wordlist for
;the presence of an element and if it is not found then the
;word will be added to the list and the list length value
;incremented.
;**************************************************************
ASSUME   CS:PCODE,DS:PDATA,ES:PEXTRA
;**************************************************************
PDATA   SEGMENT
NEWWRD  DW      0202H   :
WRDNUM  DW      24       ;List length i.e number of words
BYTNUM  DW      48       ;Number of bytes in the list
WRDLST  DW      21,23,25,27,29,31,33,35
        DW      37,39,41,43,45,47,49,51
        DW      20,40,60,800,1000,2000,4000,4400
;WRDLST is the initial list of words to be examined
PDATA   ENDS
;**************************************************************
PCODE   SEGMENT
        MOV     AX,PDATA
        MOV     DS,AX
        MOV     ES,AX   ;Data and Extra Segments overlap
        CLD
        MOV     DI,OFFSET WRDLST
        MOV     CX,WRDNUM
        MOV     AX,NEWWRD
REPNE   SCASW
        JCXZ    INSERT  ;Jump to insert new element
        JMP     LAST ;Jump as element is already present
INSERT: MOV     SI,OFFSET WRDLST
        ADD     SI,BYTNUM
        MOV     AX,NEWWRD
        MOV     [SI],AX ;New Element added to the list
        INC     WRDNUM  ;List length updated
        ADD     BYTNUM,02 ;Byte number also updated
LAST:   HLT
PCODE   ENDS
;**************************************************************
PEXTRA SEGMENT
PEXTRA ENDS
;**************************************************************
        END
```

Program 8.6

```
;       Title:    Conversion to Positive Values
;       Filename: NSTR.A86
;       Registers used: AX,BX,CX,SI,DI
;       Size:     Program 32 Bytes
;                 Data variable
;       Purpose: The examination of a series
;of signed 16 bit numbers and the substitution of
;the positive equivalent value for any negative
;values, e.g -873 would be substituted by 873.
;**********************************************
ASSUME  CS:PCODE,DS:PDATA,ES:PEXTRA
;**********************************************
PDATA   SEGMENT
TOTAL   EQU     05;N=5 five words in this example
DATS1   DW      8010H,1712H,94EFH,0A111H,5CFEH
PDATA   ENDS
;**********************************************
PEXTRA  SEGMENT
DATS2   DW      10 DUP (?)
PEXTRA  ENDS
;**********************************************
PCODE   SEGMENT
        MOV     AX,PDATA
        MOV     DS,AX
        MOV     AX,PEXTRA
        MOV     ES,AX
        CLD
        MOV     SI,OFFSET DATS1
        MOV     DI,OFFSET DATS2
        MOV     CX,TOTAL ;Registers initialised
BEGIN:  JCXZ    LAST     ;Leave when all values checked
        LODSW
        MOV     BX,AX
        RCL     BX,1
        JNC     STORE    ;Jump if value is positive
        NEG     AX       ;Convert negative to positive
STORE:  STOSW            ;Store value in data list
        LOOP    BEGIN
LAST:   HLT
PCODE   ENDS
;**********************************************
        END
```

Program 8.7 Checksum Formation for Data/Program Listing

This is the first program in this chapter to involve the use of the stack and therefore a stack segment. Register contents are pushed onto the stack to be saved for use again at a later time in the program execution. Consequently as well as initialising the stack segment register to PSTAK, the stack pointer SP must be set to a convenient offset location within the segment, i.e. STKTOP. This is because data placed on the stack loads downwards through memory, i.e. the stack pointer is decremented each time data is placed on the stack.

In this example the data or target listing is arbitrarily chosen as byte array 'TARG'. To form the checksum of this data the logical exclusive operation is performed on the current checksum with each word in turn. Hence the exclusive operation is performed on 0000H and 5D01H, and then on the result of this operation with FE38H, and then on the new result with 2255H, etc. The final checksum word is placed at the end of the listing. Because the process is performed on words it is necessary that the listing consists of an even number of bytes, and so the first part of the program does in fact ensure that this is the case. Register BX contains the number of bytes in the list, i.e. (OFFSET FIN - OFFSET TARG). If this is an odd number then the word beyond the list is set to zero by the instruction MOV [BX + SI],AX and the number of bytes is incremented to an even value. The values of both BX and SI are saved on the stack, before the exclusive-or sum is formed and retrieved after the formation to use in the storing of the checksum.

As the programs increase in complexity, the number of comments within the program listing is proportionately increased to aid comprehension.

Program 8.7

```
;       Title:   Checksum Formation
;       Filename: CHECO.A86
;       Registers used: AX,BX,SI
;       Size:    Program 52 Bytes
;                Data Depends on target program length
;       Purpose:This routine forms the checksum of a
;program/data listing which is treated as the data
;segment. The routine places the Exclusive-Or checksum
;word at the end of the target program listing.
;In this example the target listing is the array TARG.
;***********************************************************
ASSUME  CS:PCODE,DS:PDATA,SS:PSTAK
;***********************************************************
```

Program 8.7 Continued

```
PDATA    SEGMENT
TARG     DB    01H,5DH,38H,0FEH,55H,22H,0AH,88H,34H,12H
         DB    01H,02H,38H,86H,99H,0A2H,0F5H,4FH,55H,7BH
         DB    49H,8CH,66H,0D4H,87H,0A2H,55H,73H,18H,44H
         DB    0CAH,0ACH,0ADH,01H,0F5H,49H,81H,0EEH,99H,87H
         DB    23H,0F4H,0BCH,0A6H,0A7H,0EEH,12H,0B8H,0FH,22H
         DB    19H
FIN      DB    ?
PDATA    ENDS
;************************************************************
PCODE    SEGMENT
         MOV   AX,PDATA
         MOV   DS,AX
         MOV   AX,PSTAK
         MOV   SS,AX
         MOV   SP,OFFSET STKTOP
         MOV   SI,OFFSET TARG
         MOV   BX,(OFFSET FIN-OFFSET TARG) ;Count in BYTES
;If this number of bytes is odd then 00 is added to the list
;to produce an even number of bytes and the remainder of the
;program is operated using WORDS.
         MOV   AX,0        ;Initially AX contains zero
         RCR   BX,1
         JNC   REFO ;Jump if even number of bytes in listing
         RCL   BX,1
         MOV   [BX+SI],AX ;Set next word to zero
         INC   BX ;Set the number of bytes to an even value
         JMP   STOR
REFO:    RCL   BX,1
;Count value in BX is twice the number of words in listing
STOR:    PUSH  SI
         PUSH  BX
FORM:    XOR   AX,[SI] ;Form exclusive OR checksum word
         INC   SI
         INC   SI
         DEC   BX
         DEC   BX
         JNZ   FORM
         POP   BX
         POP   SI
         MOV   [BX+SI],AX ;Store checksum word at end
         HLT
PCODE    ENDS
;************************************************************
PSTAK    SEGMENT
         DW    50 DUP (?)
STKTOP   DW    ?
PSTAK    ENDS
;************************************************************
         END
```

Program 8.8 Voltage Waveform Generation using a Digital to Analogue Convertor

This voltage waveform generation program is included to introduce the concept of subroutines (procedures). A subroutine is a sequence of instructions which can be accessed by a CALL instruction from the main program as many times as required, so avoiding the constant repetition of the instruction sequence. The use of subroutines provides a much improved program structure and an opportunity to debug the program in an organised manner, i.e. each subroutine can be debugged separately. In this program the subroutine used is one which provides a variable length delay. The subroutine limits are identified using the PROC and ENDP directives accompanying the name. The use of the CALL instruction to access a subroutine requires that the return offset address should be stored on the stack. Therefore the stack segment is initialised at the beginning of the program along with the data segments. The program is essentially a matter of transmitting a maximum value, namely 0FFH, to an output port of an 8255A PPI to which is connected a DAC, delaying for a specific length of time, T1, and then transmitting a minimum value 00 to the same port and delaying for a second specific time, T2. The delay times T1 and T2 are equal and have the value T, hence a square voltage waveform is developed at the DAC output. Delay time T can be varied so changing the frequency of the square voltage waveform developed.

Program 8.8

```
;           Title:   Square Waveform Generation
;           Filename: SQUARE.A86
;           Registers used: AX,BX,CX,DX
;           Size:    Program 52 Bytes
;                    Data 4 Bytes
;           Purpose:This program outputs data to generate a
;square voltage waveform when a DAC is used at the output
;port. However the program can simply be used to
;introduce the use of subroutines (procedures) and
;to show how parameters can be passed to the
;subroutine. The subroutine used is a delay in
;which there are two parameters involved PARAM1
;and PARAM2 both of which are stored in the data
;segment.
;*************************************************************
ASSUME   CS:PCODE,DS:PDATA,SS:PSTAK
;*************************************************************
PDATA    SEGMENT
PARAM1   DW    ?
PARAM2   DW    ?
PDATA    ENDS
;*************************************************************
```

Program 8.8 Continued

```
PCODE   SEGMENT
PORT_IN         EQU     0FFFBH
PORT_OUT        EQU     0FFF9H
CRTLREG         EQU     0FFFFH
CRTLDAT         EQU     82H
        MOV     AX,PDATA
        MOV     DS,AX
        MOV     AX,PSTAK
        MOV     SS,AX
        MOV     SP,OFFSET STKTOP ;Segments initialised
        MOV     AX,CRTLDAT
        MOV     DX,CRTLREG
        OUT     DX,AL   ;Port initialisation complete
        MOV     DX,PORT_OUT
SQUARE: MOV     AL,0FFH ;Clock periods in parenthesis (4)
        OUT     DX,AL   ;Maximum value output to the DAC (8)
        CALL    DELAY1                                  ;(n)
        JMP     NEXT    ;This is included simply to ensure
;a mark to space ratio of 1:1, because the number of clock
;periods is the same as that for JMP SQUARE.           (15)
NEXT:   MOV     AL,0                                    ;(4)
        OUT     DX,AL   ;Minimum value output to the DAC (8)
        CALL    DELAY1                                  ;(n)
        JMP     SQUARE                                  ;(15)
;.............................................................
;Subroutine which provides the required delay
DELAY1  PROC    NEAR    ;Subroutine (Procedure) definition
        MOV     CX,PARAM1
OUTER:  MOV     BX,PARAM2
INNER:  DEC     BX
        JNZ     INNER
        LOOP    OUTER
        RET
DELAY1  ENDP            ;Subroutine limit
PCODE   ENDS
;*************************************************************
PSTAK   SEGMENT
        DW      10 DUP (?)
STKTOP  DW      ?
PSTAK   ENDS
;*************************************************************
        END
```

186 The 8086 and Assembly Language

Program 8.9 Read/Write Memory (RAM) Operation Check

The extra segment register is set to the lowest address of the RAM device to be checked, so up to 64 KByte can be checked at any one program execution.

The instruction STOSW is used to fill the memory device with a different data word for each word location; for example, the first three words stored are 0303H, 0606H and 0909H. Each of these words is then again loaded into the accumulator at the line labelled COMPA and then compared with the same word previously stored in memory by the instruction CMP AX,[DI]. If the these two words are not equal then JNE ERR causes a jump to an error routine, which is not included in this example. After each word has been verified as the same as that previously stored in memory, the complement of the word is formed using the instruction XOR AX,0FFFFH, and immediately stored in the same memory location. A comparison of the word in AX and the word in memory is made using SCASW. If the two words are not equal then again there is a jump to error. If no difference is detected between the two words then the data in the accumulator is restored to its previous value by the second usage of the instruction XOR AX,0FFFFH, and the cycle is repeated for the next word value. It should be noted that if the program had been written so as to fill the memory device with a constant value, e.g. 0A0AH, then the user would have no way of knowing whether a single word location or the complete device was being checked.

Program 8.9

```
;
;       Title:  RAM Test Program
;       Filename: RAMT.486
;       Registers used: AX,CX,DI
;       Size:   Program 57 Bytes
;               Data 2K Bytes
;       Purpose:In order to check a read/write 2 KByte
;RAM memory device a pattern of data is written to the
;device then read from the device and the data verified.
;The process is repeated with a different data pattern.
;***************************************************
ASSUME  CS:PCODE,ES:PEXTRA
;***************************************************
PEXTRA  SEGMENT
BEGIN   DW      ?
PEXTRA  ENDS
;***************************************************
```

Program 8.9 Continued

```
PCODE   SEGMENT
INCRE   EQU     0303H
CAPAC   EQU     1024    ;Word count value for 2 KByte RAM
        MOV     AX,PEXTRA
        MOV     ES,AX
        MOV     DI,OFFSET BEGIN
        MOV     CX,CAPAC
        MOV     AX,0    ;Initialisation complete
STORA:  ADD     AX,INCRE;New value ready to write to memory
        STOSW
        LOOP    STORA   ;RAM now filled with data pattern
        MOV     CX,CAPAC
        MOV     AX,0
        MOV     DI,OFFSET BEGIN;Re-initialisation complete
COMPA:  ADD     AX,INCRE
        CMP     AX,[DI]         ;Data verified
        JNE     ERR
        XOR     AX,0FFFFH ;Data complemented
        MOV     [DI],AX   ;Memory refilled
        SCASW             ;Data verified
        JNE     ERR
        XOR     AX,0FFFFH ;Data uncomplemented
        LOOP    COMPA
        JMP     HALT
ERR:    NOP
HALT:   HLT
PCODE   ENDS
;************************************************************
        END
```

Program 8.10 Signed Number Numerical Sorting Routine

The number of comments within the program listing plus the explanation given prior to the program under the heading 'purpose' should satisfactorily explain the program operation. However to provide futher elaboration the essential steps in the program execution are now explained. The instruction SCASW is associated with the DI register as a pointer, so the first comparison is between the first and second elements of the list. If the first element is less than the second then the jump instruction JLE NEXT is executed. The pointer value DI, now pointing to the third element as a result of the execution of the instruction SCAS, is compared with the address of the last element in DX, and as it is below this value JBE COMP causes a jump to COMP. A jump will not occur when the first element has been compared with every other element in the list. The first element can now be compared with the third element and the process repeated. When a comparison is made between the first element and an element pointed to by DI and the first element is the greater of the two, then an interchange of the elements occurs. This is carried out by the intructions XCHG AX,[BX] and MOV [SI],AX. Repetition of the process ensures that the lowest element occupies the first position in the list.

Program 8.11 Use of a USART to Communicate with a Printer

The simpler of the RS-232C serial links shown in figure 7.8 is used for communication between an 8251A USART, acting as a serial port, and a serial printer. The program involves initialising the 8251A for asynchronous communication and the use of four subroutines namely, TRANSMIT, WAITB, NLINE and SETTLE. Subroutine SETTLE provides a short delay and is used between initialisation data transmissions to the 8251A to provide time for the device to accept the data. Subroutine WAITB is used to examine the USART status register and to determine when it is ready to receive new data from the microprocessor. NLINE is a separate routine used to transmit 'line feed' and 'carriage return' to the printer at the end of each line. The comments provided in the program should enable the reader to understand the process.

Program 8.10

```
;       Title:    16 Bit Number Sorting Routine
;       Filename: WSORT.A86
;       Registers used: AX,BX,DX,SI,DI
;       Size:     Program 40 Bytes
;                 Data     Variable
;       Purpose: This routine will scan a list of 16 bit
;signed numbers and rearrange the list in numerical
;order from the lowest to the highest value.
;************************************************************
ASSUME  CS:PCODE,DS:PDATA
;************************************************************
PDATA   SEGMENT
WLIST   DW      2345,65,-564,12876,45,777,-66,-456,99,-2
        DW      -12876,3456,-88,8764
ELIST   DW      ?
PDATA   ENDS
;************************************************************
PCODE   SEGMENT
        MOV     AX,PDATA
        MOV     DS,AX
        MOV     ES,AX     ;Data and Extra segments overlap
        MOV     SI,OFFSET WLIST
        MOV     DX,(OFFSET ELIST-2)
;SI holds the address of the first word in the list and
;DX holds the address of the last word
        CLD
POINT:  MOV     DI,SI
        INC     DI
        INC     DI
COMP:   MOV     AX,[SI] ;Elements are now to be compared
        MOV     BX,DI
        SCASW
        JLE     NEXT
;If the contents of AX are greater than those of the
;location pointed to by the DI register then these two values
;should be interchanged.
        XCHG    AX,[BX]
        MOV     [SI],AX ;Elements now interchanged
;A further pair of elements are now to be compared
NEXT:   CMP     DI,DX
        JBE     COMP
;If a jump has not occurred then the next lowest element
;is to be compared with all the remaining elements
        INC     SI
        INC     SI      ;Point to the next lowest value element
        CMP     SI,DX
        JB      POINT   ;Restart if there are elemnts remaining
        HLT
PCODE   ENDS
;************************************************************
        END
```

190 The 8086 and Assembly Language

Program 8.11

```
;       Title:    Using the Serial Port
;       Filename: PRINT.A86
;       Registers used: AX,BX,CX,DX,SI
;       Purpose:  To repeatedly send a string of characters
;to a serial printer via a USART type 8251A.
;************************************************************
ASSUME CS:PCODE, DS:PDATA,SS:PSTACK,ES:PEXTRA
;************************************************************
PDATA   SEGMENT
TEXT1   DB    'A programmer of machine code
              Found his micro in the wrong mode
              He said I can't feel
              If its virtual or real
              His ignorance obviously showed'
PDATA   ENDS
;************************************************************
PSTACK  SEGMENT
FILL    DB    50 DUP (?)
STKTOP  DW    ?
PSTACK  ENDS
;************************************************************
PEXTRA  SEGMENT
PEXTRA  ENDS
;************************************************************
PCODE   SEGMENT
;Definition of constants used in the program
SDAT    EQU   0FFF0H ;8251A Serial Data Read/Write address
SMOD    EQU   0FFF2H ;8251A Mode control register address
STAT    EQU   0FFF2H ;8251A Status register address
RESET   EQU   065H   ;8251A Reset data
IDAT    EQU   0CFH   ;8251A Mode Initialisation data
;8 Bits, Parity disabled, 2 Stop Bits, Baud rate 1/64 of TxC
TXEN    EQU   25H    ;8251A Command transmit enable data
;Initialisation of segments, data/extra segments overlapping
        MOV   AX,PDATA
        MOV   DS,AX
        MOV   ES,AX
        MOV   AX,PSTACK
        MOV   SS,AX
        MOV   SP,OFFSET STKTOP
;Initialisation of the 8251A serial port
        MOV   DX,SMOD ;
        MOV   AL,RESET
        OUT   DX,AL   ;8251A Reset (RESET)
        CALL  SETTLE
        MOV   AL,25H
        OUT   DX,AL
        CALL  SETTLE
        MOV   AL,RESET
        OUT   DX,AL   ;8251A (RESET)
        CALL  SETTLE
        MOV   AL,IDAT    ~ protocol details
        OUT   DX,AL   ;8251A Asynchronous mode (MODE)
```

higher value in the array. If the value in the accumulator is above that with which it is being compared, then the instruction LOOP INCRE is the next to be executed and the parameter value in BX is again increased by ten. This process continues until the input value in the accumulator is above or equal to the value in the array with which it is being compared. In this manner the parameter passed in register BX will increase in value with increase in value of the input voltage and can be modified by altering the elements of the array identified by DVAL.

In the main section of the program the fundamental task, after the constants, segment registers and ports are initialised, is simply to repeatedly call subroutines SETD and DRIVE in that sequence. However, if the input voltage is unchanged then there is no need to call subroutine SETD. The instructions CMP AL,INVAL and JE AGAIN are used to avoid calling this subroutine.

Program 8.13 Use of Software Interrupts

This program shows the organisation involved in using interrupts. Hence the interrupt service routine is one which simply causes LEDs at an 8255A port to flash on and off alternately for a selected number of times. The main program consists of calling two subroutines, INIT and PATT, and of using INT 64 as a vectored subroutine. First the subroutine INIT is called to initialise the ports of the 8255A device. This is followed by calling subroutine PATT, which is used to set the eight LEDs to display an initial pattern decided by the constant PATTERN1. The constant is passed to the subroutine via the AX register. The software interrupt is then activated and again the subroutine PATT is called, this time to display a different pattern.

An absolute segment is used to ensure that the required vector, consisting of the IP and CS addresses, corresponding to vector type number 64 is stored at the correct memory location namely, 4 * 64. The assembler directive DD is used to initialise the address expression of the vector service routine, whose identifier is VROUTINE. This use of DD is explained in the data definition section of chapter 5. The service routine calls a delay subroutine DELAY. The constant COUNTF determines the number of times the LEDs will flash during the operation of the the service routine. The service routine is ended by the instruction IRET, the return from interrupt instruction. This ensures that the values restored from the stack to the IP and CS registers are those required for the main program to continue correctly. Finally PATTERN2 is displayed simply to indicate that the service routine is completed.

Program 8.12

```
;       Title:    Stepper Motor Speed Control
;       Filename: STEPC.A86
;       Registers used: AX,BX,CX,DX,DI
;       Size:     Program 109 Bytes
;                 Data 19 Bytes
;       Purpose: An analogue input voltage taken via an ADC
;to a port of a PPI, is used to control the step pulse
;rate to a stepper motor and hence control the speed
;of rotation of the stepper motor.
;*************************************************************
ASSUME   CS:PCODE,DS:PDATA,ES:PEXTRA,SS:PSTAK
;*************************************************************
PDATA    SEGMENT
DLENG    DW      50 ;First delay parameter
FIX      DW      03 ;Value determining the minimum number of
;steps each time the motor is driven at every access.
INVAL    DB      ?
PDATA    ENDS
;*************************************************************
PEXTRA   SEGMENT
DVAL     DB      5,10,15,20,25,30,40,50,60
&,75,90,125,150,175,200,225
;Values used in determining the second delay parameter.
PEXTRA   ENDS
;*************************************************************
PSTAK    SEGMENT
OFF      DW      10 DUP (?)
STKTOP   DW      ?
PSTAK    ENDS
;*************************************************************
PCODE    SEGMENT
;Constants used are initialised
PSET     EQU     82H
CREG     EQU     0FFFFH
IPORT    EQU     0FFFBH
OPORT    EQU     0FFF9H
;Segments are initialised
         MOV     AX,PEXTRA
         MOV     ES,AX
         MOV     AX,PDATA
         MOV     DS,AX
         MOV     AX,PSTAK
         MOV     SS,AX
         MOV     SP,OFFSET STKTOP
;Ports on the 8255A are initialised
         MOV     DX,CREG
         MOV     AL,PSET
         OUT     DX,AL
;Program to control the speed of the stepper motors
         MOV     INVAL,0
READIN:  MOV     DX,IPORT
         IN      AL,DX   ;Input data via the ADC
         CMP     AL,INVAL
```

Program 8.12 Continued

```
            JE      AGAIN     ;Jump to avoid changing delay
;parameter if input value is unchanged
            CALL    SETD      ;Set new delay constant
;dependent on new input value
AGAIN:      CALL    DRIVE     ;Drive the stepper motor
;with the number of pulses determined by constant FIX.
            JMP     READIN
;Subroutine to set a delay parameter in the BX register which is
;dependent on the input value from the ADC at IPORT.
SETD        PROC    NEAR
            MOV     DI,OFFSET DVAL
            MOV     CX,LENGTH DVAL
            MOV     BX,5
            MOV     DX,IPORT
            IN      AL,DX
INCRE:      ADD     BX,10     ;Increase delay constant
            SCASB             ;Compare set parameter with input
            JBE     LAST      :
            LOOP    INCRE
LAST:       MOV     INVAL,AL  ;Store input value
            RET
SETD        ENDP
;Subroutine to drive the stepper motor for a predetermined
;number of steps at a rate determined by the delay subroutine.
DRIVE       PROC    NEAR
            MOV     CX,FIX
OUT1:       MOV     AL,02H
            MOV     DX,OPORT
            OUT     DX,AL     ;Take O/P pin high
;           so providing rising edge of pulse
            CALL    DELAY
            MOV     AL,0
            OUT     DX,AL     ;Take O/P pin low
;so providing trailing edge of pulse
            CALL    DELAY
            LOOP    OUT1
            RET
DRIVE       ENDP
;Delay subroutine with two parameters, the first being in
;register BX and the second being variable at address DLENG.
DELAY       PROC    NEAR
            PUSH    CX
            PUSH    BX
            MOV     CX,BX     ;1st parameter passed from BX.
OUTER:      MOV     BX,DLENG  ;2nd parameter from data segment.
INNER:      DEC     BX
            JNZ     INNER
            LOOP    OUTER
            POP     BX
            POP     CX
            RET
DELAY       ENDP
PCODE       ENDS
;************************************************************
            END
```

Program 8.13

```
;       Title:  Use of Software Interrupt
;       Filename: SVECT.A86
;       Registers Used: AX,BX,CX,DX
;       Size:   Program 69 bytes
;       Purpose: To use a software interrupt INT 64
;with its service routine VROUTINE which is used to flash
;LEDS at an 8255 PPI port.
;**************************************************************
;Constant values are initialised
VECTNUM         EQU     64        ;Vector type number is 64
PORTP1A         EQU     0FFF9H
CREG            EQU     0FFFFH
INCRE           EQU     200
CDAT            EQU     82H
COUNT           EQU     10000
PATTERN1        EQU     0AAH
PATTERN2        EQU     55H
COUNTF          EQU     50
DELVAL          EQU     50000
;**************************************************************
ABSZERO SEGMENT AT  0
        ORG     4*VECTNUM ;Vector table address of type 64
        DD      VROUTINE  ;Two words reserved for IP
;and CS addresses for start of service routine VROUTINE
ABSZERO ENDS
;**************************************************************
ASSUME  CS:PCODE
PCODE   SEGMENT
        CALL    INIT
        MOV     AX,PATTERN1
        CALL    PATT
        INT     64   ;Software vector interrupt type 64
        MOV     AX,PATTERN2
        CALL    PATT
        HLT
;..............................................................
;Subroutine to output a value to LEDS at port PORTP1A and
;maintain the output for a fixed length of time.
PATT    PROC    NEAR
        MOV     BX,INCRE
NUMB:   MOV     CX,COUNT
DISP1:  MOV     DX,PORTP1A
        OUT     DX,AL
        LOOP    DISP1
        DEC     BX
        JNZ     NUMB
        RET
PATT    ENDP
;..............................................................
```

Program 8.13 Continued

```
;Subroutine to initiate ports of 8255 PPI
INIT    PROC    NEAR
        MOV     AL,CDAT
        MOV     DX,CREG
        OUT     DX,AL
        RET
INIT    ENDP
;.........................................................
PCODE   ENDS
;**********************************************************
PCODE   SEGMENT
VROUTINE        PROC    FAR
;Vector service routine to flash the LEDS on and off
        MOV     DX,PORTP1A
        MOV     CX,COUNTF
FLASH:  MOV     AL,0FFH
        OUT     DX,AL
        CALL    DELAY
        MOV     AL,0
        OUT     DX,AL
        CALL    DELAY
        LOOP    FLASH
;.........................................................
;Delay subroutine
DELAY   PROC
        PUSH    CX
        MOV     CX,DELVAL
DEL:    LOOP    DEL
        POP     CX
        RET
DELAY   ENDP
;.........................................................
        IRET
VROUTINE        ENDP
PCODE   ENDS
;**********************************************************
        END
```

198 The 8086 and Assembly Language

Questions

Write programs in 8086 assembly language to solve the following problems.

(8.1) Form the sum of a list of signed 16 bit numbers.
(8.2) Add four 32 bit unsigned numbers.
(8.3) Multiply two 16 bit signed numbers.
(8.4) Determine the number of negative elements in a 40 element array.
(8.5) Convert an input array of elements in BCD format to Gray code and output the elements in their new format.
(8.6) Search a string of information for a substring of 8 characters and record the number of times the substring is encountered.
(8.7) Produce via a DAC a triangular voltage waveform with both positive and negative going ramps.
(8.8) Detect an input byte of information at a port of an 8255A PPI device and if it is greater than 0FH generate via a DAC a voltage sawtooth waveform, otherwise generate a square voltage waveform of twice the frequency of the sawtooth waveform.
(8.9) Use software interrupts to display sequentially the numbers 1 to 20 at two 7 segment displays via an 8255A device.
(8.10) Write a program to control the following process.

System operation:

(a) System activated with mains switch.
(b) Required process selected.
(c) Pressing and releasing the process start button causes the process to begin.
(d) An input from an active fault transducer causes the corresponding light to flash ON/OFF.
(e) If the fault is cleared within a specified time then the 'fault corrected' switches can be used to restart the process.
(d) If the malfunction remains after the specified time the fault indicating light remains ON and the process is switched OFF.

System simulation:

(a) A bank of switches for process selection of 1 out of 6 processes, and 2 'fault corrected' switches.
(b) A bank of 8 switches to provide a switch for mains ON/OFF, a process start button and 6 fault transducer inputs.
(c) A bank of 8 LEDs, 1 to indicate mains ON, 1 to indicate 'process running' and 6 to indicate transducer faults.

CHAPTER 9
Introducing the 80186 and the 80286

Intel introduced the 8086 microprocessor in 1978, and in 1979 the modified version with the 8 bit data bus, the 8088, was introduced. The 8088 microprocessor has been heavily used in personal microcomputer applications. The enhanced version of the 8086, the iAPX186, appeared in 1983, to be followed in the same year by the more advanced iAPX286 microprocessor. Strictly speaking the Intel names are, as stated iAPX186 and iAPX286, but here the names are simplified to the more generally used forms 80186 and 80286.

The main advantages of the 80186 when compared to the 8086 are (1) that ten new instructions are added and (2) the requirement for supporting integrated circuit devices is reduced. The 80286 further provides hardware virtual memory support and adds a further sixteen instructions. These are associated with the virtual memory mode. However, when compared to the 80186 it provides a reduced support for integrated circuit devices. It is important to note that both the 80186 and 80286 microprocessors are software compatible with the 8086 microprocessor.

THE 80186 MICROPROCESSOR

Effectively the 80186 microprocessor consists of an 8086 microprocessor with additions to its instruction set, a clock generator, a two mode programmable timer, a programmable interrupt controller, a chip select subsystem and a two channel direct memory access system, all accommodated on a single chip. The 80186 microprocessor is enclosed in a 68 pin JEDEC type A package; the pin layout is shown in figure 9.1. The block diagram of the 80186 microprocessor is shown in figure 9.2, indicating clearly the 8086 structure plus the additional hardware. The hardware additions are linked to the EU and BIU by an internal bus. In the 8086 the effective address is calculated by microcode, i.e. a machine language stored in ROM within the microprocessor. In the 80186 the BIU contains the six byte queue and the segment registers as

200 The 8086 and Assembly Language

Top view

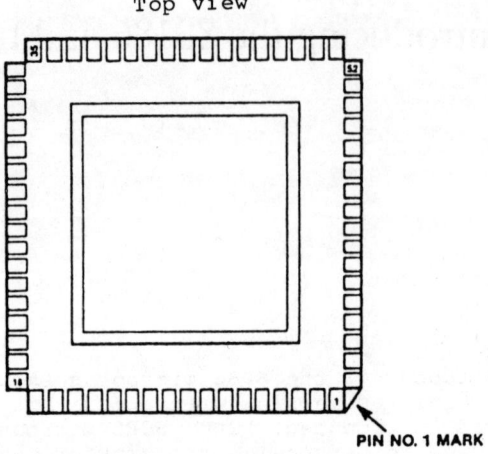

Bottom view

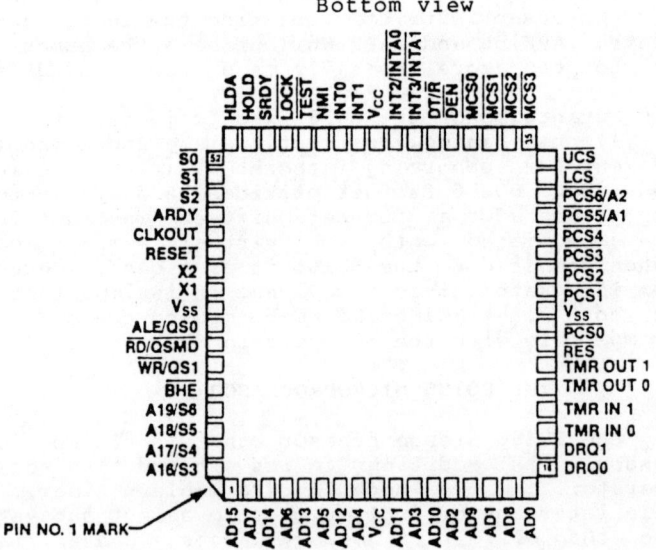

Figure 9.1 80186 Pin layout.
(Courtesy of Intel Corporation)

in the 8086, but also hardware to calculate the effective memory address. As a result of the effective memory address being produced by hardware there is an improvement in the speed of the calculation and so the 80186 microprocessor has an improved speed of operation when compared to the 8086.

80186 and 80286 Microprocessors **201**

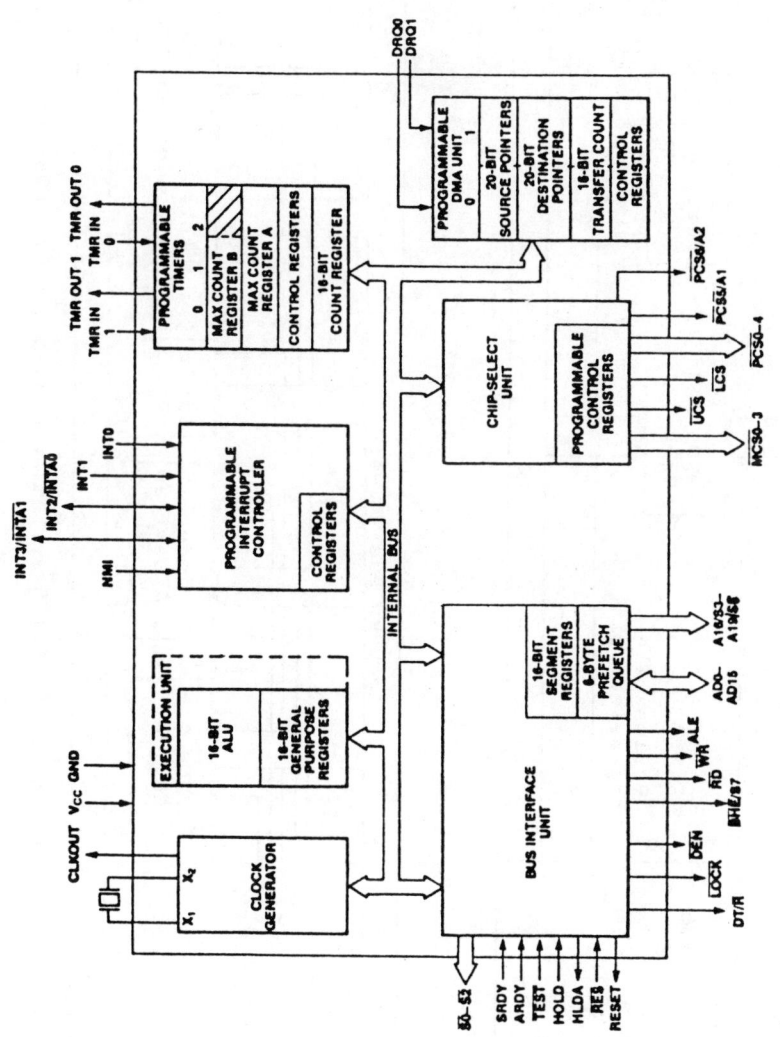

Figure 9.2 80186 Block diagram (Courtesy of Intel Corporation).

202 The 8086 and Assembly Language

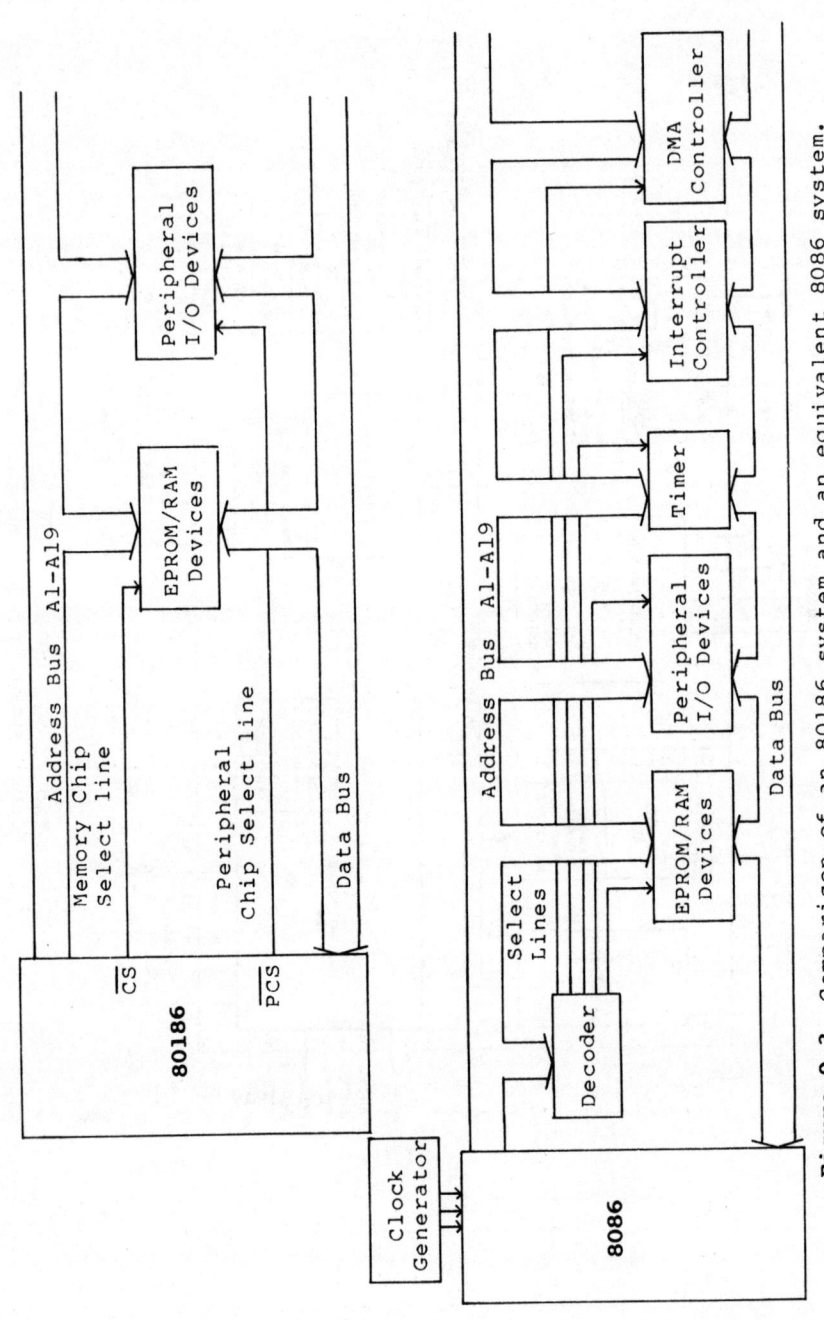

Figure 9.3 Comparison of an 80186 system and an equivalent 8086 system.

The ALU of the 8086 has been expanded in the 80186 to include facilities to deal with the new instructions. The result of having these additional integrated on-chip peripheral devices is clearly demonstrated in figure 9.3, where the number of separate circuit chips required for the 80186 system is five less than for the number required for a similar 8086 system. This type of circuit could well apply to a small stand-alone microprocessor application such as a process controller. The reduced number of chips could make the cost low enough to be attractive. The integrated on-chip peripherals of the 80186 microprocessor are now considered separately, and the method of programming these peripherals using the internal register block is also explained.

Clock Generator

The on-chip clock generator provides both internal and external clock generation at a frequency one half that of the external crystal frequency.

Programming the Internal Peripherals

Within the 80186 microprocessor there is a peripheral control register block of size 256 bytes. The 16 bit registers in the block can be written to or read by the microprocessor at any time in a program. The location of the register block can be determined by a relocation register within the block, but initially after the 80186 microprocessor is reset the relocation register is set to 20FFH, so allocating the base location of the block to FF00H in I/O space. Each of the registers is at a specific offset address with respect to the block base location. Figure 9.4 shows the map of these internal registers. As the block is initially mapped to I/O, so the registers can be treated as I/O ports. Writing information to one of the registers within the block can be done as follows assuming the base of the block to be at the reset location:

```
MOV DX,0FFA0H
MOV AX,0FE38H
OUT DX,AX
```

These instructions output the value 0FE38H to the upper memory chip select register UMCS at location 0FFA0H.

Chip Select Logic

The chip select logic provides six select outputs which can be used for three address areas. The upper chip select UCS is used for the top of the memory. The upper limit of this memory top is always FFFFFH and the lower limit is programmable. After the 80186 microprocessor is reset, execution of instructions located at memory location FFFF0H begins, so this area is normally reserved for the

204 The 8086 and Assembly Language

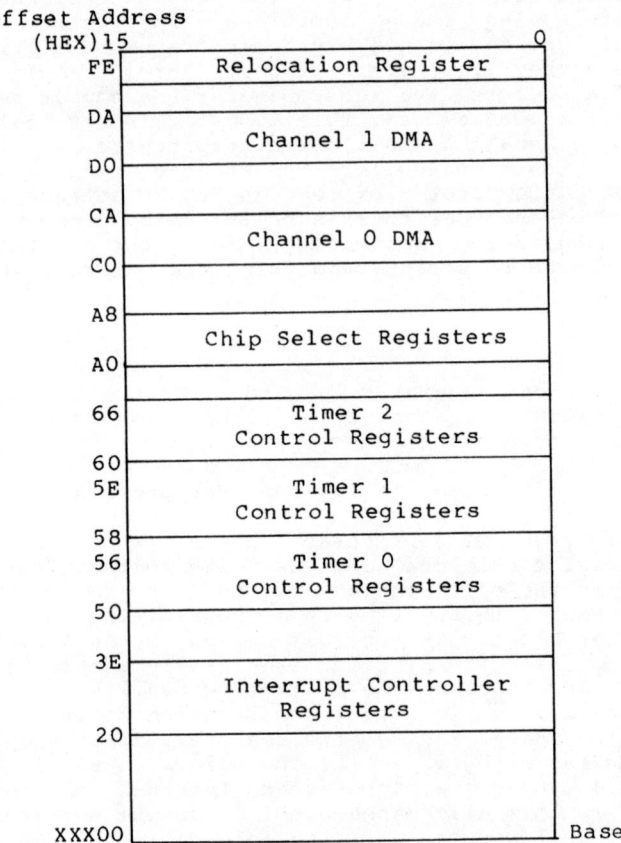

Figure 9.4 80186 Peripheral control internal register map.

systems ROM. The second chip select is used for the bottom of the memory and is called the lower chip select $\overline{LCS}$. The lower limit of the memory block defined by this chip select is always 0H. The lower limit of the block selected by $\overline{UCS}$ and the upper limit of the block selected by $\overline{LCS}$ can be programmed, so defining the size of these memory blocks. The other four chip select lines are used for mid-range memory and are known as the $\overline{MCS}$ lines. These lines are used to select one of four equal contiguous areas of memory; for example, a 32 Kbyte block is made up of four contiguous 8 Kbyte sections. The base address of the memory block and the section size can be programmed by reference to registers in the internal peripheral control register block. A typical memory chip select arrangement showing the chip select lines directly from the 80186 microprocessor is shown in figure 9.5.

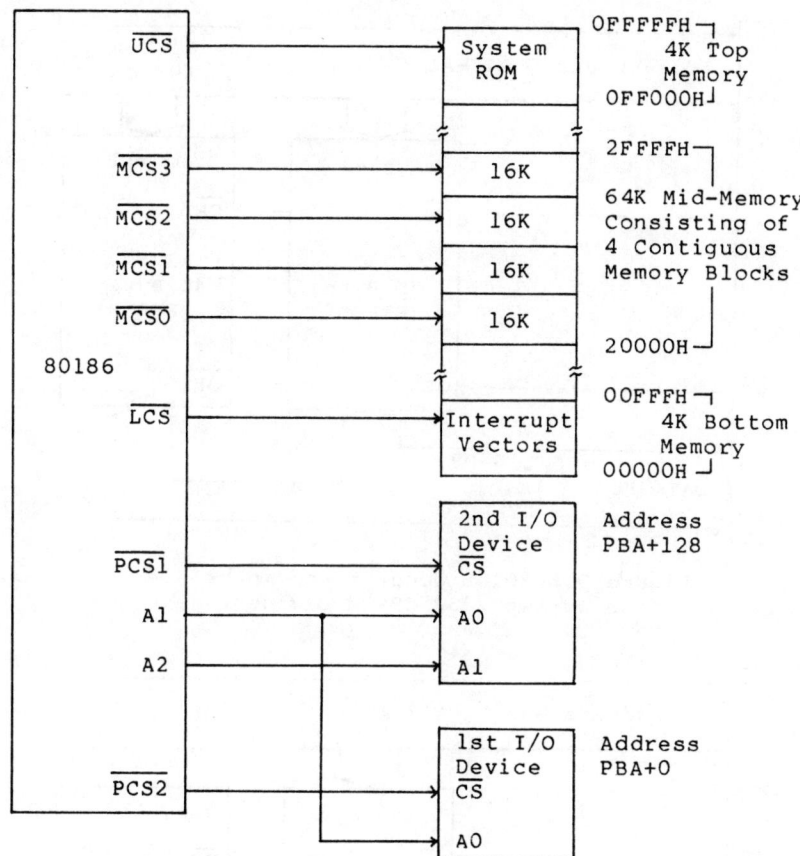

Figure 9.5 Typical 80186 memory and peripheral chip select arrangement.

The upper range interface can be extremely simple, involving only a direct connection from the $\overline{UCS}$ output of the 80186 to the chip enable inputs of the memory devices. Such an interface to two 2732 EPROM devices is shown in figure 9.6. A single memory bank selection signal is adequate as the only process taking place is that of reading even addressed words. Separate chip select lines are required for each memory bank of read/write memory. An example of this is shown in figure 9.7 where a lower range interface for the bottom of the memory is illustrated. $\overline{LCS}$ together with A0 is used to select the low memory bank, whereas LCS is used with $\overline{BHE}$ to select the high memory bank; this separate selection of the banks allows writing of bytes as well as words to memory.

206 The 8086 and Assembly Language

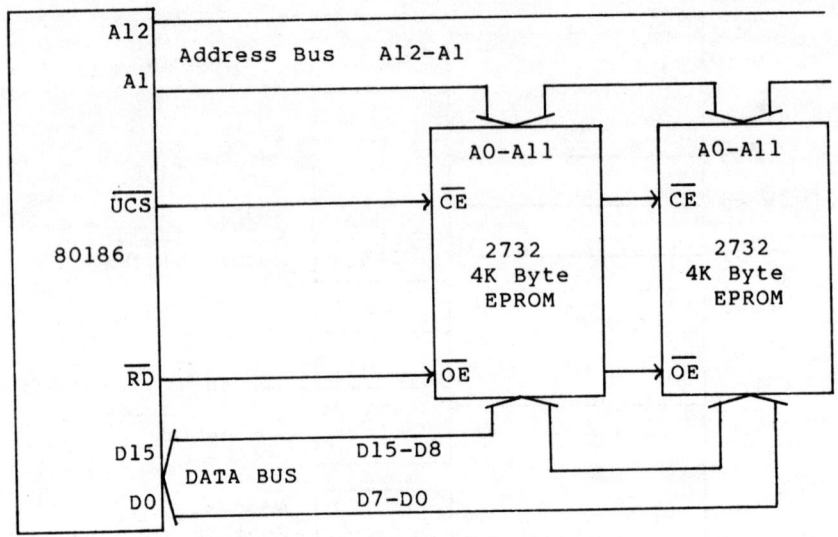

Figure 9.6 80186 Upper range interface using two 2732 EPROM devices.

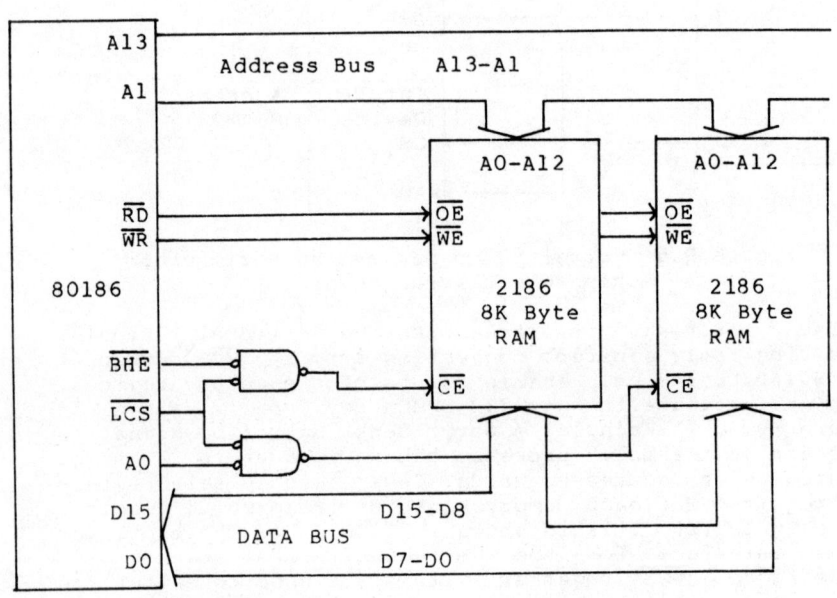

Figure 9.7 80186 Lower range interface using two 2186 RAM devices.

The two 2186 RAM devices provide a 16 Kbyte memory block, the addressing range for which is 0H to 03FFFH. For this range the $\overline{LCS}$ line will be active provided the LMCS register at I/O address 0FFA2H has been set to the value 03F8H. The instructions required to program the LMCS register when the internal register block is at the reset base location are:

```
MOV DX,0FFA2H    ;LMCS internal register address
MOV AX,03F8H     ;Data for LMCS register
OUT DX,AX
```

The integrated chip select logic also provides seven peripheral chip select lines, PCS0 to PCS6, which can be used to select interface devices. The base address of the peripheral chip selects can be programmed via an internal control register, and each chip select is active for a block of 128 bytes. $\overline{PCS0}$ is active between base address PBA and address (PBA + 127), whereas $\overline{PCS1}$ is active between addresses (PBA + 128) and (PBA + 255). An arrangement of peripheral chip select lines used with I/O devices is shown in figure 9.5. The connection of address lines A1 and A2 ensure that the I/O device interfaces have even addresses. Because of these memory and peripheral device chip select facilities, the 80186 microprocessor, when employed in a system requiring a small number of external interfaces, has eliminated the need for external decoders. The diagram of an 80186 computer arrangement shown in figure 9.8 illustrates this point.

Furthermore, the chip select logic block contains programmable wait state generators. A READY signal can be generated internally for each of the memory or peripheral chip select lines, the control of which consists in programming three READY bits labelled R0, R1 and R2 in each of the chip select control registers. The result is that there are eight possible options, 0 to 3 wait states with the external READY being active and 0 to 3 wait states with the external READY input being ignored. Hence the 80186 microprocessor can be programmed to communicate successfully with slower external devices.

Direct Memory Access Channels

A direct memory access DMA channel is one which allows data to be transferred at high speed on the microprocessor bus system between a peripheral device and main memory without the intervention of the microprocessor itself. The 80186 DMA controller provides two such channels which allow data transfer at a maximum rate of 2 Mbyte per second. The transfer can take place from memory to memory, from memory to peripheral and vice versa, and between peripherals.

208 The 8086 and Assembly Language

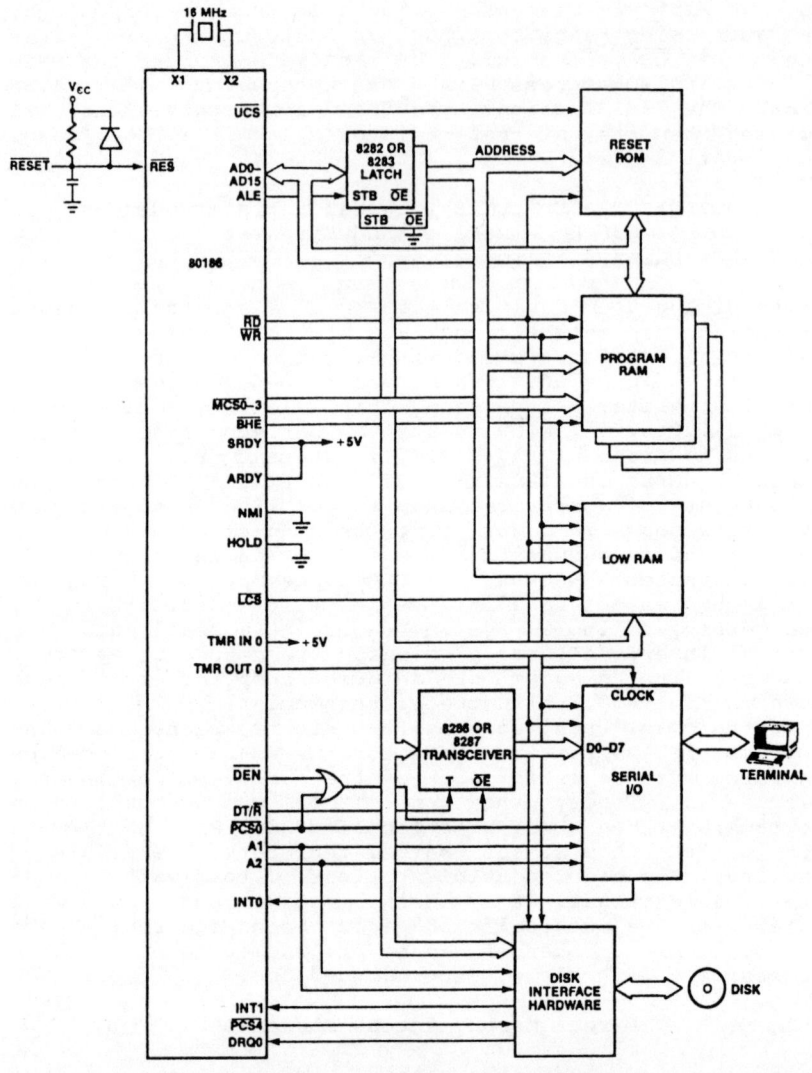

Figure 9.8 A typical 80186 computer.
(Courtesy of Intel Corporation)

For each DMA channel there are six programmable registers:

(1) Four registers, two forming a 20 bit source register and the other two forming a 20 bit destination register, each of which is automatically incremented or decremented after every data transfer.
(2) A 16 bit transfer count register specifing the number of DMA byte or word transfers to take place. This register is decremented after every data transfer.

(3) A 16 bit control word which specifies whether the transfer is in bytes or words, whether the address space is in either memory or I/O, whether the source and destination pointers should be incremented or decremented, the relative priority of the DMA channels, the interrupt logic and the mode of synchronisation.

Whenever the stop bit of a DMA control register is set, data transfer will take place on the corresponding channel. DMA requests can be generated externally by peripherals connected to 80186 inputs DRQ0 and DRQ1, and generated internally by timer 2.

Programmable Timers

Three internal 16 bit programmable timers are provided. Timers 0 and 1 can be used as external event counters, and to generate pulse outputs. They are connected to four external pins on the 80168, two inputs TMR0 IN and TMR1 IN, and two outputs TMR0 OUT and TMR1 OUT. Timer 2 is completely internal and can be used as a real time clock, a time delay generator, to activate a DMA request and as a prescaler to the other two timers. Eleven 16 bit registers can be programmed to control these timers. For each timer there is a mode/control register, a count register and a maximum count register, besides which timers 0 and 1 have a second maximun count register. The count register holds the current value of the timer, which is incremented after every timer event. When the value stored in the maximum count register is reached the timer count value is reset to zero. Timers 0 and 1 can alternate their count between two different maximum values. This gives the programmer the flexibility to change the duty cycle of the waveform. The mode control register can be checked to examine the programmed status and can be programmed for the following options:

(1) Each of the timers can be set either to halt or to continue on reaching the maximum count value.
(2) Timers 0 and 1 can be set to operate using either the internal clock at a rate of up to one-quarter the clock frequency or an external clock up to the same maximum rate. They can also be set to alternate between maximum count registers, and to retrigger on external events.
(3) Each timer can be set to generate an internal interrupt request on reaching the maximum count value.

These timer programmable options are illustrated in figure 9.9

210 The 8086 and Assembly Language

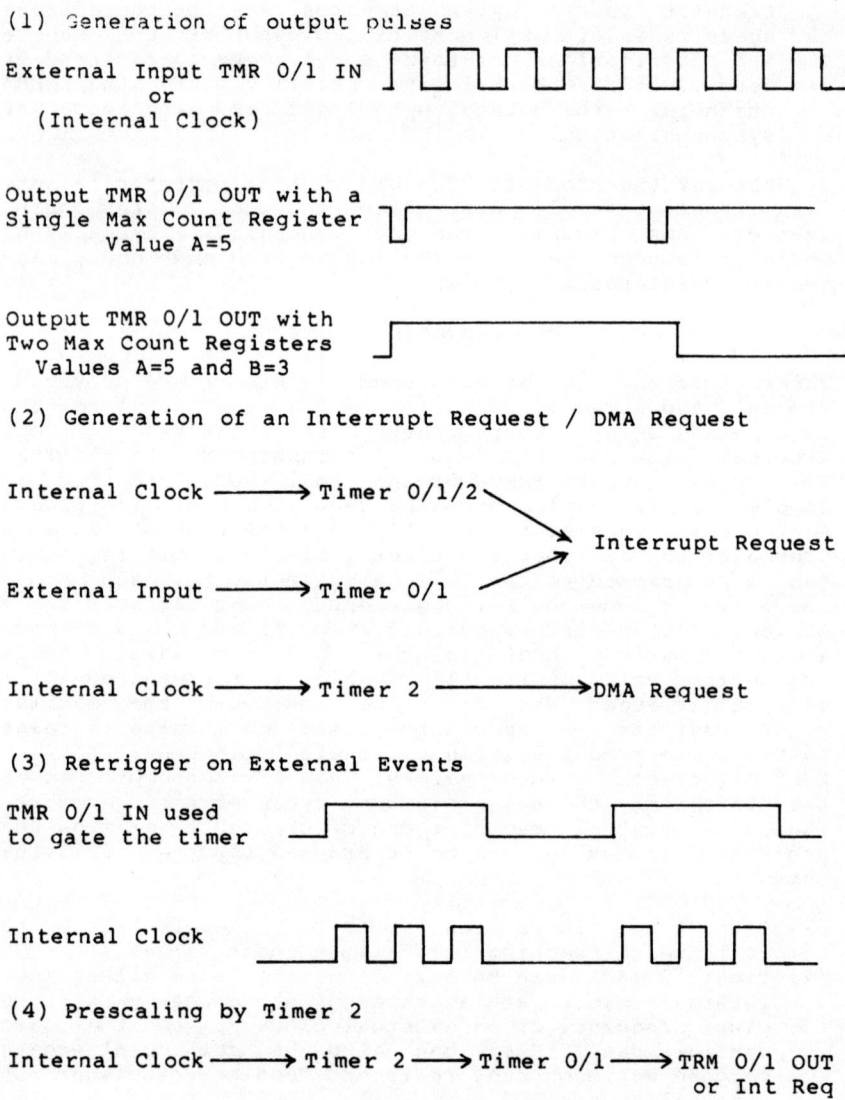

Figure 9.9 Timer operations.

Interrupts

Interrupts to this microprocessor are classified as hardware initiated interrupts, INT software interrupts or as interrupts resulting from instruction exceptions. All

80186 and 80286 Microprocessors 211

of these interrupts have a vector type which is a number used to obtain the interrupt vector location. Table 9.1 lists the interrupts.

Table 9.1 80186 Interrupts

Name	Type	Default priority hardware interrupts
Type 0 - Divide Error	0	n/a
Type 1 - Single Step	1	n/a
NMI - non-maskable	2	1
Type 3 - Breakpoint	3	n/a
INT 0 - Overflow	4	n/a
Array - BOUND instr	5	n/a
Invalid - Op-code	6	n/a
Escape - for 8087	7	n/a
Timer 0	8	2A
Reserved	9	3
DMA 0	10	4
DMA 1	11	5
INT 0 (external)	12	6
INT 1 (external)	13	7
INT 2 (external)	14	8
INT 3 (external)	15	9
Timer 1	18	2B
Timer 2	19	2C

n/a - not applicable

Interrupt Controller

This controller can operate in one of two modes, the master mode or the RMX86 compatible mode. Note that after reset the controller is in the master mode. In the master mode it behaves in a similar manner to the 8259 interrupt controller and accepts external and internal interrupts. In the RMX86 mode it behaves as a slave controller to an external master interrupt controller such as the 8259 device.

In the master mode the controller can accept interrupts from five external sources because the 80186 has five interrupt pin connections. These external interrupts can be programmed to be accepted in either a level or an edge triggered mode. One of the external interrupts is non-maskable and the other four are vectored. In this mode hardware interrupts are also accepted from internal sources such as timers and DMA channels. The hardware interrupts can be programmed into eight priority levels; table 9.1 lists the default priorities of these interrupts. They can also be individually masked and the system can be developed by cascading with a series of external slave interrupt controllers.

212 The 8086 and Assembly Language

In the RMX mode the 80186 interrupt controller acts as one of a series of slaves to an external interrupt controller. External interrupts are not recognised by the controller in this mode.

Additional Instructions

IMUL Multiplication by an immediate signed operand
IMUL result dest reg,mem/reg by data
This instruction causes multiplication of two operands. The first operand can be the contents of a register or of a memory location; the second is an immediate operand which is either a signed word or a byte sign extended to 16 bits. The 16 bit result is stored in a general purpose register.
Example 9.1
```
      IMUL   BX,SI,-350
      IMUL   CX,PPP,45
      IMUL   DX,260
```

The instruction IMUL BX,SI,-350 will multiply the contents of SI by -350 and place the result in BX. Whereas in the instruction IMUL DX,260 the contents of DX will be multiplied by the immediate operand 260 and the result placed in DX itself.

SHIFT and **ROTATE** by an Immediate Operand
SHL reg/mem,data
SAR reg/mem,data
SHR reg/mem,data
RCL reg/mem,data
RCR reg/mem,data
ROL reg/mem,data
ROR reg/mem,data
These shift and rotate operations are governed by an 8 bit unsigned immediate operand.
Example 9.2
```
      SAR  BL,3
      ROR  DX,9
      RCR  PPPP,5
```

PUSH an Immediate Operand to the top of the stack
PUSH data
This instruction causes an immediate 16 bit or sign extended 8 bit operand to be placed on the stack and the stack pointer is decremented by two.
Example 9.3
```
      PUSH 230H
      PUSH 47
```

PUSHA Pushes all eight general purpose registers on to the stack
The data pointer and index registers are saved on the stack in the order AX, CX, DX, BX, SP, BP, SI and DI, and the stack pointer is decremented by sixteen.

POPA Restores all general purpose registers from the stack.
Restores data, pointer and index registers from the stack, but the SP value is discarded.

INS/INSB/INSW String input
The instruction causes the contents of the I/O port pointed to by the DX register to be loaded to the memory location pointed to by the DI register in the extra segment. The DI register is then incremented or decremented depending on the setting of the DF direction flag as 0 or 1 respectively. For INSW the DI is changed by two, and for INSB by one. When used with the repeat prefix REP, transfer continues until CX is at zero. This is often referred to as block transfer.

OUTS/OUTSB/OUTSW String output
The contents of the location pointed to by the SI register are transferred to the port pointed to by the DX register. For the byte transfer OUTSB SI is updated by one, and for the word transfer OUTSW SI is updated by two. The index register is incremented when DF is 0 and decremented when DF is 1. This instruction can also be used with the REP prefix.

High Level Language Support Instructions

BOUND Array limits check
BOUND reg,mem
Before executing the instruction the assumed array index is placed in the first operand register. The second operand is the memory array bounds location. On execution the instruction compares the contents of the register with the memory location values, and if the register value is outside the memory limits then an out of bounds interrupt type number 5 occurs. The interrupt service routine can be used to end the program. This instruction is very useful for compiler generated code with data array applications.

ENTER Procedure entry
ENTER mem,mem
Block structured high level languages use a temporary data area relating to the calling of procedures. They are known as stack frames. The pushing and popping of these stack frames is required support for block structured languages. ENTER saves stack frame pointers from the calling procedure and allocates a new stack frame for the current procedure. The first operand specifies the memory area required and the second specifies the procedure level.

LEAVE Procedure leave
This instruction on leaving a procedure restores the calling procedure's stack frame.

THE 80286 MICROPROCESSOR

The 80286 microprocessor is a more sophisticated device than either the 8086 or the 80186. Nevertheless, it is software compatible with the 8086 microprocessor. It has built in memory management, and the facility to operate in both real memory mode and virtual memory mode. The microprocessor consists of four distinct processing sections which operate concurrently. These sections are the bus unit, the instruction unit, the execution unit and the address unit; they are shown diagramatically in figure 9.10.

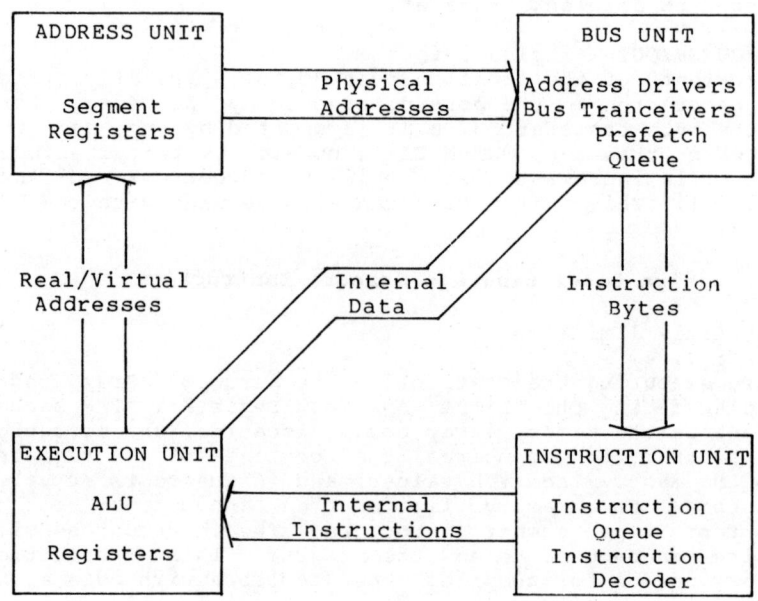

Figure 9.10 Simplified block structure of 80286 microprocessor.

The bus unit houses address latches and drivers, data transceivers and a six byte prefetch instruction queue, and provides bus control signals. The unit fetches instructions from memory and places them in the prefetch queue. The instruction unit contains an instruction decoder and a second queue three instructions in length used for decoded instructions. The action of this unit is to take instructions from the prefetch queue, decode them and place them in a second instruction queue. The execution unit contains the eight central processor registers, the microprogrammable control logic and the

80186 and 80286 Microprocessors

arithmetic logic unit, all of which together facilitate the execution of instructions. Decoded instructions are obtained by this unit from the three instruction queue in the instruction unit, and then executed. The last section in this simplified block structure is the address unit which contains the four segment registers used to evaluate the 20 bit physical addresses employed in the real memory mode, and additional logic used to evaluate the 24 bit physical addresses employed in the virtual memory mode.

The result of the division of the microprocessor into four sections which operate simultaneously is to greatly increase the speed of execution of instructions. For example, an 8 MHz version of the 80286 microprocessor has an increase in speed of operation by a factor of approximately three when compared to an 8086 microprocessor running at the same clock rate. The 80286 microprocessor incorporates 130,000 circuits on the chip and is packaged in a 68 pin JEDEC type A package.

Real Address Mode

The 80286 microprocessor operating in the real address mode is compatible with the 8086 microprocessor. In this mode the microprocessor can address up to 1 Mbyte of address space employing lines A0 to A19; lines A20 to A23 are ignored. The physical address is computed in the same manner as in the 8086 microprocessor (see figure 1.8). Again the 32 bit address pointer consists of the 16 bit segment address and the 16 bit offset address, and it is these logical addresses which are combined in the address unit to produce a 20 bit physical address for direct use with memory by the bus unit. When power is supplied to the microprocessor it automatically enters the real mode of operation. Initialisation of tables and registers for virtual mode operation take place in the real mode and then transition to the virtual mode of operation can be effected. This transition is achieved by executing the instruction LMSW (load machine status word) in which the protection enable bit is set to logic '1'.

Protected Virtual Address Mode

In the protected virtual address mode the memory management allows addressing of up to 2^{30} bytes or 1 Gbyte of virtual address space per task, supported by 2^{24} or 16 Mbyte of real address space. Virtual memory is considered to be the combination of the available real system memory and the bulk storage devices, such as disk, into a single memory space. Only the part of the program which is executing will in fact be in real memory; the remainder will be on disk.

Virtual memory management is a method of running programs, which occupy memory larger than the available real memory, by moving sections of the program back and forth between the disk and memory. This type of operation

216 The 8086 and Assembly Language

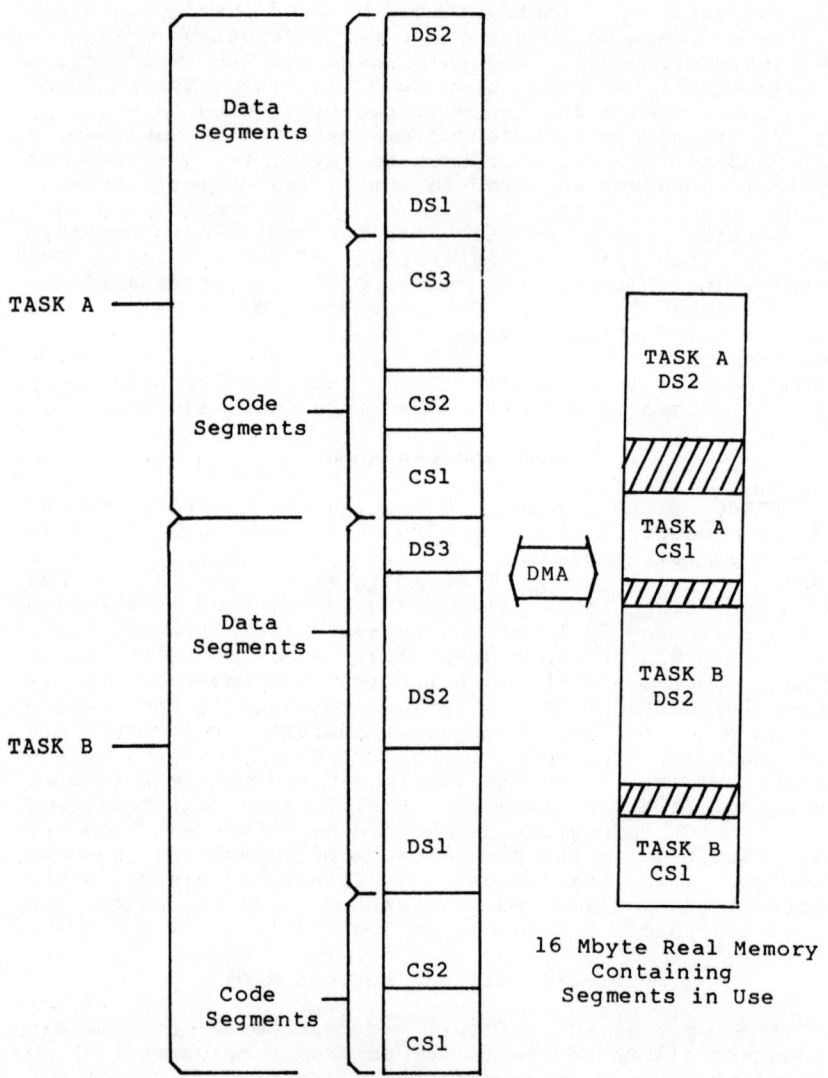

Figure 9.11 Virtual memory 1 Gbyte per task.

is conducive to multitasking as well as to the running of programs which in themselves occupy more memory than is physically available. Multitasking is the process by which

80186 and 80286 Microprocessors 217

the microprocessor can run several programs at the same time. Figure 9.11 shows the general concept of virtual memory in which program segments are moved between real memory and disk storage. The sections of the programs being accessed by the microprocessor are in real memory while the remaining program sections are still on disk.

In the virtual mode segment and offset addresses are still employed, but instead of the segment address being shifted four places left to give the segment base physical address, it is used to index a table in memory to obtain a base address, which points to a target segment. In effect, then, the segment registers are used to specify one 64 Kbyte segment from a choice of 16K (sixteen thousand) such segments. The translation from virtual to physical address is performed automatically by the 80286 microprocessor. Use of segment base addressing techniques in both real and virtual memory modes ensures that programs written for the 8086 and for the 80286 in the real mode can be used, without alteration, in the virtual mode of operation.

Address space protection is provided to enable the 80286 to be used in multi-user systems. This protection consists of the isolation of the operating system from the application programs and the isolation of users from each other. Automatic protection checking is also provided.

The 80286 register set is shown in figure 9.12. It includes the 8086 register set plus further registers to deal with virtual addressing, multitasking and software protection.

New flag bits are also included within the MSW. They are used in controlling the task-to-task transfer and to enable address space protection.

The segment registers shown in the 80286 register set of figure 9.12 have extension registers known as segment descriptor cache registers. These 48 bit segment extension registers effectively extend the segment register to hold 64 bits of information. The information within the segment descriptor cache register includes segment base address, limit parameters and protection parameters, all of which are used automatically by the microprocessor to convert a virtual address to a physical address. When a segment register is loaded, within a program, the microprocessor copies the descriptor for that segment into the associated extension cache register. The data in the segment selector contains three fields: a single bit table indicator TI to select either the global descriptor table or the local descriptor table, a two bit RPL field to select the privilege level, and a 13 bit index field which refers to the required descriptor in the table selected.

The process of loading a segment extension cache register with a segment descriptor is as follows:

(1) The segment selector is loaded into the segment register, so choosing either the LDTR or the GDTR and providing a descriptor index and a privilege level selection.

218 The 8086 and Assembly Language

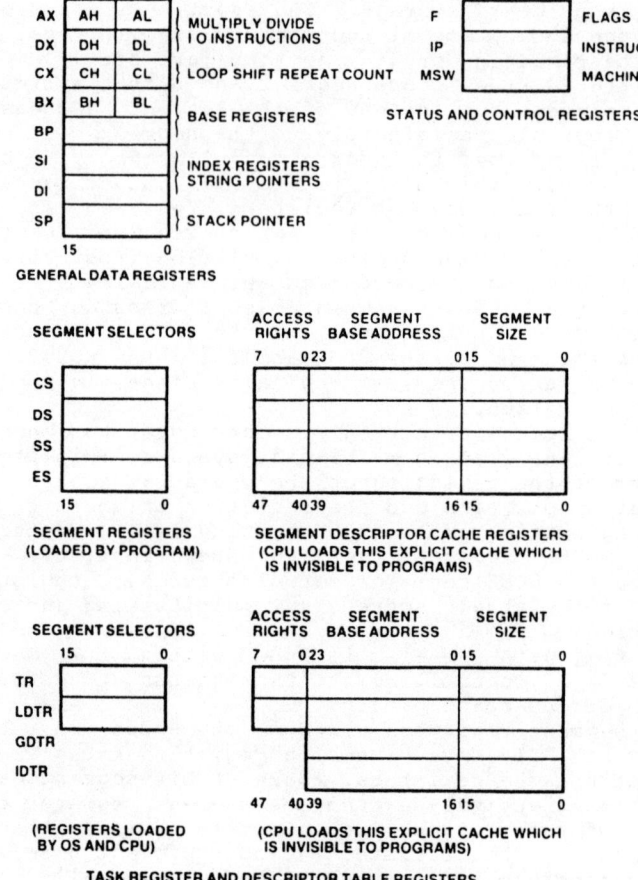

Figure 9.12 80286 Register set (Courtesy of Intel Corporation).

(2) The DTR selected indicates the base address and the length of the descriptor table.
(3) The index is added to the descriptor table base address, so selecting a descriptor.
(4) The segment access rights are verified by the microprocessor and the descriptor is copied to the segment cache register.

This process is illustrated in figure 9.13.

80186 and 80286 Microprocessors **219**

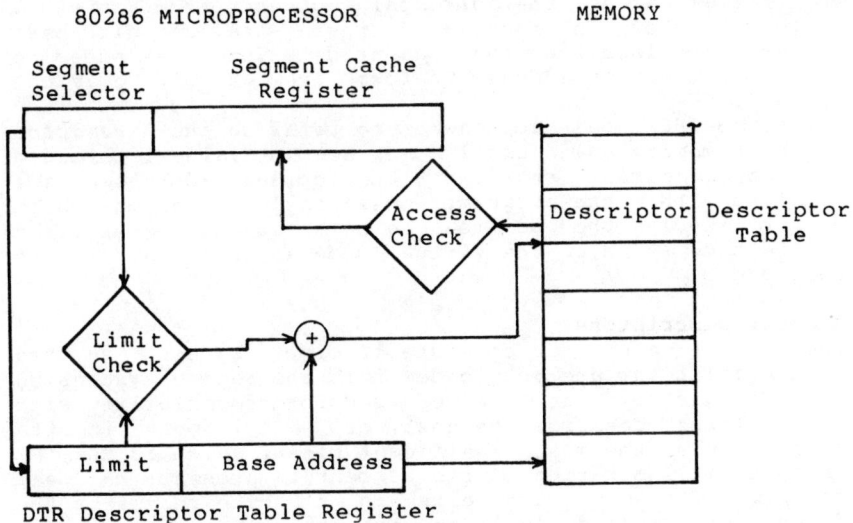

Figure 9.13 Loading the segment extension cache register.

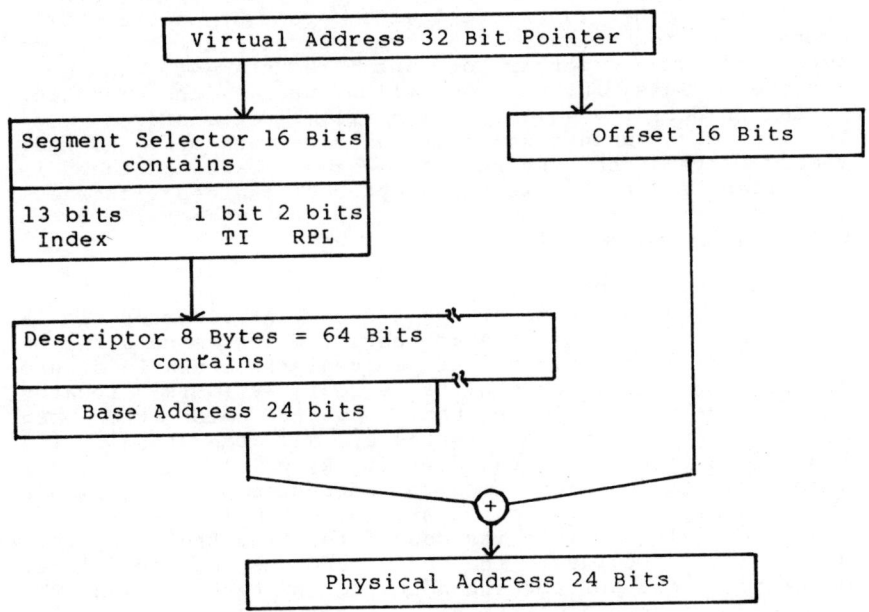

Figure 9.14 Physical address formation in virtual mode.

Calculation of a Physical Address from a Virtual Address

The formation of the physical address from a virtual address is shown in figure 9.14, where the 24 bit base address obtained from the segment descriptor has added to it a 16 bit offset address to form the 24 bit physical address.

The 80286 does not need to refer to the descriptor table in memory again until a new segment value is loaded into the segment register; the offset addresses are provided within the program. Consequently programs which do not involve the modification of a segment register run at the same speed in the virtual mode as they would in the real mode.

Segment Descriptors

The segment descriptor consists of eight bytes. The two most significant are not loaded into the segment extension cache register, but are reserved for compatibility with other microprocessors. The next, or sixth, byte is the access byte, the most significant bit of which is the (P) present bit indicating if the segment is present in real memory. The next two bits in the byte represent the descriptor privilege level and the following bit indicates whether the descriptor applies to a code/data segment or to a non-segment descriptor. Descriptor tables can contain descriptors other than those associated with segments, e.g. gate and interrupt descriptors. The next three bits of the access byte specify the segment 'type' (this is explained further in the following paragraph on the 80286 protection mechanism). The least significant bit of the byte indicates whether or not the segment has been accessed. This information will be used by the operating system in deciding which segment will be transfered back to the disk when segment exchange between disk and real memory is required. The 24 bit segment base address is specified by the next three bytes of the descriptor and the least significant byte specifies the segment limit, so defining the segment length.

Descriptor Table Registers

The table indexed in memory by the segment register is a descriptor table, the base address of which is held in the corresponding descriptor table register shown in figure 9.12. The global descriptor table register (GDTR) locates the global descriptor table, which holds the base addresses of the segments shared by all the tasks. The local descriptor table register (LDTR) points to the local descriptor table which holds the addresses of the segments which apply only to that task. The extension register of the LDTR is loaded with its descriptor from the GDT. This descriptor provides the base address of the local desriptor table LDT corresponding to the task in hand. The base address of the GDT is held in the GDTR and this is added to the index provided by the selector in the LDTR. The interrupt descriptor table register (IDTR) contains the interrupt descriptor table base address and length. The interrupt descriptor table itself contains eight byte descriptors associated with the interrupt handlers.

Multitasking
Each task has an associated task state segment which contains the information required to start and stop the task. The task register (TR) contains a global descriptor table selector for the current task state segment. When the current task is to be changed the 80286 saves the register contents in the current task state segment pointed to by the task register. It then loads the task register with the appropriate selector for the new task state segment. Then from the new task state segment it loads the 80286 registers, including the local descriptor table register. Relatively fast task switching is achieved because the amount of information to be saved is small. The new task can now begin to execute, the segment descriptors being provided by the new local descriptor table.

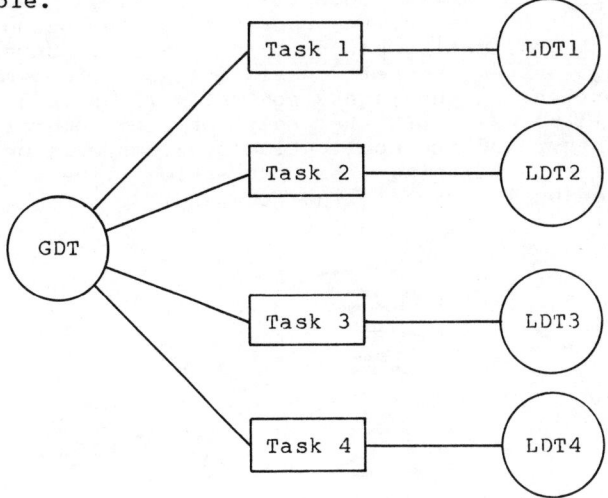

Figure 9.15 Tasks and associated descriptor tables.

The organisation of descriptor tables is usually as shown in figure 9.15 where each task has its own local descriptor table and all the tasks share the global descriptor table. A segment whose descriptor is in the global desriptor table can be accessed by every task whereas a segment whose descriptor is in a local descriptor table can be accessed only by one task. A task change is caused by an intersegment jump instruction JMP to the task state segment of a new task; the offset part of the jump's target address is ignored. The operating system can switch from the local address space of one task to that of another by changing the contents of the LDTR.

Protection Mechanism of the 80286

The protection mechanism in the virtual mode prevents an application program from modifying (a) the operating system code or data and (b) the code or data of another application program. The segment is the unit which is used in the protection mechanism.

Firstly each segment, within its segment descriptor, is allotted a segment 'type' which is effectively an access privilege. The segment types are: (1) execute only, (2) execute and read, (3) read only, and (4) read and write. Typically, a code segment would be of executable type whereas a stack segment should be of type 'read and write'. When the segment register is loaded the segment type is checked and also the fact that the segment is present in real memory is verified.

The 80286 provides four hierarchical protection or privilege levels within the virtual address space. These are shown in figure 9.16. Level 0 is the level with the highest privilege and level 3 is that level with the lowest. The simplest system involving privilege levels occupies only two levels, the operating system being in level 0 and the application programs in level 3. Usually the operating system kernel consisting of the memory management, protection and access control will be in level 0, level 1 will be used for the rest of the operating system routines, and the application programs will be at level 3. The tasks spanning the protection levels are shown separated by the radial lines.

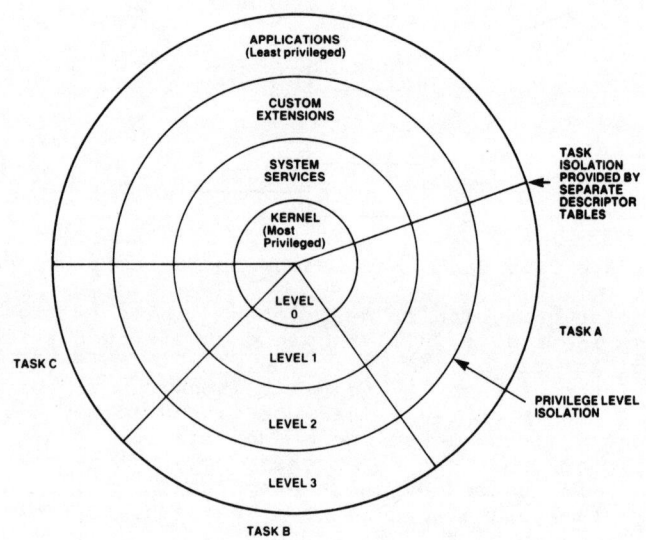

Figure 9.16 Privilege levels in the 80286 virtual mode (Courtesy of Intel Corporation).

80186 and 80286 Microprocessors **223**

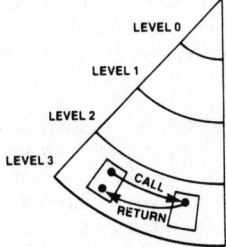
(a) Call operation within a privilege level

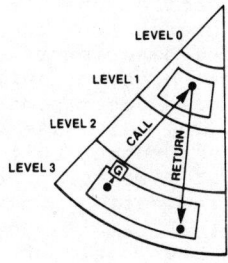
(b) Inter-privilege call within a task

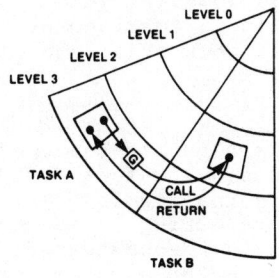
(c) Both inter-task and inter-privilege call

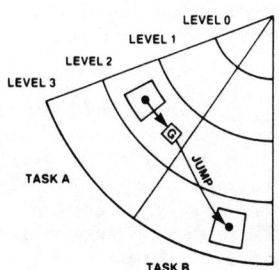
(d) Inter-task and inter-privilege transfer

Figure 9.17 Gate descriptors used in inter-task and inter-privilege level protection (Courtesy of Intel Corporation).

224 The 8086 and Assembly Language

The privilege level of each segment is defined within its segment descriptor. A program can access data at its own or a lower privilege level. However, it is allowed to call subroutines at its own or at a higher privilege level provided the called subroutine is in a segment of type 'execute'. For each privilege level there is a stack and an associated stack pointer. When a subroutine at, say, level 3 calls a subroutine at level 1, parameters from the stack of the calling subroutine are passed to the stack of the called subroutine. This restricts communication between the privilege levels to parameter passing and so ensures the protection of the higher privilege routine.

Protection is further provided by 'call gates' which are descriptors via which a program will call a subroutine. The call instruction has a virtual address with a selector which references the call gate descriptor. It is the call gate descriptor which specifies the virtual address of the point of entry in the more privileged segment. The call gate descriptors are held in the global descriptor table. The call gate descriptor has the following fields: (1) a present bit to indicate whether the segment is in system memory or on disk, (2) a destination selector field indicating the target code segment or the target task state segment, (3) a destination offset indicating the point of entry within the segment, (4) a word count field specifiying the number of parameters to be passed in the call, and (5) an access field specifying the privilege level. Figure 9.17 shows control transfer both within a task and between tasks. This clearly demonstrates that when privilege levels are crossed call gates are employed.

Virtual Memory Operation
In figure 9.18 an example is shown of the operation that occurs when a program instruction refers to a virtual address that is not present in real memory. The use of the segment descriptor fields referring to segment presence and segment access are clearly demonstrated. The real memory in the RAM of the 80286 system contains the operating system programs OS, descriptor tables, the code segment of an application program and some unoccupied space in which to load the required segment.

System Interface
The 80286 can be used in a local bus configuration which is similar to the 8086 microprocessor in maximum mode. The bus system consists of a 24 line address bus, a 16 line data bus and an 8 line control bus to interface the microprocessor to local memory and I/O components, and has the option to add the 80287 numeric processor extension device. Such a system is shown in figure 9.18. It includes an 82284 clock generator, an 82288 bus controller, 8282 latches, 8286 transceivers and an 8259A interrupt controller. One Mbyte of physical memory can be addressed in the real mode and 16 Mbytes can be addressed in the

80186 and 80286 Microprocessors **225**

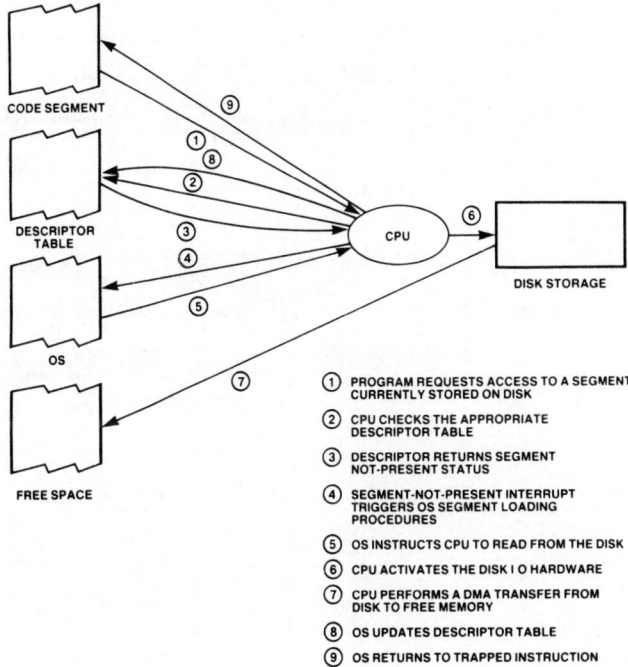

Figure 9.18 Virtual memory operation
(Courtesy of Intel Corporation).

virtual protected mode of operation, and 64 Kbytes of I/O address space can be accommodated in either mode.
The 80286 microprocessor uses pipelined addressing. This involves the overlapping of bus operations. The address of the new bus operation is made available by the microprocessor during the last clock cycle of the present bus operation and consequently address decoding can operate ahead of the bus operation. External latches can be used to hold the address for the complete bus operation. The 82288 bus controller device is used to provide control signals such as ALE, DT/R, DEN, RD and WR.

The 80287 numeric processor extension can perform calculations and data transfers concurrently with the 80286 execution of other instructions. The extension numeric processor is employed to provide a greatly enhanced facility for floating point arithmetic. Futhermore, the addition of an 82289 bus arbiter device to the system provides the 80286 with a bus interface to a multiple processor system in which it can act as an independent processor.

226 The 8086 and Assembly Language

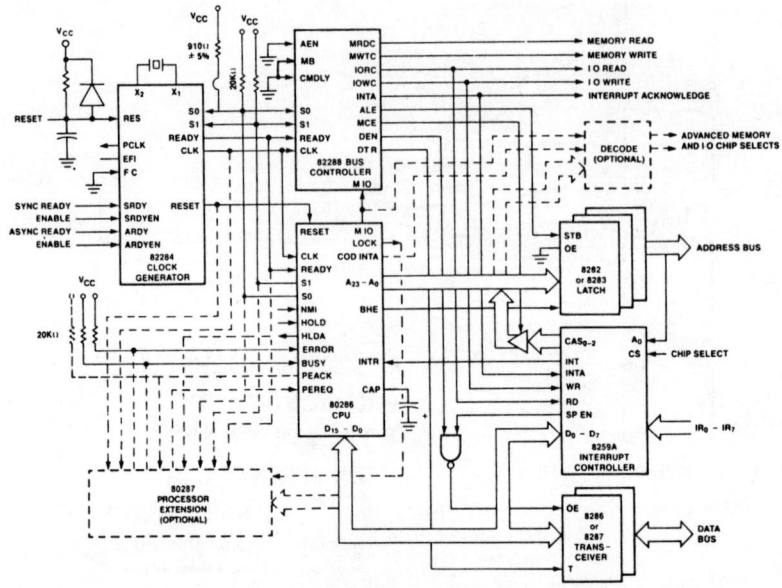

Figure 9.19 Basic 80286 microprocessor system (Courtesy of Intel Corporation).

Additional Instructions

The following sixteen instructions are included in the 80286 instruction set. These instructions are associated with the virtual mode of operation and allow the manipulation of the additional registers, the descriptor tables and the gates.

ARPL Adjust Requested Privilege Level
Adjust the RPL field of the 16 bit register or memory operand in the instruction to be the maximum of its original value and the value in the instruction.

CTS Clear the Task Switch Flag
Clear the task switch flag in the machine state byte. The hardware sets this flag at each task switch.

LGTD Load the Global Descriptor Table Register
Load the six byte base and limit information to the GDT register from the memory indicated in the instruction.

LIDT Load the Interrupt Descriptor Table Register
Load the IDT register with six bytes indicating the base and limit information for the descriptor table.

LLDT Load the Local Descriptor Table Register
Load, from a register or memory operand, the LDT with a 16 bit selector to point to one of the local descriptor tables listed in the GDT.

LMSW Load the Machine Status Word
Load the MSW from either a 16 bit register or a memory operand.

LTR Load the Task Register
Load the task register with a 16 bit selector for one of the task state segments within the GDT.

SGTD Store the Global Descriptor Table Register
Store the contents of the GDT in six bytes at the location given in the instruction.

SIDT Store the Interrupt Descriptor Table Register
Store the contents in six bytes indicated by the instruction.

SLDT Store the Local Descriptor Table Register
Store the selector of the LDT in the 16 bit register or memory operand given in the instruction.

SMSW Store the Machine Status Word
Store the MSW in the register or memory operand indicated in the instruction.

STR Store the Task Register
Store the selector for the TR in the operand indicated.

LAR Load Access Rights
Load the high byte of a sixteen bit register with the segment access byte of a descriptor table.

LSL Load Segment Limit
Load the segment size of a descriptor table into the specified register.

VERR Verify Read Access
If the segment specified in the instruction is read accessible the instruction sets the ZF; otherwise, it clears ZF.

VERW Verify Write Access
If the segment specified in the instruction is write accessible the ZF is set; otherwise, it is cleared.

Finally, table 9.2 provides a brief comparison of the 16 bit microprocessors in the 8086 family.

Table 9.2 Comparison of 16 bit microprocessors in the 8086 family.

Microprocessor	8086	80186	80286
8086 Instruction set	Yes	Yes	Yes
Extra instructions	–	10	16
Package type	40 pin DIL	68 pin JEDEC A	68 pin JEDEC A
Clock frequencies	10 MHz 8 MHz 5 MHz	8 MHz 6 MHz	8 MHz 6 MHz 4 MHz
Data bus size	16	16	16
Address bus size	20	20	24
Real address range	1 Mbyte	1 Mbyte	16 Mbyte
Virtual addressing capability	No	No	1 Gbyte per task
On-chip clock	No	Yes	No
On-chip interrupt controller	No	Yes	No
On-chip DMA controller	No	Yes	No
On-chip chip select	No	Yes	No
On-chip timer	No	Yes	No
Use with co-processors	8087 8089	8087	80287
Multi-tasking applications	No	No	Yes
Memory protection	No	No	Yes

Appendix A

```
                  Diagnostic (List) File for Program 5.1
                       10      ASSUME  CS:PROGC
                       11      ;*********************************************
                       12      PROGC   SEGMENT
0000 9090909090        13      LOOP1   MOV   AL,1234H ;Move immediate to accumulator
*** ERROR #37, LINE #13, UNDEFINED INSTRUCTION OR ILLEGAL VARIABLE DEFINITION
*** ERROR #2, LINE #13, OPERANDS DO NOT MATCH THIS INSTRUCTION
0005 9090909090        14              MOV   0300,AX ;Move AX contents to offset 300H
*** ERROR #2, LINE #14, OPERANDS DO NOT MATCH THIS INSTRUCTION
000A B3009090          15              MOV   BL,FFH  ;Set each bit in BL to '1'
*** ERROR #38, LINE #15, (PASS 2) UNDEFINED SYMBOL, ZERO USED
000E 9090909090        16              MOV   CX,BL   ;Transfer between 16 bit registers
*** ERROR #2, LINE #16, OPERANDS DO NOT MATCH THIS INSTRUCTION
0013 9090909090        17              MOV   OFFFE,BL ;Move a byte from BL to memory
*** ERROR #18, LINE #17, ILLEGAL CHARACTER IN NUMERIC CONSTANT
*** ERROR #2, LINE #17, OPERANDS DO NOT MATCH THIS INSTRUCTION
0018 9090909090        18      LOOP2:  INC   0303H    ;Increment memory location contents
*** ERROR #2, LINE #18, OPERANDS DO NOT MATCH THIS INSTRUCTION
001D 9090909090        19              SBB   0304H    ;Subtract immediate from AX
*** ERROR #2, LINE #19, OPERANDS DO NOT MATCH THIS INSTRUCTION
0022 3C009090          20              CMP   AL,AAH   ;Compare immediate AL with AAH
*** ERROR #38, LINE #20, (PASS 2) UNDEFINED SYMBOL, ZERO USED
0026 9090                21            JNZ   LOOP1    ;Conditional jump
*** ERROR #38, LINE #21, (PASS 2) UNDEFINED SYMBOL, ZERO USED
*** ERROR #2, LINE #21, (PASS 2) OPERANDS DO NOT MATCH THIS INSTRUCTION
0028 9090                22            JLE   LOOP2    ;Conditional jump
*** ERROR #38, LINE #22, (PASS 2) UNDEFINED SYMBOL, ZERO USED
*** ERROR #2, LINE #22, (PASS 2) OPERANDS DO NOT MATCH THIS INSTRUCTION
002A 9090909090        23              DIV   AX,CX    ;Divide by the word stored in CX
*** ERROR #2, LINE #23, OPERANDS DO NOT MATCH THIS INSTRUCTION
-----                  24      PROGC   ENDS
*** ERROR #86, LINE #24, MISMATCHED LABEL ON ENDS OR ENDP
                       25      ;*********************************************
*** ERROR #89, LINE #25, PREMATURE END OF FILE (NO END STATEMENT)

ASSEMBLY COMPLETE, 17 ERRORS FOUND
```

Corrected Version of Program 5.1

```
;   Title:    Assembly Language Errors Corrected
;   Filename: CORREC.A86
;   Purpose:  This is the list of instructions ERROR.A86
;each one of which has now been corrected.
;**************************************************************
ASSUME   CS:PROGC,DS:PROGD
;**************************************************************
PROGC    SEGMENT
LOOP1:   MOV   AX,1234H;Move immediate - AL replaced by AX
         MOV   LOT1,AX ;LOT1 is address identifier (300H)
         MOV   BL,OFFH ;Data begins with numeric character
         MOV   CX,BX   ;BX replaces BL for a 16 bit register
         MOV   DI,0FFFEH
         MOV   [DI],BL ;Move byte from BL to offset 0FFFEH
LOOP2:   INC   NUMB3   ;Increment variable at location 0303H
         SBB   AX,0304H;Subtract immediate from AX
         CMP   AL,0AAH ;Data begins with numeric character
         JNZ   LOOP1   ;Colon sets LOOP1 as NEAR label
         JLE   LOOP2   ;Conditional jump (: at LOOP2)
         CWD           ;Sign extend AX to DX-AX pair
         DIV   CX      ;Divide DX-AX by the word in CX
PROGC    ENDS
;**************************************************************
PROGD    SEGMENT ;Data segment used to define variables
         ORG   0300H
LOT1     DW    ? ; Word variable at LOT1 undefined
NUMB3    DB    24; Byte variable at NUMB3 has value 24
PROGD    ENDS
;**************************************************************
         END
```

Appendix B

RS-232C Interface Pin Assignments

Pin number	Description
1	Protective ground
2	Transmitted data
3	Received data
4	Request to send
5	Clear to send Channel 1
6	Data set ready
7	Logical ground
8	Data carrier detect
9	Reserved
10	for testing
11	Unassigned
12	Received line signal detector
13	Clear to send Channel 2
14	Transmitted data
15	Transmitter signal element timing
16	Received data ———Channel 2
17	Receiver signal element timing
18	Unassigned
19	Request to send Channel 2
20	Data terminal ready
21	Signal quality detector
22	Ring indicator
23	Data signal rate select
24	Transmit signal element timing
25	Unassigned

Appendix C

PROCEDURE FOR 8086 MACHINE INSTRUCTION ENCODING

The machine instruction format for the complete set of 8086 instructions is provided in table C.1. Figure 1.10 shows the general format of the 8086 machine instruction. The encoding procedure is outlined in the following steps:

(1) Obtain from the instruction encoding list of table C.1 the simplest form of object code word applicable to the instruction under consideration. The opcode bits will be present in this word.
(2) Usually if it is present the single bit W field in the encoding word can be filled in immediately, because a 16 bit operand is specified by W = 1 and an 8 bit operand by W = 0.
(3) If now in the encoding word the only remaining field to encode is the 3 bit register field, this can be completed by reference to table C.2.
(4) It may be that in the encoding word the second field which must be completed is the mode field. This field specifies whether the operand is in a register or in a memory location. Reference to table C.3 enables the selection of the bits for this field.
(5) Usually after completing the mode field the 3 bit register/memory field values must be selected, table C.4 is used.
(6) Other single bit fields can be encoded by reference to table C.5.

SINGLE OPERAND INSTRUCTIONS

The simplest instruction to encode is that with a single operand specified by a 16 bit register. The instruction to decrement the contents of a 16 bit register can be taken as an example.

Example C.1 DEC BX
By referring to the 8086/8088 instruction encoding table listed as table C.1 the instruction can be seen to be encoded to a single byte as shown below:

```
    opcode      reg
    0 1 0 0 1   - - -
```

This byte contains 5 bits which specify the opcode and a 3 bit reg field. Reference to the register field encoding table C.2, indicates that BX is specified by 011

reg field = 011   specifies register BX.

Hence encoding of instruction DEC BX results in:

```
    01001011
       4B     the HEX object code for DEC  BX
```

The address mode for this instruction can be referred to as the register address mode. Other instructions which have the same mode of addressing are: INC, PUSH, POP, XCHG.

The decrement instruction can again be used to show the encoding of a single operand instruction which involves two bytes of object code. Referring to the encoding table, it can be seen that the general form of the DEC instruction has the opcode split between the first and second bytes of the instruction.

```
    opcode w       mod opcode r/m
    1111111-       --   001   ---
```

The opcode field is 1111111 in the first byte and 001 in the second byte. Also in the first byte is the 1 bit W field, and in the second byte there are two fields the 2 bit MOD field and the 3 bit R/M field.
  The W field is a 1 bit field which specifies the width of the operand.

W = 0 specifies an 8 bit operand.
W = 1 specifies a 16 bit operand.

The MOD field is a 2 bit field which specifies whether the operand is in a microprocessor register or in a memory location. The MOD field encoding values are given in table C.3.

MOD = 11   specifies register mode.
MOD = 00   specifies memory mode with no displacement.
MOD = 01   specifies memory mode with an 8 bit displ.
MOD = 10   specifies memory mode with a 16 bit displ.

The R/M field is a 3 bit register/memory field the encoding of which depends on the value in the MOD field. The values for R/M field are given in table C4. When in the register mode denoted by MOD = 11, the R/M field acts as a register field and specifies the second register in the instruction. When MOD = 00 or 01 or 10, the R/M field acts as a memory field indicating how the effective address EA of the memory operand is calculated.

Example C.2 DEC CL
This instruction involves decrementing an 8 bit register and the encoding is not covered by the single byte instruction. Reference to the encoding table shows that the instruction DEC CL can be encoded using:

```
         w        mod      r/m
      1111111-    --       001    ---
```

Now we can establish for the instruction DEC CL the values for the three remaining fields.
W = 0 specifies an 8 bit operand (register CL).
MOD = 11 specifies the register mode (the operand is the contents of register CL).
R/M = 001 specifies the register CL.
Completing these two bytes produces:

```
         w        mod   r/m
      11111110    11 001 001
         FE          C9        the HEX object code.
```

When a single operand instruction involves effective address EA calculations more than two bytes of object code are required. In this situation the MOD field specifies a memory mode. Examination of the R/M field encoding table indicates that when dealing with the EA calculation the two bytes involving opcode can be followed by:

(a) bytes three and four indicating a direct address
(b) byte three indicating an 8 bit displacement
(c) bytes three and four indicating a 16 bit displacement
(d) no further bytes as the effective address can be obtained from the index or pointer registers.

Example C.3 DEC VARB
Consider that VARB has been designated as the identifier for the offset address 0A24H of a word variable within the current data segment. The object code information obtained from the encoding table is :

```
         w       mod   r/m     displ low     displ high
      1111111-   --    001 ---  --------      --------
```

It can be seen immediately that the the third and fourth bytes are 24H (displacement low) and 0AH (displacement high). The first two bytes can be encoded in a similar manner to the previous examples.

W = 1 specifies a 16 bit operand, because the example quotes the address as that of a word.
MOD = 00 this specification denotes a direct address this can be seen in column 1 of table C.4.
R/M = 110 this specifies a direct address when MOD = 00.

The first two bytes become:

```
opcode w      mod   r/m
11111111      00001110
   FF            0E      the HEX object code.
```

The HEX object code for the complete instruction is now given by : FF 0E 24 0A, four bytes in all. The offset address of the operand was, in this case, stipulated directly when the variable location in the data segment was designated by VARB. This type of memory addressing via a 16 bit displacement is known as direct addressing.

Example C.4 DEC [SI + 154]
Consider that the address specified by SI + 154 is the address of a byte of information, note that if the instruction is specified in this way the assembler will not know that a byte is addressed, the PTR operator should be included to avoid error. Consequently the instruction should be written as DEC BYTE PTR [SI + 154]. From the encoding table the object code information is :

```
          w      mod   r/m    displ low
       1111111-   --001---    --------
```

The third byte which represents the 8 bit displacement will be 9AH (the equivalent of the decimal value 154). The first two bytes are now encoded as follows:

W = 0 specifies an 8 bit operand.
MOD = 01 specifies an 8 bit displacement.
R/M = 100 specifies [SI + D8].

The first two bytes are:

```
          w      mod   r/m
       11111110   01001100
          FE        4C     the HEX object code.
```

The HEX object code for the complete instruction can now be given as: FE 4C 9A, forming a three byte instruction.

Example C.5 DEC [BX + DI + 146H]
Consider that the address designated by BX + DI + 146H is a byte address, so again the byte pointer operator should be included in the instruction as follows DEC BYTE PTR [BX + DI + 146H].

From the encoding table the object code is given by:

```
            w    mod  r/m    displ low    displ high
         1111111-  --001---  --------     --------
```

The third and fourth bytes are 46H and 01H respectively the low byte preceding the high byte.

W = 0 specifies an 8 bit operand.
MOD = 10 specifies a 16 bit displacement.
R/M = 001 specifies (BX) + (DI) + D16

The first two bytes are:
```
         w        mod  r/m
      1111110    10001001
         FE         89        the HEX object code.
```

The HEX object code for the complete instruction is given by: FE 89 46 01, a four byte instruction. This instruction is an example of based indexed addressing.

TWO OPERAND INSTRUCTIONS

A typical example of a two operand instruction is that dealing with subtraction, the mnemonic for which is: SUB mem/reg1,mem/reg2. The operand specified by mem/reg2 is subtracted from the operand specified by mem/reg1 and the resulting operand is specified by mem/reg1. This can also be considered as: SUB destination,source. The specification can be for either an 8 bit or a 16 bit operation. If both operands were in memory then a MOD field and an R/M field would be required to specify each operand. The machine instruction format does not provide two such tables, so it is necessary that one of the operands must be in a register. The options are:

Subtract - register operand from register operand
          - register operand from memory operand
          - memory operand from register operand

The instruction encoding table shows the following code for the subtraction instruction:

```
 opcode dw   mod reg r/m    displ low    displ high
 001010 --   --  --- ---    -------      --------
```

In the first byte there is a single bit destination field. The D field indicates which of the other fields specifies the destination of the result operand.

d = 1 specifies that the result is destined for the operand specified by the REG field.
d = 0 specifies that the result is destined for the operand specified by the MOD and R/M fields.

The REG field specifies either an 8 bit or 16 bit register.

Appendix C **237**

Example C.6 SUB AL,CH
This instruction subtracts the contents of register CH from the contents of register AL leaving the result in register AL. The encoding is as follows:

```
opcode  dw    mod reg r/m
001010  --    --  --- ---
```

D = 1 result stored in operand specified by REG field.
W = 0 specifies 8 bit operand.
REG = 000 specifies AL register as destination of result.
MOD = 11 specifies the register mode.
R/M = 101 specifies CH register.

Hence the encoding produces:

```
opcode  dw    mod reg r/m
001010  10    11  000 101
  2A              C5         the HEX object code
                             for SUB AL,CH.
```

A second encoding method can be used for this register mode. In this case D = 0 and the register holding the result is specified by MOD and R/M fields.

W = 0 again specifies an 8 bit operand.
REG = 101 specifies CH register.
MOD = 11 again specifies register mode.
R/M = 000 specifies AL register.

```
opcode  dw    mod reg r/m
001010  00    11  101 000
  28              E8         this is an alternative
                             HEX object code for SUB AL,CH.
```

Example C.7 SUB CL,[BP + 2]
This instruction subtracts the contents of the memory location, indicated by the base pointer plus the displacement, from the contents of the the CL register. Encoding the instruction as:

```
opcode  dw    mod reg r/m    displ low
001010  --    --  --- ---    --------
```

D = 1 indicates that the result is destined for the CL register which is specified by the reg field.
W = 0 specifies an 8 bit operand.
REG = 001 specifies CL register.
MOD = 01 specifies memory mode with an 8 bit displacement.
R/M = 110 specifies [BP + D8] as the effective address.

```
opcode  dw    mod reg r/m    displ low
001010  10    01  001 110    00000010
  2A              4E            02       the HEX
object code for the instruction SUB CL,[BP + 2].
```

238 The 8086 and Assembly Language

Example C.8 SUB [DI],BX
In this example the contents of a register BX are subtracted from the contents of a memory location pointed to by the DI register and the result resides in that memory location. The object code information is:

```
        opcode  dw      mod reg r/m
        001010  --      --  --- ---
```

D = 0 indicates result in memory location specified by MOD
    and R/M fields.
W = 1 specifies a 16 bit operand.
REG = 011 specifies register BX.
MOD = 00 indicates memory mode but no displacement.
R/M = 101 specifies [DI] as effective address.

```
        opcode  dw      mod reg r/m
        001010  01      00  011 101
           29                1D           the HEX object code
                                          for SUB [DI],BX.
```

Example C.9 RCL BX,1
This instruction rotates the contents of the specified register left through the carry flag by the specified number of bits. Reference to the encoding table results in the following:

```
        opcode  vw      mod opcode r/m
        110100  --      --   010    ---
```

V = 0 specifies rotate count is one.
W = 1 specifies a 16 bit operand.
MOD = 11 specifies register mode.
R/M = 011 specifies BX register.

```
        opcode  vw      mod opcode r/m
        110100  01      11   010    011
           D1                 D3            the HEX object code.
                                            RCL BX,1.
```

Notice that the previously unconsidered single bit V field was involved in this instruction. The V field specifies whether the number of bits to be shifted or rotated is one (V = 0) or is contained in the CL register (V = 1).

Example C.10 SUB [SI],8FH
This instruction involves the subtraction of immediate data 8FH from the contents of memory location addressed by the source index register SI and leaving the result in this location. From the encoding table we have:

```
                sw      mod    r/m     data low
        100000  --      --  101  ---   --------
```

W = 1 specifies 16 bit operand.

S = 1 specifies sign extension of 8 bit immediate data.
MOD = 00 specifies memory mode and no displacement.
R/M = 100 specifies (SI) as effective address.

```
           sw      mod     r/m      data low
  100000  11     00 101   100      10001111
    8A              2C               8F           the HEX
         object code for the instruction SUB (SI),8FH.
```

This example involved the single bit sign extending S field. Notice that although the instruction deals with a data word only a byte of data is required in the instruction, because of the S field presence.

There are often two methods which can be used to encode a particular instruction. The first method employs the general form and the second method the shortened form of encoding. As an example the instruction DEC BX can be encoded using the general form for the decrement instruction, and this produces the two byte hexadecimal code FF CB; whereas using the shortened form produces the single byte hexadecimal code 4B (as evaluated in example C.1). It is reasonable to expect the assembler to select the shortened form automatically.

Table C.1 8086 Instruction encoding.

Data Transfer

MOV = move
Register/memory to/from register
| 1 0 0 0 1 0 d w | mod reg r/m |

Immediate to register/memory
| 1 1 0 0 0 1 1 w | mod 0 0 0 r/m | data | data if w = 1 |

Immediate to register
| 1 0 1 1 w reg | data | data if w = 1 |

Memory to accumulator
| 1 0 1 0 0 0 0 w | addr-low | addr-high |

Accumulator to memory
| 1 0 1 0 0 0 1 w | addr-low | addr-high |

Register/memory to segment register
| 1 0 0 0 1 1 1 0 | mod 0 SR r/m |

Segment register to register/memory
| 1 0 0 0 1 1 0 0 | mod 0 SR r/m |

240 The 8086 and Assembly Language

PUSH = Push
Register/memory
| 1 1 1 1 1 1 1 1 | mod 1 1 0 r/m |

Register
| 0 1 0 1 0 reg |

Segment register
| 0 0 0 reg 1 1 0 |

POP = Pop
Register/memory
| 1 0 0 0 1 1 1 1 | mod 0 0 0 r/m |

Register
| 0 1 0 1 1 reg |

Segment register
| 0 0 0 reg 1 1 1 |

XCHG = Exchange
Register/memory with register
| 1 0 0 0 0 1 1 w | mod reg r/m |

Register with accumulator
| 1 0 0 1 0 reg |

IN = Input to AL/AX from
Fixed port
| 1 1 1 0 0 1 0 w | port |

Variable port (DX)
| 1 1 1 0 1 1 0 w |

OUT = Output from AL/AX to
Fixed port
| 1 1 1 0 0 1 1 w | port |

Variable port (DX)
| 1 1 1 0 1 1 1 w |

XLAT = Translate byte to AL
| 1 1 0 1 0 1 1 1 |

LEA = load EA to register
| 1 0 0 0 1 1 0 1 | mod reg r/m |

LDS = load pointer to DS
| 1 1 0 0 0 1 0 1 | mod reg r/m |

LES = load pointer to ES
| 1 1 0 0 0 1 0 0 | mod reg r/m |

LAHF = load AH with flags
| 1 0 0 1 1 1 1 1 |

Appendix C **241**

SAHF = store AH into flags
| 1 0 0 1 1 1 1 0 |

PUSHF = push flags
| 1 0 0 1 1 1 0 0 |

POPF = pop flags
| 1 0 0 1 1 1 0 1 |

Arithmetic

ADD = Add
Register/memory with register to either
| 0 0 0 0 0 0 d w | mod reg r/m |

Immediate to register/memory
| 1 0 0 0 0 0 s w | mod 0 0 0 r/m | data | data if s:w = 01 |

Immediate to accumulator
| 0 0 0 0 0 1 0 w | data | data if w = 1 |

ADC = Add with carry
Register/memory with register to either
| 0 0 0 1 0 0 d w | mod reg r/m |

Immediate to register/memory
| 1 0 0 0 0 0 s w | mod 0 1 0 r/m | data | data if s:w = 01 |

Immediate to accumulator
| 0 0 0 1 0 1 0 w | data | data if w = 1 |

INC = Increment
Register/memory
| 1 1 1 1 1 1 1 w | mod 0 0 0 r/m |

Register
| 0 1 0 0 0 reg |

AAA = ASCII adjust for add
| 0 0 1 1 0 1 1 1 |

DAA = Decimal adjust for add
| 0 0 1 0 0 1 1 1 |

SUB = subtract
Register/memory with register to either
| 0 0 1 0 1 0 d w | mod reg r/m |

Immediate from register/memory
| 1 0 0 0 0 0 s w | mod 1 0 1 r/m | data | data if s:w = 01 |

Immediate from accumulator
| 0 0 1 0 1 1 0 w | data | data if w = 1 |

SBB = subtract with borrow
Register/memory and register to either

| 0 0 0 1 1 0 d w | mod reg r/m |

Immediate from register/memory

| 1 0 0 0 0 0 s w | mod 0 1 1 r/m | data | data if s:w = 01 |

Immediate from accumulator

| 0 0 0 1 1 1 0 w | data | data if w = 1 |

DEC = decrement
Register/memory

| 1 1 1 1 1 1 1 w | mod 0 0 1 r/m |

Register

| 0 1 0 0 1 reg |

NEG = Change sign

| 1 1 1 1 0 1 1 w | mod 0 1 1 r/m |

CMP = Compare
Register/memory and register

| 0 0 1 1 1 0 d w | mod reg r/m |

Immediate from register/memory

| 1 0 0 0 0 0 s w | mod 1 1 1 r/m | data | data if s:w = 01 |

Immediate from accumulator

| 0 0 1 1 1 1 0 w | data |

AAS = ASCII adjust for subtract

| 0 0 1 1 1 1 1 1 |

DAS = Decimal adjust for subtract

| 0 0 1 0 1 1 1 1 |

MUL = Multiply (unsigned)

| 1 1 1 1 0 1 1 w | mod 1 0 0 r/m |

IMUL = Integer multiply (signed)

| 1 1 1 1 0 1 1 w | mod 1 0 1 r/m |

AAM = ASCII adjust for multiply

| 1 1 0 1 0 1 0 0 | 0 0 0 0 1 0 1 0 |

DIV = Divide (unsigned)

| 1 1 1 1 0 1 1 w | mod 1 1 0 r/m |

IDIV = Integer divide (signed)

| 1 1 1 1 0 1 1 w | mod 1 1 1 r/m |

AAD = ASCII adjust for divide

| 1 1 0 1 0 1 0 1 | 0 0 0 0 1 0 1 0 |

CBW = Convert byte to word
| 1 0 0 1 1 0 0 0 |

CWD = Convert word to double word
| 1 0 0 1 1 0 0 1 |

Logic

NOT = Invert
| 1 1 1 1 0 1 1 w | mod 0 1 0 r/m |

SHL/SAL = Shift logical/arithmetic left
| 1 1 0 1 0 0 v w | mod 1 0 0 r/m |

SHR = Shift logical right
| 1 1 0 1 0 0 v w | mod 1 0 1 r/m |

SAR = Shift arithmetic right
| 1 1 0 1 0 0 v w | mod 1 1 1 r/m |

ROL = Rotate left
| 1 1 0 1 0 0 v w | mod 0 0 0 r/m |

ROR = Rotate right
| 1 1 0 1 0 0 v w | mod 0 0 1 r/m |

RCL = Rotate through carry left
| 1 1 0 1 0 0 v w | mod 0 1 0 r/m |

RCR = Rotate through carry right
| 1 1 0 1 0 0 v w | mod 0 1 1 r/m |

AND = And
Register/memory and register to either
| 0 0 1 0 0 0 d w | mod reg r/m |

Immediate to register/memory
| 1 0 0 0 0 0 0 w | mod 1 0 0 r/m | data | data if w = 1 |

Immediate to accumulator
| 0 0 1 0 0 1 0 w | data | data if w = 1 |

TEST = And function to flags, no result
Register/memory and register
| 0 0 0 1 0 0 d w | mod reg r/m |

Immediate data and register/memory
| 1 1 1 1 0 1 1 w | mod 0 0 0 r/m | data | data if w = 1 |

Immediate data and accumulator
| 1 0 1 0 1 0 0 w | data | data if w = 1 |

OR = Or
Register/memory and register to either

| 0 0 0 0 1 0 d w | mod reg r/m |

Immediate to register/memory

| 1 0 0 0 0 0 0 w | mod 0 0 1 r/m | data | data if w = 1 |

Immediate to accumulator

| 0 0 0 0 1 1 0 w | data | data if w = 1 |

XOR = Exclusive or
Register/memory and register to either

| 0 0 1 1 0 0 d w | mod reg r/m |

Immediate to register/memory

| 1 0 0 0 0 0 0 w | mod 1 1 0 r/m | data | data if w = 1 |

Immediate to accumulator

| 0 0 1 1 0 1 0 w | data | data if w = 1 |

String Manipulation

REP = Repeat

| 1 1 1 1 0 0 1 z |

MOVS = Move byte/word

| 1 0 1 0 0 1 0 w |

CMPS = Compare byte/word

| 1 0 1 0 0 1 1 w |

SCAS = Scan byte/word

| 1 0 1 0 1 1 1 w |

LODS = Load byte/word to AL/AX

| 1 0 1 0 1 1 0 w |

STOS = Store byte/word from AL/AX

| 1 0 1 0 1 0 1 w |

Control Transfer

CALL = Call
Direct within segment

| 1 1 1 0 1 0 0 0 | disp-low | disp-high |

Indirect within segment

| 1 1 1 1 1 1 1 1 | mod 0 1 0 r/m |

Direct intersegment

| 1 0 0 1 1 0 1 0 | offset-low | offset-high |
| | seg-low | seg-high |

Indirect intersegment

| 1 1 1 1 1 1 1 1 | mod 0 1 1 r/m |

Appendix C **245**

JMP = Unconditional jump
Direct within segment

| 1 1 1 0 1 0 0 1 | disp-low | disp-high |

Direct within segment-short

| 1 1 1 0 1 0 1 1 | disp |

Indirect within segment

| 1 1 1 1 1 1 1 1 | mod 1 0 0 r/m |

Direct intersegment

| 1 1 1 0 1 0 1 0 | offset-low | offset-high |
| | seg-low | seg-high |

Indirect intersegment

| 1 1 1 1 1 1 1 1 | mod 1 0 1 r/m |

RET = Return from call
Within segment

| 1 1 0 0 0 0 1 1 |

Within segment adding immediate to SP

| 1 1 0 0 0 0 1 0 | data-low | data-high |

Intersegment

| 1 1 0 0 1 0 1 1 |

Intersegment adding immediate to SP

| 1 1 0 0 1 0 1 0 | data-low | data-high |

JA/JNBE = Jump if above/neither below nor equal

| 0 1 1 1 0 1 1 1 | disp |

JAE/JNB = Jump if above or equal/not below

| 0 1 1 1 0 0 1 1 | disp |

JB/JNAE = Jump if below/neither above nor equal

| 0 1 1 1 0 0 1 0 | disp |

JBE/JNA = Jump if below or equal/not above

| 0 1 1 1 0 1 1 0 | disp |

JC = Jump if carry is set

| 0 1 1 1 0 0 1 0 | disp |

JCXZ = Jump if CX register is zero

| 1 1 1 0 0 0 1 1 | disp |

JE/JZ = Jump if equal/zero

| 0 1 1 1 0 1 0 0 | disp |

JG/JNLE = Jump if greater/neither less nor equal

| 0 1 1 1 1 1 1 1 | disp |

246 The 8086 and Assembly Language

JGE/JNL = Jump if greater or equal/not less than
| 0 1 1 1 1 1 0 1 | disp |

JL/JNGE = Jump if less/neither greater nor equal
| 0 1 1 1 1 1 0 0 | disp |

JLE/JNG = Jump if less or equal/not greater than
| 0 1 1 1 1 1 1 0 | disp |

JNC = Jump if no carry
| 0 1 1 1 0 0 1 1 | disp |

JNE/JNZ = Jump if not equal/not zero
| 0 1 1 1 0 1 0 1 | disp |

JNO = Jump if no overflow
| 0 1 1 1 0 0 0 1 | disp |

JNP/JPO = Jump if no parity/parity odd
| 0 1 1 1 1 0 1 1 | disp |

JNS = Jump if no sign (jump if positive)
| 0 1 1 1 1 0 0 1 | disp |

JO = Jump if overflow is set
| 0 1 1 1 0 0 0 0 | disp |

JP/JPE = Jump if parity is set/even
| 0 1 1 1 1 0 1 0 | disp |

JS = Jump if sign is set
| 0 1 1 1 1 0 0 0 | disp |

LOOP = Loop CX times
| 1 1 1 0 0 0 1 0 | disp |

LOOPZ/LOOPE = Loop while zero/equal
| 1 1 1 0 0 0 0 1 | disp |

LOOPNZ/LOOPNE = Loop while not zero/equal
| 1 1 1 0 0 0 0 0 | disp |

INT = Interrupt
type specified
| 1 1 0 0 1 1 0 1 | type |

type 3
| 1 1 0 0 1 1 0 0 |

INTO = Interrupt on overflow
| 1 1 0 0 1 1 1 0 |

IRET = Interrupt return
| 1 1 0 0 1 1 1 1 |

Processor Control

CLC = Clear carry
`1 1 1 1 1 0 0 0`

CMC = Complement carry
`1 1 1 1 0 1 0 1`

STC = Set carry
`1 1 1 1 1 0 0 1`

CLD = Clear direction
`1 1 1 1 1 1 0 0`

STD = Set direction
`1 1 1 1 1 1 0 1`

CLI = Clear interrupt
`1 1 1 1 1 0 1 0`

STI = Set interrupt
`1 1 1 1 1 0 1 1`

HLT = Halt
`1 1 1 1 0 1 0 0`

WAIT = Wait
`1 0 0 1 1 0 1 1`

LOCK = Bus lock prefix
`1 1 1 1 0 0 0 0`

SEGMENT = Segment override prefix
`0 0 1 reg 1 1 0`

ESC = Escape (to external device)
`1 1 0 1 1 x x x | mod yyy r/m`

Table C.2 Register field (REG) encoding.

REG	W=0	W=1
000	AL	AX
001	CL	CX
010	DL	DX
011	BL	BX
100	AH	SP
101	CH	BP
110	DH	SI
111	BH	DI

Table C.3 Mode field (MOD) encoding.

Code	Mode explanation
00	Memory mode with no displacement (16 bit displacement when R/M=110)
01	Memory mode with 8 bit displacement
10	Memory mode with 16 bit displacement
11	Register mode

Table C.4 Register/memory field (R/M) encoding.

	MOD			EFFECTIVE ADDRESS CALCULATION		
R/M	W=0	W=1	R/M	MOD=00	MOD=01	MOD=10
000	AL	AX	000	(BX)+(SI)	(BX)+(SI)+D8	(BX)+(SI)+D16
001	CL	CX	001	(BX)+(DI)	(BX)+(DI)+D8	(BX)+(DI)+D16
010	DL	DX	010	(BP)+(SI)	(BP)+(SI)+D8	(BP)+(SI)+D16
011	BL	BX	011	(BP)+(DI)	(BP)+(DI)+D8	(BP)+(DI)+D16
100	AH	SP	100	(SI)	(SI)+D8	(SI)+D16
101	CH	BP	101	(DI)	(DI)+D8	(DI)+D16
110	DH	SI	110	Direct Addr	(BP)+D8	(BP)+D16
111	BH	DI	111	(BX)	(BX)+D8	(BX)+D16

Table C.5 Single-bit field encoding.

Field	Value	Function
S	0	No sign extension
	1	Sign extend 8 bit immediate data to 16 bits if W=1
W	0	Instruction operates on data byte
	1	Instruction operates on data word
D	0	Instruction source specified in REG field
	1	Instruction destination specified in REG field
V	0	Shift/rotate count is one
	1	Shift/rotate specified in CL register
Z	0	Repeat/loop while zero flag is clear
	1	Repeat/loop while zero flag is set

Table C.6 Segment register field encoding.

Segment Register	Field
ES	00
CS	01
SS	10
DS	11

ADDRESSING MODES AND THE OBJECT CODE

The study of the encoding procedure highlights the various memory addressing modes available with the 8086 microprocessor. Figure C.1 shows in detail the relationship between the addressing modes and the machine instruction format required to obtain that type of addressing mode.

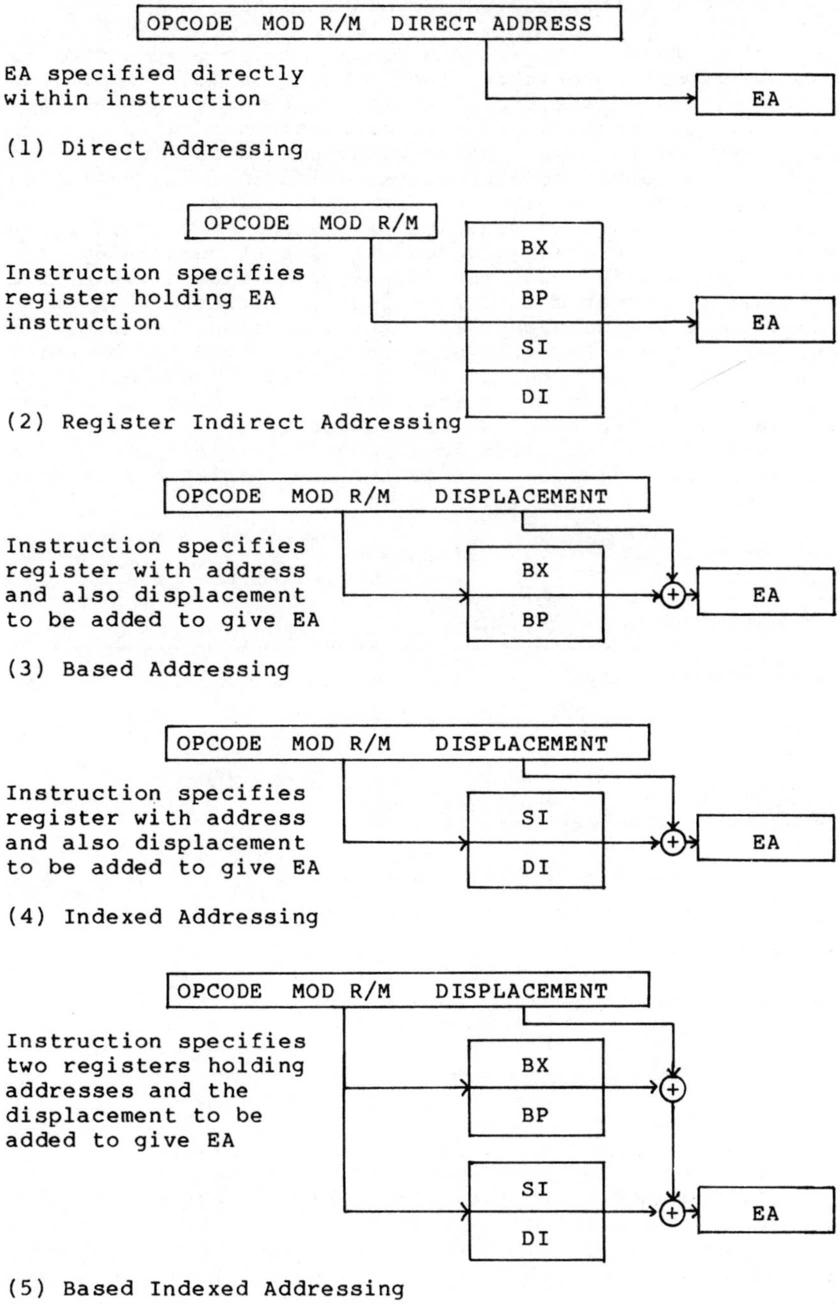

OPCODE MOD R/M DIRECT ADDRESS
EA specified directly within instruction
EA
(1) Direct Addressing
OPCODE MOD R/M
Instruction specifies register holding EA instruction
BX
BP
SI
DI
EA
(2) Register Indirect Addressing
OPCODE MOD R/M DISPLACEMENT
Instruction specifies register with address and also displacement to be added to give EA
BX
BP
EA
(3) Based Addressing
OPCODE MOD R/M DISPLACEMENT
Instruction specifies register with address and also displacement to be added to give EA
SI
DI
EA
(4) Indexed Addressing
OPCODE MOD R/M DISPLACEMENT
Instruction specifies two registers holding addresses and the displacement to be added to give EA
BX
BP
SI
DI
EA
(5) Based Indexed Addressing

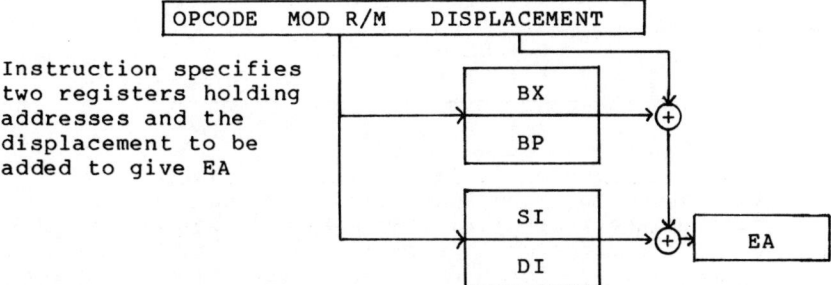

Figure C.1 Memory addressing modes.

250 The 8086 and Assembly Language

INSTRUCTION EXECUTION TIMES

The time taken to execute a particular instruction is usually given in terms of the number of clock periods which elapse during the execution of the instruction. For example, an 8086 microprocessor running at a clock frequency of 5 MHz has a clock period of 200ns, so an instruction requiring four clock periods for its execution will take 800ns. As has been discussed in the section on addressing modes in chapter 1, when an operand is in memory there are a large number of ways of generating the effective memory address EA. A clear indication of the methods of generation of the effective address EA is shown in figure C.1. The number of clock periods required to calculate the EA will need to be included in the total time for the execution of the instruction. These effective address calculation times are given in table C.7. An indication of the range of the number of clock periods for each instruction is given in chapter 3. Table 3.1 provides the number of clock periods for the variations of each instruction.

Table C.7 Effective address calculation time.

Effective address components		No of clock periods
Displacement only		6
Base or Index register only	(BX,BP,SI,DI)	5
Base or Index register + displacement	(BX,BP,SI,DI)	9
Base + Index register	BP + DI, BX + SI BP + SI, BX + DI	7 8
Base + Index register + displacement	BP + DI + Displ BX + SI + Displ BP + SI + Displ BX + DI + Displ	11 12

The ADD instruction can be used as an example to show the evaluation of the number of clock periods for each variation of the instruction. By reference to tables 3.1 and C.7, the clock periods can be evaluated. The results of the evaluations, for a range of instruction examples, are given in table C.8.

Appendix C **251**

Table C.8 Clock periods for addition instructions.

	Clock periods	Operands
ADD AX,CX	3	register,register
ADD CX,[SI]	9 + EA(5) = 14	register,memory
ADD AX,[BX+DI]	9 + EA(8) = 17	register,memory
ADD VAL1,CX	16 + EA(6) = 22	memory,register
ADD [SI+128],CX	16 + EA(9) = 25	memory,register
ADD CX,1234H	4	register immediate
ADD [BP+SI+02],4321H	17 + EA(12) = 29	memory,immediate
ADD [BX+SI],62000	17 + EA(7) = 24	memory,immediate

Appendix D

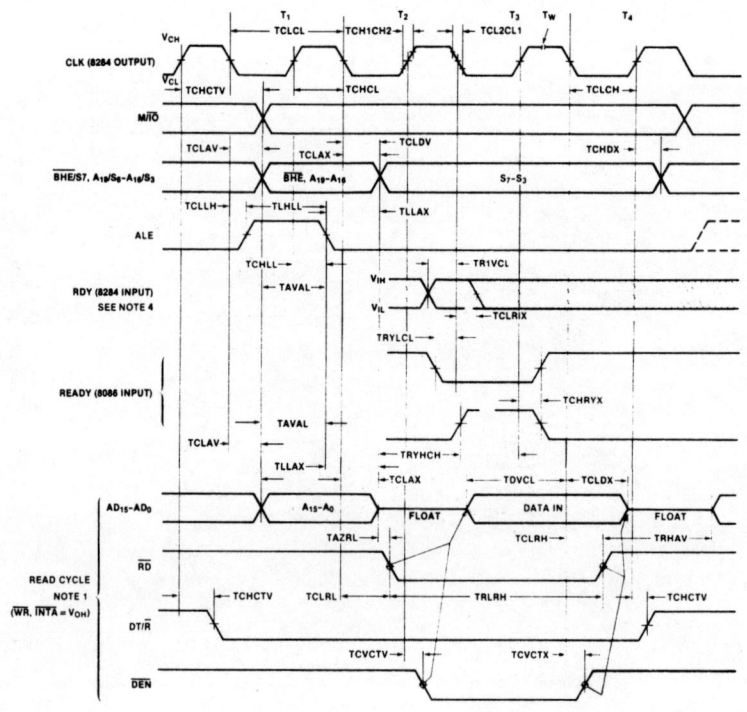

Figure D.1 8086 Bus timing for minimum mode system (Courtesy of Intel Corporation).

Appendix D **253**

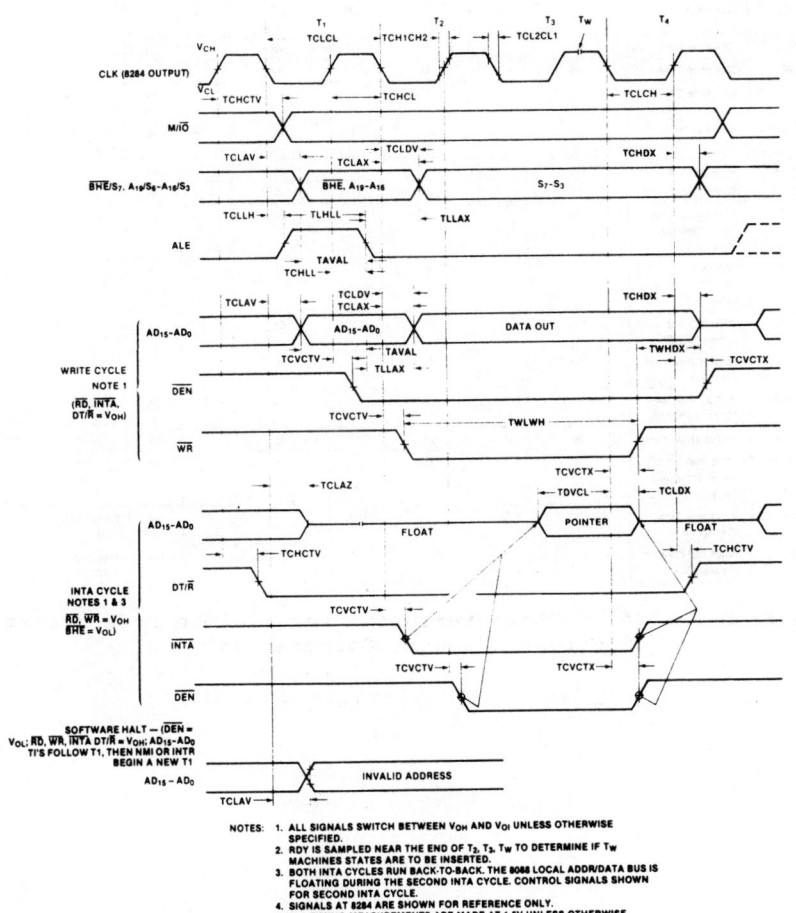

Figure D.1 8086 Bus timing for minimum mode system (Courtesy of Intel Corporation)

254 The 8086 and Assembly Language

Symbol	Parameter	8086 Min.	8086 Max.	8086-1 (Preliminary) Min.	8086-1 (Preliminary) Max.	8086-2 Min.	8086-2 Max.	Units	Test Conditions
TCLCL	CLK Cycle Period	200	500	100	500	125	500	ns	
TCLCH	CLK Low Time	118		53		68		ns	
TCHCL	CLK High Time	69		39		44		ns	
TCH1CH2	CLK Rise Time		10		10		10	ns	From 1.0V to 3.5V
TCL2CL1	CLK Fall Time		10		10		10	ns	From 3.5V to 1.0V
TDVCL	Data in Setup Time	30		5		20		ns	
TCLDX	Data in Hold Time	10		10		10		ns	
TR1VCL	RDY Setup Time into 8284A (See Notes 1, 2)	35		35		35		ns	
TCLR1X	RDY Hold Time into 8284A (See Notes 1, 2)	0		0		0		ns	
TRYHCH	READY Setup Time into 8086	118		53		68		ns	
TCHRYX	READY Hold Time into 8086	30		20		20		ns	
TRYLCL	READY Inactive to CLK (See Note 3)	-8		-10		-8		ns	
THVCH	HOLD Setup Time	35		20		20		ns	
TINVCH	INTR, NMI, TEST Setup Time (See Note 2)	30		15		15		ns	
TILIH	Input Rise Time (Except CLK)		20		20		20	ns	From 0.8V to 2.0V
TIHIL	Input Fall Time (Except CLK)		12		12		12	ns	From 2.0V to 0.8V

Figure D.2 8086 AC Characteristics for minimum mode system (Courtesy of Intel Corporation).

Appendix D **255**

Symbol	Parameter	8086		8086-1 (Preliminary)		8086-2		Units	Test Conditions
		Min.	Max.	Min.	Max.	Min.	Max.		
TCLAV	Address Valid Delay	10	110	10	50	10	60	ns	
TCLAX	Address Hold Time	10		10		10		ns	
TCLAZ	Address Float Delay	TCLAX	80	10	40	TCLAX	50	ns	
TLHLL	ALE Width	TCLCH−20		TCLCH−10		TCLCH−10		ns	
TCLLH	ALE Active Delay		80		40		50	ns	
TCHLL	ALE Inactive Delay		85		45		55	ns	
TLLAX	Address Hold Time to ALE Inactive	TCHCL−10		TCHCL−10		TCHCL−10		ns	
TCLDV	Data Valid Delay	10	110	10	50	10	60	ns	*C_L = 20-100 pF for all 8086 Outputs (In addition to 8086 self-load)
TCHDX	Data Hold Time	10		10		10		ns	
TWHDX	Data Hold Time After WR	TCLCH−30		TCLCH−25		TCLCH−30		ns	
TCVCTV	Control Active Delay 1	10	110	10	50	10	70	ns	
TCHCTV	Control Active Delay 2	10	110	10	45	10	60	ns	
TCVCTX	Control Inactive Delay	10	110	10	50	10	70	ns	
TAZRL	Address Float to READ Active	0		0		0		ns	
TCLRL	RD Active Delay	10	165	10	70	10	100	ns	
TCLRH	RD Inactive Delay	10	150	10	60	10	80	ns	
TRHAV	RD Inactive to Next Address Active	TCLCL−45		TCLCL−35		TCLCL−40		ns	
TCLHAV	HLDA Valid Delay	10	160	10	60	10	100	ns	
TRLRH	RD Width	2TCLCL−75		2TCLCL−40		2TCLCL−50		ns	
TWLWH	WR Width	2TCLCL−60		2TCLCL−35		2TCLCL−40		ns	
TAVAL	Address Valid to ALE Low	TCLCH−60		TCLCH−35		TCLCH−40		ns	
TOLOH	Output Rise Time		20		20		20	ns	From 0.8V to 2.0V
TOHOL	Output Fall Time		12		12		12	ns	From 2.0V to 0.8V

Figure D.2 8086 AC Characteristics for minimum mode system (Courtesy of Intel Corporation).

Appendix E

	0 0000	1 0001	2 0010	3 0011	4 0100	5 0101	6 0110	7 0111	8 1000	9 1001	A 1010	B 1011	C 1100	D 1101	E 1110	F 1111
0 000	NUL	SOH	STX	ETX	EOT	ENQ	ACK	BEL	BS	HT	LF	VT	FF	CR	SO	SI
1 001	DLE	DC1	DC2	DC3	DC4	NAK	SYN	ETB	CAN	EM	SUB	ESC	FS	GS	RS	US
2 010	SP	!	"	#	$	%	&	'	(	)	*	+	,	-	.	/
3 011	0	1	2	3	4	5	6	7	8	9	:	;	<	=	>	?
4 100	@	A	B	C	D	E	F	G	H	I	J	K	L	M	N	O
5 101	P	Q	R	S	T	U	V	W	X	Y	Z	[	\	]	^	_
6 110	`	a	b	c	d	e	f	g	h	i	j	k	l	m	n	o
7 111	p	q	r	s	t	u	v	w	x	y	z	{			}	~	DEL

The ASCII Character Set

The code for an ASCII character can be obtained in either binary or hex by reading the number in the first column at the side of the row and then the number in the first row at the top of the column. From the table the binary code for ! can be seen to be 0100001B, and the hex code for K to be 4BH.

Index

AAA, 29
AAD, 29
AAM, 30
AAS, 30, 176
ADC, 30
ADD, 31
Address generation, 9, 220
Address timing, 131
Addressing modes, 13, 248
ALU, 19,
AND, 32, 82
Arithmetic instructions, 73
ASCII code, 80, 145, 256
Assembler, 27, 90
Assembler controls, 108
Assembler directives, 97
Assembler errors, 108
Assembler operators, 102
ASSUME directive, 98
Auxiliary carry flag, 6

Baud rate, 145
BCD arithmetic, 80, 176
BHE, 22, 121
BIU, 18,
Bus contention, 133
Bus cycle, 113
Bus demultiplexing, 112
Bus timing, 252
Byte PTR, 104,

CALL, 32, 184, 190
Carry flag, 6, 74
CBW, 34
Chip select logic, 203
CLC, 34
CLD, 34

CLI, 34
CMC, 35
CMP, 35, 76
CMPS, 36, 84
Conditional jump
  instructions, 43, 86
Co-processor, 135, 225
CWD, 37

DAA, 37
DAS, 37
Data bus, 2, 23
  buffering, 115
Data bus transceivers, 115
Data definition, 99
Data manipulation
  instructions, 81
Debugging, 93
DEC, 37
Descriptor, 217, 223
Descriptor cache
  register, 217
Descriptor tables, 220
Direct addressing, 14
Direct memory access, 24, 207
DIV, 38
Divide by zero, 157
Division, 78
DMA, 24, 207
Doubleword, 37

EA - Effective address, 16
Editor, 91
8088 Microprocessor, 25
80186 Microprocessor, 199, 228
80286 Microprocessor, 214, 228

258 The 8086 and Assembly Language

8251A Communication
  Interface, 146, 150
  programming of, 149
8255A Programmable
  Interface, 136, 142
  programming of, 138
8259A Interrupt
  Controller, 160
  programming of, 163
  interface, 163
8282 Octal Latch, 113
8284 Clock Generator, 114
8286 Transceiver, 115
EQU directive, 97
Errors - assembly, 108
EU - Execution Unit, 19
EVEN directive, 101
EXTRN directive, 101

Flags, 5

GROUP directive, 102

HLT, 40

IBM PC, 93
IDIV, 40
Immediate addressing, 13
IMUL, 41
IN, 41, 135
INC, 42
Indexed addressing, 14
Indirect addressing, 14
Instruction encoding, 232
Instruction fetch, 17
Instruction bytes, 63
Instruction periods, 63
Instruction mnemonic, 27
Instruction operands, 27
INT, 42
Interrupt 8086, 154
    80186, 210
Interrupt acknowledge,160
Interrupt enable
    flag, 7, 158
Interrupt sequence, 159
Interrupt type
    number, 155,193
Interrupt vector, 155, 193
Intersegment, 33, 45, 54
INTO, 42

Intrasegment, 33, 44
I/O instructions, 41, 135
I/O interface, 135
IRET, 43

Jump instructions, 44

LABEL directive, 101
LAHF, 45
LDS, 46,69
LEA, 46
LES, 46
Linker, 91
List (LST) file, 90, 173
LODS, 47, 84, 179
LOOP, 47

Macro, 105
MASM, 93
Maximum mode, 25
Memory bank, 121
Memory mapped I/O, 136
Minimum mode, 23, 116
Modem, 148
MOV, 48,68
MOVS, 48, 85, 171
MUL, 49
Multiplexing, 23
Multiplication, 78
Multitasking, 221

Name directive, 102
NEG, 49, 179
NOT, 50, 82
Non-maskable interrupt, 159

Object code, 12, 91, 248
Offset address, 8
OFFSET operator, 103, 182
OR, 50,82
ORG directive, 101, 196
OUT, 51, 135
Overflow flag, 6, 75

Parity flag, 6
POP, 51, 71, 194
Privilege levels, 222
PROCEDURE directive, 100
Protection mechanism, 222
PUBLIC directive,
PUSH, 52, 71, 194
PUSHF, 53

Index

RAM interface, 127
RCL/RCR, 53, 83
Read bus cycle, 116
   timing, 132
Relocatable object
  code, 91
Register set, 3, 218
  segment, 3, 11, 16
  general, 4
  index, 4
  pointer, 4
Register addressing, 14
REP, 53, 85, 171
RET, 54, 190
ROM interface, 124
ROL/ROR, 54, 83
RS-232C interface, 145

SAHF, 55
SAL/SAR 56, 83
SBB, 56
SCAS, 57, 84, 179, 186
Segmentation, 7, 94
Segment register, 3, 11, 16
  initialisation, 107
SEGMENT/ENDS directive, 97,
SHL, 56
SHR, 58
Sign flag, 6
Signed binary, 74
Single-step, 157
Stack, 71
Status flags, 6
STC, 58
STD, 58
STI, 59
STOS, 59, 84, 186
String instructions, 84
SUB, 59
Subroutine, 184

TEST, 60
Timers, 209
Trap flag, 7, 157

UART, 144
USART, 144, 149, 188

Virtual memory, 215, 224

Word PTR, 104
Write bus cycle, 118

XCHG, 61, 188
XLAT, 61, 70
XOR, 62, 82, 183, 186

Zero flag, 6